Movement Experiences
for the Mentally Retarded
or Emotionally Disturbed Child

Consulting Editors

Eloise M. Jaeger and
Robert D. Clayton

Movement Experiences

for the Mentally Retarded or Emotionally Disturbed Child

Joan May Moran
*Director Physical Education and Recreation
for the Handicapped
University of Utah*

Leonard Harris Kalakian
Mankato State College

BURGESS PUBLISHING COMPANY • MINNEAPOLIS, MINNESOTA

Editors of this book were Robert E. Lakemacher,
Alice R. Lanyk and Thomas M. Newcomb.
Designed by Dennis Tasa, production was
supervised by Morris Lundin. Line drawings by
A. Bruce Fredrick and D. Tasa, photos by the
authors. Type set in Palatino by The Type House
and printed by The Colwell Press.

3   4   5   6   7   8   9   0

To Charles, who has painfully, but perseveringly come to know and understand the value and importance of movement in rehabilitation. And to Lisa and all of God's other "special" children in our society, this book is dedicated.

Preface

According to information reported in 1970,[1] on the basis of a compilation of multiple studies of incidence from Title V State Reports, it is estimated that there are 7,083,599 handicapped school-aged children in the United States. These statistics are further broken down as follows:

Speech impaired 2,440,515

Mentally retarded 1,697,620

Emotionally disturbed 1,387,920

Learning disabled 697,620

Hard of hearing 348,645

Crippled and other health impaired 348,645

Visually impaired 69,729

Deaf 52,297

Multi-handicapped 40,938

All too frequently, severely emotionally disturbed children, because of their lack of response in a testing situation, are incorrectly

---

[1]John A. Nesbitt, The handicapped child: Therapeutic recreation service needs in program, manpower and research, *Therapeutic Recreation Journal*, 1970, 4 (Second Quarter), 33-40.

classified as mentally retarded. The emotionally disturbed child possesses limited, inflexible, restricted behavior that impairs adaptation to changing environments and reduces behavioral freedom. The mentally retarded child possesses impairments in adaptive behavior which make it difficult for him to maintain himself independently and to meet the demands of his environment. These similar impairments in adaptive behavior may be one of the reasons for the difficulty in correctly classifying the emotionally disturbed child. This is the basic rationale for including movement experiences for the mentally retarded and/or emotionally disturbed child in one text. Additional characteristics of the mentally retarded or emotionally disturbed child can be found in Chapter II, The Status of Physical Education/Recreation for the Mentally Retarded and Emotionally Disturbed and Chapter V, Play Therapy.

Numerous teaching and learning problems are imposed on the mentally retarded or emotionally disturbed child who also possesses a physical disability. The teacher of these multi-handicapped children must be extremely flexible and creative in developing individualized movement experiences for these children. The authors have not included the multi-handicapped in this text. The teacher of these children is referred to adapted physical education textbooks for additional information needed for planning the physical education/recreation program for the multi-handicapped child in his classroom.

Movement experiences for the mentally retarded or emotionally disturbed child, as included in this text, are all of those activities which involve movement of the entire body or its various parts — alone, in combination with another child or group of children, and with or without the use and/or manipulation of small or large equipment. Such movement experiences enable the mentally retarded and/or emotionally disturbed child to develop his physical, social, and emotional self, thereby making him better able to cope with and function in his "real" environment. These movement experiences should be a part of every mentally retarded or emotionally disturbed child's physical education and recreational pursuits.

This text has been written as a tool for use by the educator in providing individualized and meaningful movement experiences for those children in our society who are mentally retarded or emotionally disturbed.

January 1974   *Joan M. Moran*
                                                      Leonard H. Kalakian

Contents

Chapter I.   Physical Education and Recreation
                 Movement Experiences — A Rationale   **1**

Chapter II.   The Status of Physical Education / Recreation
                 for the Mentally Retarded and
                 Emotionally Disturbed   **5**

Chapter III.   Basic Physical and Motor Fitness   **25**

Chapter IV.   Basic Motor Patterns and Skills   **49**

Chapter V.   Play Therapy   **77**

Chapter VI.   Movement Education   **111**

Chapter VII.   Music, Rhythms, and Dance   **139**

Chapter VIII.   Perceptual-Motor Development   **237**

Chapter IX.   Developmental Gymnastics   **255**

Chapter X.   Swimming and Water-Related Activities   **291**

Chapter XI.   Integrating Movement Experiences
                 with Other School Subjects   **339**

Chapter XII.   Innovative Equipment   **355**

                 Index   **381**

Chapter I

Physical Education and Recreation Movement Experiences — A Rationale

The philosophy which suggests that each individual is entitled to an education commensurate with his potential is a relatively recent phenomenon. Educational opportunities stemming from this philosophy have only recently begun to be extended to the handicapped. Among such opportunities are activities of a physical education and recreation nature.

For many years physical educators and recreators have programmed activities for individuals whose handicaps were primarily physical. Programming such experiences for the mentally retarded and/or emotionally disturbed, however, has only recently become a major professional trend in physical education and recreation.

Physical educators, recreators, and indeed, many special educators have come to recognize the potential of physically and motorically based learning experiences in teaching the mentally retarded and/or emotionally disturbed. It is generally accepted that such individuals are more like their normal peers physically and motorically than in any other respect. The overriding implication is that vast opportunities for successful experiences may lie in waiting for mentally retarded and/or emotionally disturbed individuals through physical education and recreation pursuits. Such individuals who heretofore have experienced repeated failure in classroom-oriented tasks often find new reassurance and unexpected success in movement experiences.

1

Historically, programs for the mentally retarded and/or emotionally disturbed have tended to be primarily therapeutic in nature. Special programs have often tended to concentrate solely upon the disability in question rather than upon the total needs of the whole individual. This picture, however, has gradually begun to change largely through the efforts of certain physical educators and recreators. In programming movement experiences for the mentally retarded and/or emotionally disturbed, these physical educators and recreators have endeavored to capitalize upon the apparent inherent highly motivating nature of physical education and recreation experiences. In working with such handicapped individuals, they have endeavored to provide what has come to be known as education *through* the physical. This philosophy recognizes that the development of physical and motor proficiencies is among physical education's and recreation's unique and traditionally most important contribution to the individual's growth and development. In addition, however, there exists the belief that many concomitant values and learnings may be derived from movement experiences. Included among such outcomes are social development, self-image enhancement, attention span lengthening, enhanced sequential-thinking abilities, and heightened perceptual awareness.

The development of social awareness is among the important concomitant outcomes of participation in physical education and recreation experiences. The socialization process may be enhanced as movement experiences tend to bring the mentally retarded and/or emotionally disturbed individual into direct contact with others. This consideration takes on increasing importance with the awareness that the social contacts of the handicapped often tend to be inordinately limited by the handicapping condition. Movement experiences can be structured to the extent that individuals may work singly, in parallel, in pairs, or in groups depending upon the dictates of any given situation. Initially, movement experiences may be selected which require little social adaptation. As the individual's potential for socialization begins to unfold, he may take part in activities requiring increasing degrees of social awareness and interpersonal cooperation. In addition, movement experiences are often capable of providing the common ground upon which the mentally retarded and/or emotionally disturbed may successfully interact with their normal peers.

Movement experiences occurring through physical education and recreation may effectively enhance self-image among the mentally retarded and/or emotionally disturbed. Because physical education and recreation activities tend to be relatively concrete, and because such individuals function most effectively when dealing in concrete terms, movement experiences often provide them with heightened and unexpected measures of success. The opportunity to experience success and to enjoy the feeling of having done something well is especially important among the mentally retarded and/or emotionally disturbed whose encounters with success tend to be limited. Being successful at something, and especially being successful at something valued by oneself and others, creates a potent force in the enhancement of self-worth feelings. Should such success experiences occur under the auspices of the school, the individual may experience heightened levels of motivation to learn which may carry over into other learning areas. This phenomenon perhaps explains in part why some children with learning difficulties have exhibited increased levels of academic achievement following successful encounters with movement experiences.

A common characteristic among mentally retarded and/or emotionally disturbed children is the relatively short attention span. Short attention spans may stem from a variety of causes including a general lack of comprehension, frustrations resulting from repeated failure, inability to perceive purpose or value in the subject matter, or various combinations of the above. Physical education and recreation activities, because they are relatively concrete experiences, tend to facilitate comprehension among such children. Frustrations from failure tend to be reduced, because the threat of repeated failure becomes less ominous and perhaps even secondary. The relative concreteness of movement experiences, coupled with the relative ease with which success and enjoyment are experienced, facilitates the individual's ability to find purpose in what he is doing.

Movement experiences may facilitate the development of sequential-thinking abilities to the extent that such experiences require the individual to think in terms of sequences of movement. Many of the activities presented in subsequent chapters (Developmental Gymnastics; Music, Rhythms, and Dance; Movement Education; Play Therapy) require sequential thinking as an integral part of the movement experience. The need to foster sequential-thinking abilities assumes an air of increased importance when one recognizes sequential thinking's major role in virtually all facets of learning.

Motor planning, closely allied with sequential thinking, involves the ability to plot out in advance the movement patterns which one wishes to execute. One may assume generally that activities which foster motor planning also require sequential thinking. Certain learning theorists suggest that motor planning is the first form of planning experienced by the child, and that motor-planning competence may be prerequisite to the development of planning and sequential-thinking competence in subsequent, more advanced academic tasks.

Heightened perceptual awareness is thought to be closely allied with movement experiences. Theories of perceptual-motor development suggest that all learning involves perception, and that initial perceptual abilities evolve from the child's active (motoric) exploration of the environment. A more thorough explanation of perceptual-motor theory and the development of perceptual competence appears in Chapter VIII, Perceptual-Motor Development.

Movement experiences programmed through physical education and recreation offer vast potential for enriching the lives of the mentally retarded and/or emotionally disturbed. To deny such opportunities would be to deny successful learning experiences, sheer enjoyment in learning, and performance levels which sometimes equal or at least often approximate those of normal peers. Though much remains to be learned in this relatively new field, knowledge seems ever expanding. Perhaps a guiding philosophy has been most aptly articulated by author Pearl S. Buck, who believes that the quality of a civilization may be best judged by the way in which it treats its less fortunate members. In this respect, significant progress has been made in programming learning experiences for the mentally retarded and/or emotionally disturbed, yet what appears even more obvious is that the effort has barely begun.

Chapter **II**

The Status of Physical Education/Recreation for the Mentally Retarded and Emotionally Disturbed

The mental illness in children which we classify today as an emotional disturbance is a twentieth-century phenomenon, but mental retardation has always existed in society. Emotionally disturbed children, until the past few decades, have been treated as mentally retarded. Even today, in many cases the severity of the emotional disturbance leads to an incorrect diagnosis of mental retardation.

The recent compilation of multiple studies of incidence from Title VI State Reports, as shown in the Preface, estimates the number of school-aged handicapped children to be 7,083,599. Approximately 1,387,920 of these children are emotionally disturbed and 1,697,620 are mentally retarded (Nesbitt, 1970).

Characteristics — Emotional Disturbances

Authorities are not in complete agreement as to the cause of emotional disturbances in children. It is generally agreed, however, that they are caused by organic and/or environmental influences which occur early in the life of the child. Emotionally disturbed children are considered to possess limited, inflexible, restricted behavior that impairs adaptation to changing environments and reduces behavioral freedom. As a group these children possess deficiencies in at least one of the following categories:

1. Inability to establish and maintain adequate interpersonal relationships with peers and adults.
   a. Deficient social skills, inability to conform to group patterns, little social conscience.
   b. Demands constant attention or appears antisocial and plays alone.
   c. Follows rather than leads.
2. Inability to respond appropriately in day-to-day life situations. Inappropriate emotional responses.
   a. Unhappiness or depression.
   b. Inconsistencies in response.
   c. Rigidity in expectations of everyday living.
   d. Carelessness, irresponsibility, apathy, low capacity to delay gratification.
3. Inability to learn at a rate commensurate with his intellectual, sensory-motor, and physical development.
   a. Extreme difficulty in the learning process.
      1) Poor work habits.
      2) Lack of motivation.
      3) Disruptive class behavior.
      4) Lack of involvement.
      5) Inability to follow directions or seek help.
      6) Short attention span.
   b. Clumsy and awkward movement patterns.
      1) Poor motor coordination.
      2) Difficulty in making space and time assessments.
4. A variety of excessive behavior patterns.
   a. Hyperactivity.
   b. Hostility.
   c. Fears or fantasy life.
   d. Poor self-concept.
   e. Unhappy and insecure within himself.
   f. Depression and withdrawal.

If the emotionally disturbed child is to benefit from physical education/recreation experiences he MUST experience success in these activities. In addition, the teacher must support the efforts of the child and the environment must be structured with rules and routines established to facilitate appropriate actions and behavior.

Characteristics — Mental Retardation

Mental retardation is not a disease entity but a combination of symptoms derived from many causes, some inherent in the individual and others environmentally induced or determined. The American Association on Mental Deficiency (AAMD) defines mental retardation as follows:

Mental retardation refers to subaverage general intellectual functioning which originates during the developmental period and is associated with impairment in adaptive behavior.

According to this definition, to be classified as mentally retarded an individual must demonstrate deficiency in *both* adaptive behavior and measured intelligence. This definition can be further clarified as follows:

Subaverage general intellectual functioning refers to performance that is greater than one standard deviation below the population mean of the age group involved on measures of a standard IQ test. AAMD suggests the Stanford-Binet intelligence test for this purpose.

The developmental period extends to approximately sixteen years of age.

Adaptive behavior refers to the effectiveness of the individual in maintaining himself independently and in meeting the demands of his environment. It is a very general dimension, composed of all aspects of behavior which determine an individual's competence in dealing with his world. AAMD suggests levels of adaptive behavior be classified by standard deviation units of the Vineland Social Maturity Scale.

Mental retardation is a dynamic concept that can be changed. It is possible for an individual to meet criteria of mental retardation at one time in life and not another. This is especially true with the high grade mental retardate. Frequently these children are not known to be retarded before they enter school, primarily because of their ability to achieve academically up to grade six, and are assimilated into society after graduation.

Many different systems are used to classify the mentally retarded individual.

Psychological Classification

The psychological classification of the American Association on Mental Deficiency identifies different degrees of mental retardation in terms of sigma scores on a psychological examination or IQ test. The Stanford-Binet test of intelligence is usually used for this purpose and identifies these groups as follows:

1. *Profoundly retarded*, IQ 00-19 — requires complete custodial care.
2. *Severely retarded*, IQ 20-35 — can be trained to care for some of his bodily needs; develops some language; has great difficulty in social and occupational areas.
3. *Moderately retarded*, IQ 36-51 — usually unable to master academic skills; can be trained to perform daily routines; can usually perform in a sheltered workshop.
4. *Mildly retarded*, IQ 52-67 — has some degree of educability in terms of reading and writing; is educable in the area of social and occupational competence.

5. *Borderline retarded,* IQ 68-83 — difficult to classify; usually capable of competing with most children in activities other than academic; some are placed in special classes while the majority remain in regular classes in the public schools; many in this category come from culturally deprived areas.

Etiological Classification

Another means of classification of the mentally retarded is according to cause or etiology. These groups are identified as follows:

1. *Organic brain injury* — pathology to the central nervous system.
2. *Cultural familial* — environmentally induced or determined.
3. *Hereditary influences* — example: Down's Syndrome, chromosome imbalance.
4. *Physiological disturbances*—example: Phenylketonuria (PKU), amino acid imbalance.

Educational Classification

Educators frequently classify the mentally retarded into three groups as follows:

1. *Totally dependent,* IQ 00-24 — incapable of being trained for economic usefulness, social participation or total self-care. These children require complete supervision and care throughout their lives because they cannot care adequately for their personal needs, protect themselves, or communicate effectively with others.
2. *Trainable,* IQ 25-49 — can be taught to speak understandably, to play simple games, to perform routine tasks under close supervision, and to develop some self-care skills in providing for their personal needs. These children rarely learn useful reading, writing, or spelling skills. They require partial supervision throughout life. The ultimate goal in working with the trainable retardate is to develop skills necessary for adequate social adjustment and integration in the home or neighborhood and economical usefulness in the home or sheltered workshop.
3. *Educable,* IQ 50-79 — general intellectual functioning which is below the average of the general population, predicted or demonstrated inability to cope with the regular school curriculum at the typical age, potential for achievement of a minimal but significant level of basic academic skills when provided with a curriculum and teaching techniques appropriate to their level and rate of intellectual development, and potential for achievement of those social and occupational skills essential to independent adult living. The educable retardate may be expected to maintain independent living in the community and is capable of learning some academic skills. It is anticipated that current

trends toward the normalization of the mentally retarded into the mainstream of society will eventually result in the disappearance of those children classified as educable or borderline retarded.

Because mentally retarded individuals are limited in the intellectual sphere, they must draw heavily on motor activity for recreational experiences. Therefore, programs of physical education should teach carry-over, recreational motor skills applicable to adult living. In addition to providing leisure activity for the mentally retarded, recreational activity of a physical nature can contribute to the physical, social, and psychological aspects of self-satisfying living for these individuals.

Physical Education/Recreation 1800-1950

In the early 1800s there existed a general apathy toward the mentally retarded members of our society. The severely retarded were merely locked in institutions and forgotten.

The first partial success in the education and rehabilitation of the mentally retarded came in the early nineteenth century with the work of Jean-Marc Itard. In 1801 Itard published his description of Victor, the Wild Boy of Aveyron. This is probably the first record of a systematic effort to educate a child who fell well below the normal in intelligence. Itard undertook this task in 1799. His work with the boy included a variety of sensory experiences, but he was more concerned with limited sensory and sensory motor units of training than he was with large muscle and gross motor involvement.

Edovard Seguin, who trained under Dr. Itard, advocated the bombardment of the central nervous system through sensory and sensory-motor stimulation. He also advocated physical training in the rehabilitation process and introduced many physical education and physical recreation programs into the institutions and schools where he worked.

During the middle of the nineteenth century, schools for the mentally retarded began appearing. Emphasis was placed on education over pure custodial care. But educational attempts were directed toward the needs of society and not those of the mentally retarded individual. The works of Itard and Seguin were continued and expanded, but the physical education aspects were modified and greater emphasis was placed on recreation. Through the first part of the twentieth century the role of physical education/recreation for the retarded was played down primarily due to the changing philosophy of education.

Prior to World War I interest in programs emphasizing the education and rehabilitation of the mentally retarded began to appear. These programs, however, never materialized because all of the energies of society were consumed in a global conflict.

The first studies dealing with the motor ability of mentally retarded individuals appeared in this country in 1919. During the 1920s physical education was considered an adjunct of the education and rehabilitation programs for the mentally retarded. Work-centered recreation programs designed to maintain the child's morale, preserve order, prevent boredom, and alleviate behavior problems were an outgrowth of physical education. Physical education and recreation were used as tools primarily to obtain order and control, with little or no concern placed on rehabilitation and development.

In 1930 the White House Conference on Child Care and Protection passed a "Bill of Rights of the Handicapped." This bill stirred new interests in finding more creative methods to rehabilitate the handicapped. Studies of motor abilities of the mentally retarded began to increase in number, and the philosophy of physical education/ recreation for these children began to change from that of a fringe benefit or means of social control to that of an educational attribute contributing to the total adjustment of the child.

After World War II (1946) parents vitally concerned for the wellbeing of their mentally retarded children formed a "Parent Movement." This group gave birth to the National Association for Retarded Children. A phenomenal growth of interest was created at all levels of government. A changing concept in the institutionalized care of the mentally retarded began to appear. This was accompanied by a broadening in the scope and purpose of services to the mentally retarded at all levels and in all phases of their development.

Physical Education 1950 to Present

The physical education research reviewed from 1950 to the present has been summarized in three general categories which include:
1. Motor performance in mentally retarded and emotionally disturbed children.
2. Motor activity and intellectual functioning of mentally retarded and emotionally disturbed children.
3. Motor activity and social competence of mentally retarded and emotionally disturbed children.

An entire text could be written to analyze and summarize all of the experimental and descriptive research dealing with the various aspects of motor activity and their effects upon the mentally retarded and/or emotionally disturbed child. Therefore, only a small sampling of major works are cited here. For a more complete, in-depth study of research findings the reader should refer to the references cited at the end of this chapter.

A very limited number of research studies were found in the area of physical education for the emotionally disturbed child. Except where specifically cited, therefore, all of the following research deals with the mentally retarded child.

Motor Performance

Summaries of research by Stein (1963) and Malpass (1963) support the contention that the mentally retarded, when considered as a group, are less proficient in motor skills and physical fitness performance than normal children. The results of an investigation by Cratty (1966) indicate that educable and trainable youth exhibit motor deficiencies. The child with Down's Syndrome exhibits gross deficiencies in balance and the educable child is significantly higher in motor performance than the trainable child.

Studies cited in *Physical education and recreation for handicapped children: Proceedings of a study conference on research and demonstration needs* (AAHPER, 1969) indicate that the emotionally disturbed child is lower than normal in hand-eye coordination, exhibits deficits in body image and self-concept and scores below normal on measures of strength, power, agility, coordination, balance, and speed. As a group, emotionally disturbed children exhibit motor competencies typical of much younger children.

A study by Francis and Rarick (1959) indicates that the motor performance of mentally retarded children is two to four years behind that of normal children of the same chronological age. Although the mentally retarded child follows the same developmental pattern as the normal child, this pattern is at a lower level when compared to normal children of the same chronological age. The performance of the mentally retarded remained relatively fixed with age. The mentally retarded child, therefore, fell further behind the normal child as he grew older. The nonorganic educable retardate does not, however, show deficiencies in motor skill development. This research has been supported by Howe (1959) and Rarick, Widdop, and Broadhead (1970).

Oliver (1958), Gearheart (1964), Corder (1966 and 1969), and Solomon and Prangle (1967) conducted research which gives clear evidence that physical fitness and motor skills can be improved through participation in physical education programs. All of these studies, however, used a relatively small number of subjects, covered only a short period of time, and used a rather traditional activity program.

A study conducted by Chasey (1971) indicates that overlearning is an important variable in the retention of gross motor skills by mentally retarded children.

Motor Activity and Intellectual Functioning

Studies comparing motor activity and cognitive functions indicate a low, but at times significant, correlation between these two attributes. In general, however, the findings of investigations made to determine the causative effects of a physical activity program on measures of intelligence point to the need for delineating more precisely the nature of the population to whom motor activities are applied and for the better control of the variables which might have influenced change (Corder, 1966; Leighton, Cupp, Prince, Philabaum, and McLarren, 1966; Oliver, 1958; Solomon and Prangle, 1967; Moran, 1971).

Studies of retardates have been carried out in which a score in a simple motor task (vertical jump test) has been contrasted to IQ, with no significant relationship obtained. When a score of a four-count task (squat thrust test) was compared to an IQ test, a moderate relationship emerged. These findings suggest that some normal motor activities are too complicated for mentally retarded children, because they involve some degree of thought and the ability to remember a series of directions. In this respect, the performance of complex motor task can be related to intelligence test tasks (Fait and Kupferes, 1956).

Oliver (1958) found that he could significantly improve intelligence test scores and motor proficiency of educationally subnormal adolescent boys from residential schools in England after subjecting them to a ten-week, two-hour and forty-minute a day, progressive and systematically planned program of recreational skills and fitness activities. Oliver speculated that this improvement resulted from a heightened motivational state and an improved self-concept. The weaknesses in Oliver's work included his failure to control for the Hawthorne effect and his failure to write down the detailed curriculum used in the study, making it impossible to replicate the research.

Corder (1966) investigated the effects of a systematic and progressive program of physical education on the intellectual development, and social status of educable mentally retarded boys. Corder's study contained three groups of eight boys each: a training group, an officials group, and a control group. The control group remained in the classroom, while the training group participated in one hour of daily activity, five times a week, for four weeks. The officials group was inserted to interact socially with the experimental group as an attempt to anticipate and control for the Hawthorne effect. The training group made significant gains in IQ scores over the control group, but not over the officials group, indicating that the Hawthorne effect was probably operating. However, since there was no difference between the officials group and the control group, the Hawthorne effect plus additional factors must have been functioning, accounting for the gain scores made by the training group. The training group made significant gains over the other two groups in all physical fitness test items. There were, however, no differences in the three groups on the pre and posttests used to measure social status.

Hayden's (1966) data collected on trainable mentally retarded subjects, Shoman's (1966) data collected on profound, severe, moderate, and mild mentally retarded subjects, and Stein's (1966) data collected on educable mentally retarded subjects all indicate no significant relationship between intelligence quotient and physical fitness or motor skill.

Solomon and Prangle (1967) found that improvement in a population of twenty-four experimental group and eighteen control group educable mentally retarded boys, subjected to a special physical education program, was obtained only in motor ability, with IQ and other measures of school achievement remaining unaffected. The experimental group participated in a structured physical education program consisting of forty-five minutes of daily calisthenics, relays, stunts, and games for eight weeks. Although improvement was significant only in motor ability, it was interesting to note that this significant improvement in levels of physical fitness remained significant over a six-week postexperiment follow-up period.

Rarick and Broadhead (1967) investigated the role of physical education activity programs on the modification of the motor, intellectual, social, and emotional behavior of 275 educable mentally retarded children and 205 minimally brain-injured children. The children were equated and randomly assigned to an individualized physical education program, a group-oriented physical education program, an art program (to control the Hawthorne effect), or a control group. The investigation involved exposure to a thirty-five-minute daily program of activity over a twenty-week period of time. Significant positive changes in motor, intellectual, and emotional behavior occurred in the children exposed to one of the three specially planned experimental programs. The physical education programs were superior in modifying motor performance, the art program was superior in modifying emotional behavior, and all three experimental programs were equal in modifying intellectual behavior. A follow-up study conducted by Rarick, Widdop, and Broadhead (1970) supports these results and indicates that, among educable mentally retarded children of the same chronological age and sex, low positive relationships exist between tests of physical ability and measures of intelligence.

Broadhead's (1968) study with educable mentally retarded children and minimally brain-injured children included a thirty-five-minute daily program of planned activity. The teachers used in the instructional program were specially trained. Desirable results recorded as a result of participation in this planned physical education program were obtained in motor, intellectual, and emotional behavior.

Chasey and Wyrick (1970) used a group of twenty educable mentally retarded children in an experimental group and twelve educable mentally retarded children in a control group when studying the effects of a gross motor developmental program on form perception skills. The experimental group participated in a fifteen-week physical development program consisting of gymnasium and playground activities involving conditioning, coordination, gymnastics, and modified sports.

Both groups were involved in some form of activity (three or four subjects per one major student) one hour per day, five days per week. Test results indicated that gross motor developmental programs do not improve form perception skills. In this study both groups improved significantly between pre and posttests.

Goodwin (1970) compared the effects of selected physical education programs on trainable mentally retarded children as it pertained to their physical fitness, IQ, and social maturity. Three groups of ten subjects each were included, two experimental groups and one control group. One experimental group was given a traditional physical education program and the other was provided with a movement exploration program. These two groups met for thirty minutes of daily activity, five days per week for ten weeks. A motivational "award" factor was introduced prior to the testing sessions. Results of the findings of the study, within its limitations, indicated that levels of physical fitness, IQ, and social maturity can be improved in the trainable mentally retarded by the application of either a traditional physical education program or a movement exploration program, with the movement exploration program being slightly superior in improving IQ.

Moran (1971) compared the effects of the front crawl swimming stroke versus conventional developmental tasks on the intelligence quotient and social competence of twenty trainable mentally retarded children ranging in chronological age from five years four months to seven years one month. The children were equated into two groups. The experimental and control groups met for thirty minutes of activity, twice weekly, for ten weeks. An attempt was made to control for the Hawthorne effect by utilizing the same teacher aides to provide instruction to both groups and on a one-to-one basis. Results of the findings of this study, within its limitations, indicated that the front crawl swimming stroke was superior over conventional developmental tasks in the development of the intelligence quotient (.05 level of significance) as measured by the Peabody Picture Vocabulary Test, but that both programs were equally effective in the development of social competence (.01 level of significance) as measured by the Vineland Social Maturity Scale.

Motor Activity and Social Competence

Studies comparing motor activity and social competence are inconsistent in their findings and infrequent in their occurrence in available literature. This research does indicate, however, that motor activity holds great promise for helping mentally retarded children achieve increasing levels of independence and social competence.

Nunley (1965) studied eleven teenage trainable mentally retarded children, pre and posttested them, and subjected them to a daily, forty-five-minute physical education program. Although no tests of statistical significance were applied, the gain scores showed obvious improvement in adjustment and socialization, along with improvement in strength and endurance.

Corder's (1966), Shoman's (1966), and Stein's (1966) studies have been previously cited. All three of these studies showed no significant relationships between motor activity and social competence. Corder's (1969) study did indicate, however, that physical education programs can improve self-concept in mentally retarded children.

Harrison, Lecrone, Temerlin, and Trousdale (1966) investigated the effects of music and exercise upon the self-help skills of nonverbal retardates. Results of this investigation indicate a significantly greater improvement in self-help skills of the nonverbal retardates who participated in a combination of music and exercise treatment.

Jurcisin (1968) investigated institutionalized severely mentally retarded children. Evidence presented in this investigation tends to indicate that a four-week adapted physical education program, in conjunction with the utilization of a "Brief Persistence Technique" by the staff on a twenty-four-hour basis, assists in improving self-sufficiency, physical fitness, and socialization of severely mentally retarded boys.

Goodwin's (1970) study, as previously cited, indicated that levels of social maturity can be improved in trainable mentally retarded subjects. This was accomplished through both a traditional physical education program and a movement exploration program.

Moran's (1971) study, as previously cited, indicated that levels of social competence, as measured by the Vineland Social Maturity Scale, can be improved in trainable mentally retarded children participating in either conventional developmental tasks or the front crawl swimming stroke.

Auxter, Zahar, and Ferrini (1967) indicate that programs of physical activity may enhance the capacity to positively alter body image in emotionally disturbed children.

Research Needs

Although an increasing number of studies have been conducted in physical education for the mentally retarded child over the past several years, the research in all areas of physical education for the emotionally disturbed child is negligent. More well-planned, carefully controlled, scientifically experimental research is needed.

Longitudinal studies are needed to determine the effects of physical activity on all aspects of the intellectual, psychological, emotional, social, and physical development of the mentally retarded and/or emotionally disturbed child. Studies need to be conducted to determine the best teaching methods to facilitate the learning of motor skills in these children and to determine the effect of participation upon self-concept, body image, confidence, desire, level of aspiration, and competitive spirit. In addition, studies need to be conducted to determine curricular content, techniques, approaches, equipment, supplies, facilities, and adaptations needed for effective programming of physical education for the mentally retarded and/or emotionally disturbed child.

Recreation 1950 to Present

Research in the area of recreation for the disadvantaged is extremely limited. In the 1950s most of the existing recreation programs for the handicapped were conducted in state hospitals, state schools, or special schools. In addition, volunteer programs were sponsored by the American Red Cross and the Veterans Administration.

In 1961 President John F. Kennedy appointed the "President's Panel on Mental Retardation" to develop a program that could be implemented in an effective attack on mental retardation and to provide impetus and direction for treatment programs, rehabilitation, and education of the mentally retarded. Recreation was included as one of the program goals.

> The retarded child, like other children, needs opportunity for healthy, growth-promoting play. The adolescent's vital need for successful social interaction and recreational experience is frequently intensified by isolation resulting from parental overprotection, the numerous failure experiences in school and occupational pursuits, and by his exclusion by normal groups from everyday play group and social activities. For the retarded adult, opportunity and constructive use of leisure time may prove a major factor in maintaining community adjustment. [President's Panel, October 1962]

At the time of the "President's Panel" only a small proportion of public recreational agencies in the United States offered program services for the mentally retarded, either in integrated or separate groups.

Surveys conducted by Mumford (1961), Thompson (1969), co-sponsored by the National Recreation Association and the National Association for Retarded Children (Marson, 1965), Andres (1967), and Peters (1967) indicate that there has been an increase in recreational programs and services for the mentally retarded and emotionally disturbed, but that a great lag exists in the development of these services in the community setting in relation to overall population increases and shifts. These surveys indicate that approximately 25 to 35 percent of public agencies, local parks, and recreation departments offer some type of recreation programs to meet the leisure needs of handicapped children. This percentage runs higher for larger cities. In communities which do provide recreation services for the handicapped, the proportion of resources directed to these services are very small, but they are much greater for children than adults and the mentally retarded receive more attention than the emotionally disturbed. Only a small proportion of the number of handicapped children needing recreation, however, are actually being served through these programs. The personnel directing these programs have limited professional preparation in service to the handicapped and the quality of the programs offered and their effect on the development of the handicapped child are largely undetermined. It was also noted in these surveys that most recreational services for the mentally retarded or emotionally disturbed child are too much dependent on voluntary agencies.

The "Resumes of Projects for Handicapped Children Funded under PL 89-313 Amendment to Title I, ESEA, for the Fiscal Year 1967" (AAHPER, 1969) indicates that school centered recreational projects for the handicapped were conducted in special resident or day schools or as adjuncts to the exceptional education classes. Of the 48,263 children receiving recreational services in these special programs, 28,031 were mentally retarded and 5,214 were emotionally disturbed.

The Division of Training Programs, Bureau of Education for the Handicapped (BEH), is presently administering a program authorized by Public Law 90-170, Mental Retardation Amendments of 1967, Title V, The Training of Physical Educators and Recreational Personnel for Mentally Retarded and Other Handicapped Children (H.E.W., 1969). In 1967 this public law provided federal funds to support six recreation grants, one combination physical education/recreation grant, and two summer short courses. In 1968 BEH funded 121 projects, 58 percent of which were related to recreational services. This included thirty projects, totaling $800,000, in leisure education and related services. Fifteen of these projects were in institutions or centers for the handicapped. In 1968 the Hospital Improvement Program (HIP) funded 102 projects, six of which were exclusively recreation oriented. (Hillman, 1969.) For the fiscal year 1973 BEH projects have expanded to include thirty-two physical education/recreation department awards. The total government support of these programs, including special projects, exceeds $1 million.

Although a wide gap still exists between the recreational services provided for and those needed by the mentally retarded and/or emotionally disturbed child, some progress is being made. This can be attributed to federal support of programs, to parents movements (as citizens and taxpayers) demanding "recreation rights" for their children, to state legislation (thirty-two states in 1969) making it mandatory that all new construction of public buildings and facilities be designed so that they are accessible to and usable by the handicapped, and to an increasing concern on the part of recreation specialists and administrators with the large gap caused by the lack of adequate recreational services in the "total" rehabilitation of the mentally retarded and/or emotionally disturbed child.

In 1970 Mumford conducted a follow-up of her 1961 survey. This study indicated that participation in recreation programs for the handicapped in the state of California increased in six years by 155 percent. The programs, however, became increasingly dependent upon volunteers and an increase of 103 percent in volunteer leadership was reported.

The current trend is to integrate the handicapped into regular recreational activities in the community. A five-year study conducted by Pumphrey, Goodman, Kidd, and Peters (1970) indicated that three-fourths of the mentally retarded children placed in ongoing leisure time activities at a community center had done at least minimally well. Although leaders rated the social behavior of retarded members as significantly different from that of normal children in the same groups, differences were manageable and often diminished with continued exposure to normal children.

Community teamwork is essential if public recreation departments are to be successful in meeting the leisure needs of the mentally retarded and/or emotionally disturbed child. Much research is needed so that recreational services for these children can be strengthened and expanded. Recreation is an important "tool" in their total rehabilitation. One institution receiving a grant to study the problem of its returnees reported that 52 percent of the mentally retarded returnees came back to the institution because of their inability to handle leisure time, not because of difficulty adjusting to their employment situations (McGriff, 1970).

Research Needs

Recreation research in the 1970s is needed to consolidate efforts and facilitate program planning for the mentally retarded and/or emotionally disturbed child. Effective models for coordinating inter-agency recreational programs, which will not only meet the mentally retarded or emotionally disturbed child's leisure needs, but also stretch the recreation dollar, are needed. Research should be conducted to assess and evaluate the effectiveness of integrated versus noninte-grated recreation programs in "total" rehabilitation. The problem of transportation to recreational sites must be solved. Municipal recreational agencies must become involved in programs for the mentally retarded and/or emotionally disturbed child, and techniques which will utilize all community resources in the most efficient and economical manner must be developed. Research should also be conducted to determine the most effective method for delivery of recreational services to these children, utilizing available manpower in the most functional manner.

SELECTED REFERENCES

American Association for Health, Physical Education and Recreation and the National Recreation and Park Association. *Physical education and rec-*

reation for handicapped children: Proceedings of a study conference on research and demonstration needs. Washington, D.C.: Bureau of Education for the Handicapped, Department of Health, Education and Welfare, 1969.

Andres, Catherine. The status of municipal recreation for the mentally retarded. Master's project, University of Minnesota, 1967.

Auxter, D. M., E. Zahar, and L. Ferrini. Body image development of emotionally disturbed children. *American Corrective Therapy Journal*, 1967, **21**, 154-155.

Barsch, Ray H. *Achieving perceptual-motor efficiency*, Vol. 1. Seattle: Special Child Publications, 1965.

Benoit, E. Paul. The play problems of retarded children. *American Journal of Mental Deficiency*, 1955, **60**, 41-55.

Benoit, J. Paul. Extending the mind through the body. *Journal of Health, Physical Education and Recreation*, April 1966, **37**, 28-30.

Beter, Thais R. The effects of a concentrated physical education program and an auditory and visual perceptual reading program upon academic achievement, intelligence and motor fitness of educable mentally retarded children. Doctoral dissertation, Louisiana State University, 1969.

Broadhead, Geoffrey D. The role of educational physical activity programs in the modification of selected parameters of the behavior of educable mentally retarded children and minimally brain injured children of elementary school age. Doctoral dissertation, University of Wisconsin, 1968.

Brown, Billy Jo. Some relationships between intellectual, social and physical variables and physical performance of trainable retarded subjects. Doctoral dissertation, University of Cincinnati, 1969.

Bureau of Education for the Handicapped, U. S. Office of Education, Department of Health, Education and Welfare. *Resumes of projects for handicapped children funded under the P.L. 89-313 Amendment to Title I, ESEA F.Y.*, 1968.

Carlson, Bernice W. and David R. Ginglend. *Play activities for the retarded child*. New York: Abingdon Press, 1961.

Chaney, Rex. The effects of a selected recreational activity on the IQ scores, social adjustment, and physical coordination of the educable mentally retarded child. Doctoral dissertation, Indiana University, 1969.

Chasey, William C. The effect of motor development on school readiness skills of educable mentally retarded children. *American Corrective Therapy Journal*, 1970, **24** (6), 180-183.

Chasey, William C. Overlearning as a variable in the retention of gross motor skills by the mentally retarded. *Research Quarterly*, 1971, **42** (2), 145-149.

Chasey, William C. and Waneen Wyrick. Effects of a gross motor developmental program on form perception skills of educable mentally retarded children. *Research Quarterly*, 1970, **41**, 345-352.

Corder, W. Owens. Effects of physical education on the intellectual, physical, and social development of educable mentally retarded boys. *Exceptional Children*, 1966, **32**, 357-364.

Corder, W. Owens. Effects of physical education on the psycho-physical development of educable mentally retarded girls. Doctoral dissertation, University of Virginia, 1969.

Cratty, Bryant J. The perceptual motor attributes of mentally retarded children and youth. Monograph, Mental Retardation Services, Board of Los Angeles County, California, August, 1966.

Cratty, Bryant J. *Motor activity and the education of retardates.* Philadelphia: Lea and Febiger, 1969.

Cratty, Bryant J. and Sister Margaret Mary Martin. *The effects of a program of learning games upon selected academic abilities in children with learning difficulties,* Part I. Washington, D.C.: Office of Education, Bureau of Handicapped Children, 1970.

Cratty, Bryant J. and Sister Mark Szczepanik. *The effects of a program of learning games upon selected academic abilities in children with learning difficulties,* Part II. Washington, D.C.: Office of Education, Bureau of Handicapped Children, 1971.

Delacato, Carl H. *The treatment and prevention of reading problems.* Springfield, Ill. Charles C. Thomas, Publisher, 1959.

Dewey, Margaret. The autistic child in a physical education class. *Journal of Health, Physical Education and Recreation,* 1972, **43** (4), 79-80.

Fait, Hollis F. and Harriet J. Kupferes. A study of two motor achievement tests and its implication in planning physical education activities for the mentally retarded. *American Journal of Mental Deficiency,* 1956, **60**, 729-732.

Fisher, Kirk L. Effects of a structured program of perceptual motor training on the development and school achievement of educable mentally retarded children. Doctoral dissertation, Pennsylvania State University, 1969.

Francis, R. J. and G. L. Rarick. Motor characteristics of the mentally retarded. *American Journal of Mental Deficiency,* 1959, **63**, 792-811.

Funk, Dean C. The effects of a physical education program on the educational improvement of trainable mentally retarded children. Doctoral dissertation, University of Oregon, 1969.

Galvin, John and Peter A. Witt. Recreation for the conduct disorder child. *Exceptional Children,* Summer 1969, 787-791.

Gearheart, Bill R. A study of a physical education program designed to promote motor skills of educable mentally retarded children enrolled in special education classes in Cedar Rapids, Iowa. Doctoral dissertation, Colorado State College, 1964.

Getman, G. N. The visuomotor complex in the acquisition of learning skills. In *Learning disorders,* Vol. 1, ed. J. Hellmuth, pp. 49-76. Seattle: Special Child Publications, 1965.

Giles, Marian T. Fine motor development of retarded and nonretarded children. Doctoral dissertation, Colorado State College, 1969.

Goheen, Royal L. The development and evaluation of three types of physical education programs for educable mentally retarded boys. Doctoral dissertation, Bowling Green State University, 1969.

Goodwin, Lane A. The effects of two selected physical education programs on trainable mentally retarded children. Doctoral dissertation, University of Utah, 1970.

Haley, Betty B. The effects of individualized movement programs upon emotionally disturbed children. Doctoral dissertation, Louisiana State University, 1969.

Hardt, Lois J. An investigation of effective behavior changes through recreation. Doctoral dissertation, New York University, 1965.

Harrison, W., H. Lecrone, M. Temerlin, and W. Trousdale. The effects of music and exercise upon the self-help skills of non-verbal retardates. *American Journal of Mental Deficiency*, 1966, **71**, 279-282.

Hayden, Frank J. *Physical fitness for the mentally retarded.* Ontario, Canada: Metropolitan Toronto Association for Retarded Children, 1964.

Hayden, Frank J. Nature of physical performance in the trainable retarded. Symposium presented at the meeting of the Joseph P. Kennedy, Jr. Foundation, Boston, April 1966.

Hillman, William A., Jr. Federal support of recreation services related to mental retardation. *Therapeutic Recreation Journal,* 1969, **3** (Third Quarter), 6-12.

Hillman, William A., Jr. Recreation in comprehensive planning for the mentally retarded. *Challenge,* May 1968.

Hilsendager, Donald R., Harold K. Jack and Lester Mann. The buttonwood farms project: A physical education-recreation program for emotionally disturbed and mentally retarded children. *Journal of Health, Physical Education and Recreation,* 1968, **39**, 46-48.

Homer, Rouse. Physical education and exceptional children. *Peabody Journal of Education,* 1960, **37**, 340-342.

Howe, C. The comparison of motor skills of mentally retarded and normal children. *Exceptional Children,* 1959, **23**, 352-354.

Itard, Jean-Marc. *The Wild Boy of Aveyron.* New York: Appleton-Century-Crofts, 1962.

Jurcisin, George. The role of brief persistence in motivation of severely retarded boys. Doctoral dissertation, Ohio State University, 1968.

Kephart, Newell C. Perceptual-motor aspects of learning disabilities. *Exceptional Children, 1964,* **31**, 201-206.

Kiphard, Ernst J. Behavioral integration of problem children through remedial physical education. *Journal of Health, Physical Education and Recreation,* 1970, **41**, 45-47.

Leighton, Jack, Marion Cupp, Alfred Prince, Donald Philabaum and George McLarren. The effect of a physical fitness development program on self-concept, mental age, and job proficiency in the mentally retarded. *Journal of Physiology and Mental Rehabilitation,* 1966, **20**, 4-11.

Logan, Annette and Doris Berryman. A national survey of existing recreational services to disabled children and youth. Ongoing, in depth national survey being conducted by New York University, partially supported by the Children's Bureau, U.S. Department of Health, Education and Welfare.

McGriff, Vern H. Social groupings enhance recreation opportunities for retarded children. *Journal of Health, Physical Education and Recreation,* January 1970, **41**, 85-87.

Malpass, L. F. Motor skills in mentally deficiency. *Handbook of Mental Deficiency,* ed. N. R. Ellis. New York: McGraw-Hill Book Co., 1963.

Mann, Lester and Donald W. Hilsendager. The four phases: A new conceptual approach to physical education for emotionally disturbed children. *American Corrective Therapy Journal,* 1968, **22** (2), 42-46.

Mann, Lester and Donald W. Hilsendager. Physical recreation an old-new dimension in helping the emotionally disturbed child. *American Corrective Therapy Journal*, 1968, **22** (4), 131-135.

Marson, Ruth. National survey of community recreation services to the mentally retarded and physically handicapped. Master's thesis, New York University, 1965.

Mitchell, Helen Jo and William A. Hillman, Jr. The municipal recreation department and recreation services for the mentally retarded. *Therapeutic Recreation Journal*, 1969, **3** (Fourth Quarter), 32-39.

Moran, Joan M. The effects of the front crawl swimming stroke on trainable mentally retarded children. Doctoral dissertation, University of Utah, 1971.

Mumford, Barbara C. Current practices in the conduct of public recreation programs for the handicapped in the state of California, 1961. Pilot follow-up study, 1970. In *Papers on program development in recreation and physical activity for the handicapped*, comp. and ed. by John A. Nesbitt, 1971.

Nesbitt, John A. Training and research in therapeutic recreation service for handicapped children: A new era begins. *Therapeutic Recreation Journal*, 1969, **3** (Second Quarter), 3-9.

Nesbitt, John A. The handicapped child: Therapeutic recreation service needs in program, manpower and research. *Therapeutic Recreation Journal*, 1970, **4** (Second Quarter), 33-40.

New Jersey Association for Retarded Children. *Resources for the retarded in New Jersey*. Fifth ed. New Brunswick, N.J.: Standard Press, 1965, pp. 83-99.

Nunley, R. L. A physical fitness program for the mentally retarded in the public schools. *Physical Therapy*, 1965, **19**, 946-954.

Okada, Doris M. The effects of perceptual and perceptual motor training on the visual perception, auditory perception and language performance of institutionalized educable mental retardates. Doctoral dissertation, New York University, 1969.

Oliver, James N. The effect of physical conditioning exercises and activities on the mental characteristics of educationally subnormal boys. *British Journal of Educational Psychology*, 1958, **28**, 155-165.

Painter, Genevieve. Effects of a rhythmic and sensory-motor activity program on perceptual-motor-spatial abilities of kindergarten children. *Exceptional Children*, 1966, **33**, 113-116.

Peters, Martha. *A study of recreation services for the ill and disabled in the state of Illinois*. Field Service, Department of Recreation and Park Administration, University of Illinois, November 1967.

Poindexter, Hally B. Motor development and performance of emotionally disturbed children. *Journal of Health, Physical Education and Recreation*, 1969, **40**, 69-71.

President's Panel on Mental Retardation. *A proposed program for national action to combat mental retardation*. Washington, D.C.: U.S. Government Printing Office, October 1962.

Pumphrey, Muriel, Mortimer Goodman, John Kidd and Edward Peters. Participation of retarded children in regular recreational activities at a community center. *Exceptional Children*, 1969/70, **36**, 453-458.

Rarick, G. L. and G. D. Broadhead. The effects of individualized versus group oriented physical education programs on selected parameters of the development of educable mentally retarded and minimally brain injured children. Madison, Wis.: Department of Physical Education, University of Wisconsin, 1967.

Rarick, G. L., H. J. Widdop and G. D. Broadhead. The physical fitness and motor performance of educable mentally retarded children. *Exceptional Children*, 1970, **36**, 509-519.

Robarge, Arthur J. The effects of social reinforcement and competition on the motor performance of emotionally disturbed and normal children. Doctoral dissertation, University of Connecticut, 1970.

Seguin, Edovard. *Idiocy — Its treatment by the physiological method*. New York: Columbia University Press, 1907.

Sengstock, Wayne L. and Julian U. Stein. Recreation for the mentally retarded: A summary of major activities. *Exceptional Children*, 1967, **33**, 491-497.

Sharpe, Gary D. Effectiveness of specified physical educational programs and establishment of selected motor performance norms for the trainable mentally retarded. Doctoral dissertation, University of Missouri, 1968.

Shoman, Alice M. Movement patterning of a motor skill with mentally retarded children. Doctoral dissertation, University of Utah, 1966.

Smith, Etoyal G. A comparison of two methods of teaching motor skills to trainable retarded children. Doctoral dissertation, University of Alabama, 1969.

Solomon, Amiel and Roy Pangle. *The effects of a structured physical education program on physical, intellectual, and self-concept development of educable retarded boys*. Nashville, Tenn.: George Peabody College for Teachers, 1966.

Solomon, Amiel and Roy Prangle. Demonstrations of physical fitness improvement in the EMR. *Exceptional Children*, 1967, **34**, 177-181.

Solomon, Amiel H. Motivational and repeated trial effects on physical proficiency performances of the EMR and normal boys. Doctoral dissertation, George Peabody College for Teachers, 1969.

Stein, Julian U. Motor function and physical fitness of the mentally retarded. *Rehabilitation Literature*, 1963, **24**, 230-242.

Stein, Julian U. What research says about psychomotor function of the retarded. *Journal of Health, Physical Education and Recreation*, April 1966, **37**, 36-40.

Stein, Julian U. Physical fitness in relation to intelligence quotient, social distance, and physique of intermediate school mentally retarded boys. Doctoral dissertation, George Peabody College, 1966.

Taylor, George R. The relationship between varying amounts of physical education upon the development of certain motor skills in trainable mentally retarded children. Doctoral dissertation, Catholic University of America, 1969.

Thompson, Morton. The status of recreation for the handicapped as related to community and voluntary agencies. *Therapeutic Recreation Journal*, 1969, **3** (Second Quarter), 20-23.

Throne, John. Everybody's problem. *Journal of Health, Physical Education and Recreation*, April 1966, **37**, 24-25.

Troth, William B. Procedures and generalizations for remediation in motor coordination and perceptual training for the mentally retarded. *Training School Bulletin*, 1967, **64**, 77-80.

U.S. Department of Health, Education and Welfare, The Secretary's Committee on Mental Retardation. *Recreation programs for the mentally retarded.* Mental Retardation Report, May 31, 1967, No. 67-6, Washington, D.C.

Webb, Ruth C. Is movement necessary in the development of cognition? *Mental Retardation*, August 1971, 16-17.

Webb, Wellington. Physical education classes for the emotionally disturbed child. *Journal of Health, Physical Education and Recreation*, 1972, **43** (5), 79-81.

Williams, Harriet G. Learning. *Journal of Health, Physical Education and Recreation*, 1968, **39** (9), 28-31.

Witt, Peter A. A historical sketch of recreation for the mentally retarded (1920-1968). *Mental Retardation*, February 1971, 50-53.

Chapter

Basic Physical and Motor Fitness

A major goal of physical education programs for the mentally retarded and/or emotionally disturbed is, or should be, the promotion and maintenance of physical fitness. From the outset of any discourse on physical fitness, it is of major importance to recognize that the term physical fitness is a global one. Physical fitness is a rather complex phenomenon which encompasses a broad spectrum of mutually exclusive entities. These many entities or components of physical fitness are related only to the extent that collectively they represent a barometer of the individual's physical well-being. They are NOT interrelated to the extent that being physically fit with regard to any one entity in any way assures physical fitness in another entity.

The separate entities or components of physical fitness are categorized under two major headings.

Organic Performance	Motor Performance
Strength	Balance
Flexibility	Agility
Muscular Endurance	Speed
Cardiovascular Endurance	Coordination
	Reaction Time

Organic Performance Items

Strength — maximal or near maximal muscular exertion of relatively brief duration. Duration is brief of necessity because of the intense, concentrated muscular effort required. An example of strength activity is pushing a stalled automobile. An example of strength activity in physical education is performing pull-ups (chin-ups), especially when the maximum number possible for the individual is fewer than ten.

The inclusion of muscular strength activities in programs for the mentally retarded and/or emotionally disturbed is of profound importance because a certain amount of strength is required in virtually everything one does. In many instances minimum levels of strength are required before acceptable levels of skill can evolve. For example, before a child can jump with even minimum efficiency, he must possess sufficient muscular strength to propel himself from the surface and to absorb the impact of landing. Inadequate performances oftentimes attributed to low skills are, in reality, attributable to insufficient strength. One should bear in mind that without sufficient strength, performing even the simplest of activities would be difficult if not impossible.

Strength activities are those which concentrate muscular effort on a particular part of the body (e.g. the arms, legs, trunk, back). The concentration of muscular effort must be sufficiently intense to soon result in a decreased capacity to perform. Less intense activity generally is not sufficiently strenuous to stimulate strength development.

Various weights may be used in strength conditioning programs when there exists a need to increase exercise intensity. With commercially produced weights often unavailable, the teacher may improvise weights from logs or plastic bleach bottles filled with sand (see Chapter XII, Innovative Equipment). Rubber inner tube circles may be utilized whereby stretching the rubber stimulates the increased resistance of lifting a weight (see Chapter XII, Innovative Equipment). Chairs, particularly the folding variety because of their compactness, make excellent weights. Either unopened or opened cans filled with concrete may serve as improvised weights. Many teachers use hard cover school books as weights because of their ready accessibility.

The activities shown on p. 27 are suggested as examples of strength exercises utilizing improvised weights.

Flexibility — the ability of body segments to move through normal ranges of motion. Flexibility, like strength, can be a major determiner of success in the performance of many physical education and recreation activities. Many activities which require flexibility whether in physical education, recreation, or in one's daily routine cannot be performed comfortably or are performed at risk when flexibility is lacking.

The unexpected stretching of muscles beyond normal ranges of motion can lead to serious consequences ranging from discomfort to

Step on tube, flex arm

Like shooting a bow and arrow

Place tube around feet, lock knees, pull backward

Arms hold firm, extend neck backward (or sideways)

Examples of Strength Exercises with Inner Tube Strips

the need for surgical repair. Flexibility activities should be a part of the mentally retarded and/or emotionally disturbed child's physical education and recreation experience to an extent that the risk of torn muscles (muscle strains) is absolutely minimized. Such activities are of special importance to handicapped children whose tendencies toward sedentary living often result in inordinate flexibility losses.

Muscles remain flexible only so long as flexibility is required of them. Thus it is important that flexibility activity be pursued on a long range (lifetime) basis in order that desirable patterns of flexibility might be maintained. Inactivity fosters flexibility losses which, in turn, reduce one's capacity to enjoy movement experiences. This cycle may continue until one's lack of flexibility actually begins to dictate one's movement patterns. Much of the flexibility loss which comes with advancing age may well be more a function of inactivity than of age.

In fostering flexibility through exercise, it is important that muscles be extended TO, but NOT THROUGH, the threshold of discomfort. Unless some discomfort is experienced, muscles are not being stretched sufficiently to enhance flexibility. Yet, it is possible to overextend muscles to the point of injury when one stretches much beyond the initial discomfort sensation.

The activities shown on p. 29 are suggested as examples of flexibility exercises.

Muscular Endurance — submaximal muscular effort which extends over a relatively long period of time. Muscular endurance activities do not entail all-out exertions of effort. Rather, they require a continuing persistence of effort. Many activities of the kind seen in industry, sheltered workshops, domestic upkeep, as well as in physical education and recreation are of the muscular endurance type. Lifting medium-heavy weights or meeting medium-heavy resistance of any kind over an extended period of time involves the need for muscular endurance.

Many of the activities used to enhance strength can, with brief alteration, be used to build muscular endurance. Recall that in strength-building activities, the weight used or resistance encountered is of sufficient magnitude to require immediate, near maximal exertion. Because of the activity's intensity, its duration is brief. Activity of this sort may be utilized to enhance endurance merely by reducing the weight used or resistance encountered, and by simultaneously increasing the duration of the activity. As fatigue gradually sets in and the capacity to perform diminishes, one's muscular endurance capability, through being repeatedly taxed, can be steadily enhanced.

Cardiovascular Endurance — the ability of the heart, lungs, and circulatory system to adapt to the demands of prolonged, total body physical exertion. This component of physical fitness is perhaps the most important fitness component of all. It involves the functional integrity of vital organs which govern overall health and life itself. With cardiovascular disease being the number one cause of death in the

Spread legs
as far as possible,
use hands for
support

Touch toes, but
don't bend knees

Try doing a split,
use hands for support

Bend
right

Bend
left

Bend
backward

Examples of Flexibility Exercises

United States and with such disease being the very antithesis of a life abounding in breadth, it behooves the teacher of mentally retarded and/or emotionally disturbed children to actively assist the children in the development and maintenance of cardiovascular fitness. Any activity which is taxing enough to significantly elevate the heart rate for periods in excess of five minutes may be considered cardiovascular activity. Cardiovascular development may be enhanced most effectively when bouts of exercise are encountered a minimum of three times weekly. Typical cardiovascular endurance activities include walking, running, jogging, swimming, and bicycling. Many of the basic motor skills (Chapter IV), when utilized in games of low organization and played for extended periods of time, may promote cardiovascular fitness. Rhythm and dance activities (Chapter VII) may also have cardiovascular fitness value, especially when such activities extend over a period of minutes with little or no rest.

Motor Performance Items

Balance — the ability to maintain a proper relationship between one's points of support (i.e. hands, feet) and one's center of gravity. Balance may be either static or dynamic. Static balance involves balancing in a stationary position. Dynamic balance involves balance when the body is in motion. Both kinds of balance are important to the extent that the need for each is encountered in everyday movement patterns. Children with good balance may be enabled to move with greater effectiveness because of the confidence which good balance inspires. The performance of virtually every movement pattern in physical education, recreation, and in daily life requires good balance, and is enhanced as one's balance improves.

Balance may be developed using the kind of equipment illustrated in Chapter XII (Innovative Equipment) and through developmental gymnastics activities (Chapter IX). Examples of activities designed to improve both static and dynamic balance are shown on p. 31.

Agility — the ability to rapidly and effectively change directions. Agility is an extremely important component of physical fitness, especially in activities where the need to alter quickly the direction of one's movement occurs rapidly, unexpectedly, and often. Agility is important as a means of sidestepping unexpected danger (e.g. jumping from the path of an oncoming car). Agility may be promoted through a variety of low organized games, tag games, and relays. Any activity which requires rapid movement coupled with frequent direction changes may be expected to enhance agility development.

Speed — the ability to rapidly traverse straight, short distances. Speed involves running almost exclusively since running generally is the fastest mode of locomotion. All activities which require quickness in the form of running may be expected to facilitate the realization of one's potential for speed.

One point of
support (swan)

Stand on right foot
(left foot forward),
stand on left foot
(right foot forward)

Balance on
knees

Three points of
support

Balance on
hips

Balance on
one knee and foot

With hands on hips,
walk on tiptoes down
a line on the floor

Two points of
support

Examples of Balance Activities

For the purpose of enhancing speed, the distances run should seldom exceed forty to fifty yards. These distances are long enough to permit the attainment of maximum possible speed, yet short enough to avoid cardiovascular endurance demands.

Coordination — the harmonious teamwork of individual muscles and muscle groups in the production of skilled movement patterns. Coordination involves the ability of muscles to contract with proper intensity, at the opportune moment, and in proper sequence. Coordination is a twofold function of practice and properly directed effort resulting from good instruction.

Reaction Time — the elapsed time between the monitoring of a stimulus by the nervous system and the initiation of the organism's response to that stimulus. Reaction time is the component of physical fitness probably least affected by practice and instruction. While it can be improved somewhat and kept in tune through practice, reaction time must not be expected to improve drastically.

Activities requiring the pursuit of one's reaction time potential bear an important nonphysical (cognitive) value to the extent that rapid reaction time involves the ability to concentrate upon the task at hand. In so doing, an individual must filter out extraneous stimuli in order to monitor, process, and respond to the appropriate stimuli. Brief attention spans and an inability to concentrate on appropriate tasks are behavior patterns commonly observed in mentally retarded and/or emotionally disturbed children. Physical education and recreation activities requiring good reaction time for successful participation provide a highly motivating means of increasing both the attention span and the ability to concentrate upon a single task at hand.

Having now defined and briefly expounded upon each of the components or entities of physical fitness, it is now possible to see the basic difference between the two major fitness categories, organic performance and motor performance.

Organic performance fitness components represent the functions of body systems, namely the circulatory, respiratory, and muscular systems. The development of organic performance fitness is not directly associated with the development of any skill. There are indirect relationships, however, since those who are skilled tend to gravitate toward movement activities which in turn, stimulate organic performance fitness. Organic fitness is not something which one learns, as one would learn a motor skill. Rather, it is something which one trains for.

Conversely, the development of motor performance fitness components is closely aligned with the development of skill. For example, one learns the skills of attaining balance and developing speed. One learns the skills of changing directions rapidly, hence agility. The term coordination implies skill, and reaction time, like most skills, is a learned behavior. Thus motor performance fitness components differ from organic counterparts to the extent that the former are directly learned while the latter are primarily trained for.

There is one additional component of physical fitness which does not fall exclusively under either major category. The component is termed *power* or *explosive strength*. It involves the speed at which muscles are able to contract. Power is really a combination of the motor performance item *speed* and the organic performance item *strength*. Power is the component utilized when one throws, kicks, begins to run, or propels oneself from the surface as in a jump or leap.

It is important to reiterate that proficiency in any one component of fitness does not necessarily guarantee proficiency in any other component of fitness. It is also important to recognize that when physical fitness is the primary concern, activities should be selected with a view to specifically what component of fitness is being enhanced. The activities selected may well be of value in a number of respects; however, it is important to recognize the specific fitness value of the activity when fitness is the primary objective.

The teacher should consider keeping a card file consisting of activities which may be used in the child's physical education and recreation experience. The potential fitness value of each activity in addition to other potential values should be included on each card.

The teacher should keep complete performance records for each child. A substantial portion of the performance record would naturally include the child's performance and progress relative to each fitness component. Cumulative records should be kept to chart advances made by the child over a period of months and years. Data recorded may come from specific physical and motor performance tests or from anecdotal records kept by the teacher.

Measures of Physical Fitness

The following items commonly appear in many physical fitness test batteries and are applicable to performance levels exhibited by mentally retarded and/or emotionally disturbed children.

Pull-ups and Arm Hangs (Strength)

In performing pull-ups certain standardization procedures are required in order to assure the validity, reliability, and objectivity of test results. Diameter of the pull-up bar should be constant for all performers. Everyone's palms should face the same direction when gripping the bar. Note that it is more difficult to execute a pull-up when palms face away from the performer. A complete pull-up is one in which the chin is level with the bar at the top of the exercise, and the arms are fully extended at the bottom. When pull-ups are executed as a fitness test item the teacher should not permit the child to rest in the hanging position between each repetition. The child's score should be the number of correctly completed pull-ups.

Many mentally retarded and/or emotionally disturbed children simply do not possess adequate strength to execute even a single

Pull-Up

pull-up. For these children, the pull-up may be modified. One means of modifying the pull-up is to lower the bar so that the body leans back with heels touching the ground on the mat in front of the bar. The body is held rigid and pull-ups are performed while the heels never leave the ground. All of the standardization procedures suggested for the regular pull-up apply in performing the modified pull-up. In addition, the arms should approximate a ninety-degree angle to the body in the hanging position. This may necessitate some adjustment of the bar from child to child.

For children who can perform neither the regular pull-up nor the modified pull-up, there are the flexed arm and extended arm hangs. It should be noted that the flexed arm hang is somewhat more difficult than the extended arm hang.

In the flexed arm hang, the size of the bar and direction of palm placement should be standard for all children. The child is assisted into the flexed arm hang position and, when ready, is released. His score is the amount of time which he is able to hold his chin level with the height of the bar.[1]

The extended arm hang is similar to the flexed arm hang except that in the latter the child hangs in full arm extension.[2]

---

[1]National norms for this test item for educable mentally retarded children are available. Refer to the American Association for Health, Physical Education and Recreation, *Special Fitness Test for the Mentally Retarded.*

[2]Norms for this item for severely retarded children are available from the Hayden Test, *Physical Fitness for the Mentally Retarded.*

Modified Pull-Up   *Flexed Arm Hang*

Extended Arm Hang

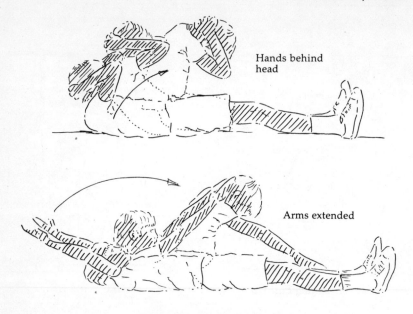

Hands behind
head

Arms extended

*Sit-Ups (Hands Clasped Behind
Head; Arms Extended)*

Sit-ups (Strength)

Sit-ups may be performed either with hands clasped behind the
head or with arms reaching forward to touch the toes as the child sits
up. The latter style of sit-up is easier to execute, because the arms
forward position shifts the torso's center of gravity nearer the hip
joint. It is desirable to have a partner hold down the performer's feet.

Note that any fitness test item which purports to measure muscular strength may, in reality, be measuring muscular endurance if the
individual is able to execute more than ten repetitions of any given
exercise. Likewise, the ability to hang for an extended period of time
may well tax one's capacity for muscular endurance rather than
strength.

Toe Touch (Flexibility)

Construct or secure a sturdy bench. Attach a yardstick to the end of
the bench with the one-inch end of the stick touching the floor. The
child stands on the end of the bench, flexes at the hips, and attempts to
reach as far down as possible. The child should not be permitted to
bend his knees or bounce in attempting to earn a good score. Where
time permits, the best of three efforts should be recorded.

For children who may feel insecure in their ability to balance

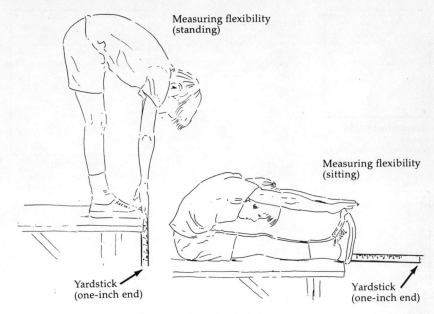

Measuring flexibility
(standing)

Measuring flexibility
(sitting)

Yardstick
(one-inch end)

Yardstick
(one-inch end)

Flexibility

on the bench, essentially the same test may be taken from a sitting position on the floor. Construct or secure a small box. Affix the yardstick to the box so that the distance of the one-inch end of the yardstick to the foot surface edge of the box is identical to the distance between the top of the bench and the floor. In taking the test from the sitting position, the teacher should be sure that the child's feet remain flat against the surface of the box. As in the test which utilizes the bench, the child should neither bounce nor bend his knees in attaining his best possible score. Where time permits, the best of three efforts should be recorded.

Running (Cardiovascular Endurance)

Although running is but one of many possible ways to measure cardiovascular endurance, it is perhaps the most convenient and certainly most widely used. Measures of cardiovascular endurance for the handicapped traditionally have been less intense than those for normal individuals. The 300-yard run-walk which appears on two standardized fitness tests for the mentally retarded is the most commonly used cardiovascular endurance measure.[3]

---

[3]The American Association for Health, Physical Education and Recreation, *Special Fitness Test for the Mentally Retarded*. The Hayden Test, *Physical Fitness for the Mentally Retarded*.

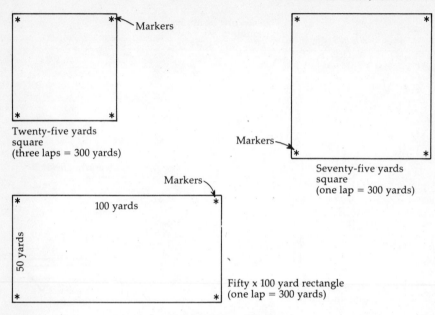

Twenty-five yards
square
(three laps = 300 yards)

Markers

Seventy-five yards
square
(one lap = 300 yards)

Markers

100 yards

50 yards

Fifty x 100 yard rectangle
(one lap = 300 yards)

300-Yard Run-Walk

Any configuration which enables the test to start and finish on the same line is acceptable. Plastic bleach bottles filled with sand or logs may be used to mark the start-finish line and the corners. The above configurations are commonly used.

Stork Stand (Static Balance)

The stork stand may be performed with the following variations, depending on the balance capabilities of the children being tested: hands on hips or hands free to balance; eyes closed or eyes open. In performing the stork stand, the child may stand either flat footed or on the toe. In order to facilitate the comparison of test results each child should, of course, perform the same skill (e.g. stork stand, flat footed, hands free to balance, eyes open). The performances are timed with the longest elapsed time indicating the best balance.

Balance Beam (Dynamic Balance)

Walking the balance beam forward, backward, and sideways provides a means of assessing balance when the child is in motion. To some extent, judgments made of beam-walking efficiency are subjective. For example, a rating scale may be used whereby the child is given a score ranging from one to four depending upon the quality of his performance. Naturally, the performance characteristics required to receive

Tiptoe,
hands on hips

Flat foot,
hands on hips

Tiptoe
hands free to
balance

Flat foot,
hands free to
balance

Stork Stand

any given numerical rating should be clearly enumerated in advance to assure validity, reliability, and objectivity. Roach and Kephart have developed one such rating scale in the Purdue Perceptual-Motor Survey.[4] The Roach and Kephart scale may be used as is or, if more appropriate, as a guideline in developing a rating scale of one's own.

Obstacle Run (Agility)

Sand-filled bleach bottles, logs, or similar obstacles are evenly spaced in zigzag fashion for a distance of approximately thirty to forty feet. The child weaves in and out of the obstacles all the way out and all the way back. The performance is timed with the shortest time indicating the best performance. The width of the zigzag should be such that the child takes no more than three or four steps before having to initiate the next direction change.

Shuttle Run (Agility)

A shuttle run involves running back and forth between two lines which are approximately twenty-five to thirty feet apart. On the line opposite the starting line place two small rubber or plastic toys side by side. From the starting line, the child runs to the far line, picks up one

---

[4]E. G. Roach and N. C. Kephart, *The Purdue Perceptual-Motor Survey.* Columbus, Ohio: Charles E. Merrill Publishing Co., 1966.

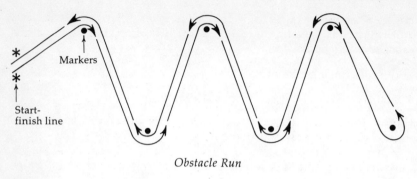

Obstacle Run

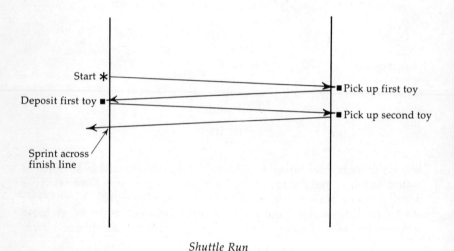

Shuttle Run

toy, then races back and deposits the toy on the starting line. He immediately returns to the far line, retrieves the second toy, and runs back across the finish line as quickly as possible. The performance is timed with the shortest time indicating the best performance.

Sprint or Dash Running (Speed)

The most commonly used means of assessing speed is a brief sprint or dash. The distance should not exceed fifty yards, and may be somewhat shorter with smaller, younger, marginally skilled, or marginally motivated children. The major objective is to see how rapidly the child can run in a straight line from one point to another. For some children it may be desirable to mark a straight line or lanes the entire distance of the dash. This will provide the child with a concrete means of staying on course. The finish line should be plainly marked so that the children know how far to run. In some instances, it is desirable to have an assistant just beyond the finish line both to encourage the child and to point out the finish line.

Throwing (Coordination)

Throwing is a relatively sophisticated skill requiring the combined effort of both upper and lower extremities. The joint actions instrumental in initiating a successful throw must occur at the proper moment and in the precise sequence.

A restraining line should be provided from which all throws are measured. The child should be given ample room behind the restraining line to comfortably initiate the throw, but should be encouraged to release the ball with the lead foot as near the restraining line as possible.

Two assistants should be on the field; one to retrieve the thrown ball and one to mark the spot where the ball lands. The child should be given a minimum of three trys to assure that the best throw has been recorded. Measure performances to the nearest foot.

Standing Long Jump (Power or Explosive Strength)

The child stands on a restraining line and attempts to jump as far forward as possible. The object is to land on the feet without falling backward onto the hands. Measure the distance between the restraining line and the part of the body touching the ground nearest the restraining line. Ideally, this measurement is from the restraining line to the child's heels. Should the child fall back on a hand, the measurement would then be from the restraining line to the hand. Adhesive tape may be placed on the floor and marked off in feet and inches to facilitate measurement.[5]

Vertical Jump (Power or Explosive Strength)

This item is similar to the standing broad jump, but is a less complex skill. It is less complex, because the child need not project his center of gravity off balance forward in executing the skill. For this reason, the vertical jump is perhaps the better of the two measures when dealing with marginally skilled or timid children.

The child stands facing a wall, reaches as high as possible with both hands, and a mark is made on the wall at the top of the fingertips. He then jumps as high as possible, and a mark is made on the wall at the highest point of reach. Measure the distance between the lower and upper marks.[6]

---

[5]National norms for this item for educable mentally retarded children are available. Refer to the American Association for Health, Physical Education and Recreation, *Special Fitness Test for the Mentally Retarded.*

[6]Norms for this item for severely retarded children are available from the Hayden Test, *Physical Fitness for the Mentally Retarded.*

Standing Long Jump

Mark highest
point of reach
standing

Mark highest
point of
reach at top
of jump

Vertical Jump

Fitness Games and Activities

A number of games of low organization, those having a minimum number of rules, provide excellent fitness development opportunities for mentally retarded and/or emotionally disturbed children. When fitness is the primary objective, activities should be selected according to which component or components of fitness they develop. By knowing the nature of any given game or activity and by knowing the kinds of experiences which promote each component of physical fitness, the teacher may soon develop a working file of activities categorized according to fitness value.

The following is a brief example of games and activities selected for specific fitness value:

Squirrels in Trees

Children are designated as being either squirrels or trees. Two children comprise one tree. Trees face each other and clasp hands with arms extended. One squirrel is permitted inside each tree. Squirrels without trees are interspersed in the midst of the activity. When the teacher calls out, *"Squirrels change,"* the trees raise arms on one side, and all squirrels run to get into a tree. Only one squirrel is allowed per tree, so naturally some squirrels are always left in the middle. The object of the game is for the squirrel not to get caught without a tree. The

Squirrels in Trees

teacher should change designation often so that all trees have opportunities to be squirrels.

Potential fitness values include the development of reaction time (moving quickly on command, *"squirrels change"*), agility (changing directions rapidly in search of an unoccupied tree), and explosive strength (powerfully thrusting oneself into motion from a stationary start).

Jump the Shot

The children form a circle. A child in the center of the circle swings a weighted rope around the circle. Note that a dampened towel wadded up and tied to the rope may serve as a safe yet sufficiently heavy weight. The child in the center of the circle gradually lets the rope out until children in the circle are required to jump over the shot. The shot should swing midway between the ankle and knee. A child who entangles the rope by failing to jump in time must take the child's place in the center and swing the shot until another child misses.

Potential fitness values include the development of leg strength and power (jumping), reaction time (properly timing the jump), balance (taking off and landing with weight squarely centered over the feet), and cardiovascular endurance (elevated heart rate resulting from intense, prolonged participation).

Jump the Shot

Loose Caboose

Children are interspersed around the activity area in lines (trains) three deep. The second child in line places his hands on the shoulders of the child at the head of the line. Likewise, the third child in line places his hands on the shoulders of the second child in line. The child at the end of each line is designated as a caboose. The remaining children interspersed throughout the activity area are designated as loose cabooses. The object of the game is for a loose caboose to attach onto the end of one of the trains. The three children forming the train move about in an attempt to keep the loose caboose from attaching. If the loose caboose successfully attaches onto the back of the line (hands on shoulders contact or if his pursuit causes the hand-shoulder contact of the line to break) he becomes a part of the train. The child at the head of the line becomes the new loose caboose.

Potential fitness values include the development of reaction time (loose caboose reacting to movement of the train and vice versa), agility (changing directions rapidly either to contact or avoid contact), and cardiovascular endurance (elevated heart rate resulting from intense, prolonged participation).

Loose caboose   Train

Loose Caboose

Inch Worm

The child assumes a push-up position, keeps the hands in a stationary support position, and walks forward until a sharp inverted *V* or pike position is reached. The feet then become stationary and the hands walk forward until the push-up position has been reassumed. The child continues to repeat the entire movement pattern and thus progresses across the floor in "inch worm" fashion. Note that the inch worm activity can become a relay for more advanced children.

Potential fitness values include the development of flexibility in the hips (stretching in the pike position), muscular endurance (submaximal but prolonged activity for the arms and legs), and coordination (the alternation of arm support while feet move and feet support while arms move).

Feet walk toward line, arms remain stationary

X

X = Reference point

X

Arms walk forward, feet remain stationary

X

Inch Worm

Tag

A variety of tag activities can be played, most of which require a good deal of running. Tag games must have boundary lines in order to prevent the game from becoming a chase between two children away off in the distance. Also, more than one person may be designated as being *IT* in a tag game, thus involving more pursuit.

Potential fitness values include the development of speed (chasing and being chased), agility (having to change directions rapidly to tag or to avoid being tagged), and cardiovascular endurance (elevated heart rate resulting from intense, prolonged participation).

Note that in as few as five relatively simple activities, each entity of physical fitness has been touched upon. This brief selection of elementary (low-organized) activities is presented to reinforce the fact that the ofttimes limited capabilities of mentally retarded and/or emotionally disturbed children need not prevent the realization of physical fitness in accordance with potential.

Chapter IV

Basic Motor Patterns and Skills

Proficiency in performing motor skills provides the mentally retarded and/or emotionally disturbed with a primary means of approximating the performance levels of their normal peers. Though performance levels often fall below those of their normal peers, such handicapped individuals more closely approximate normals in physical and motor performance measures than in any other single measure. This reality opens a broad avenue for the achievement of success by individuals whose successful encounters with learning tend to be rather limited. For mentally retarded and/or emotionally disturbed children who commonly experience frustrations from failure to learn in classroom settings, the relative ease with which their motor skills develop provides a refreshing measure of success. Such success experiences may be used as extremely potent tools in the enhancement of the child's self-image. Having succeeded in doing something valued by himself as well as by others, the child soon may begin to develop a better opinion of himself. An enhanced level of self-esteem may not only heighten motivation to learn additional motor skills, but may in fact have carry-over value for improving one's attitude toward learning in general.

Two time-honored clichés suggest that all children love to play and that play comes naturally for children. The credibility of such statements is most certainly questionable when dealing with mentally retarded and/or emotionally disturbed children. Play, even by oneself, is not particularly rewarding if few skills for play exist. Play with others almost invariably requires some quantity and quality of motor skill. Whether or not one enjoys play depends to a large degree upon whether one possesses the motor skills potentially capable of making play enjoyable. See Chapter V, Play Therapy.

The possession of a broad spectrum of motor skills increases the child's opportunities to become actively involved in play experiences with others. Active and regular participation in play experiences creates a most effective medium through which socialization processes become activated. Proficiency in motor skills and the play experiences which motor skills invoke may help supplant the child's ego-centered behavior patterns with a desire to cooperate with others and become part of a larger group.

Basically, there are two major categories of motor skills: phylogenetic and ontogenetic. Phylogenetic skills are those skills which are virtually instinctive. Such skills are a part of one's biological heritage, and seem to develop naturally among all members of the species. Phylogenetic skills often appear even in the absence of formal instruction provided the environment abounds in opportunity for such skills to appear and be practiced. Because mentally retarded and/or emotionally disturbed children are often deprived of ample opportunity to learn phylogenetic skills naturally, and because such skills do improve with practice, their inclusion in the child's physical education and recreation experiences is most certainly warranted.

The following enumeration and ensuing discussion of phylogenetic skills is by no means exhaustive, but includes those skills commonly encountered in physical education, recreation, and daily life experiences. They include: crawling and creeping, walking, running, hopping, skipping, sliding, galloping, leaping, jumping, kicking, ball bouncing, throwing and catching, pushing, pulling and lifting, and carrying.

Crawling and Creeping

Crawling is forward motion on the stomach which involves the entire body in contact with a surface. It is a smooth and coordinated movement. The right hand and left leg work simultaneouly and the left hand and right leg follow in the same manner. Each side of the body operates as an independent unit, with action alternating from left to right along a forward path. The head can either rotate slightly from side to side, looking at the forward hand as it strikes the floor, or be kept up to guide the direction of locomotion.

During creeping the trunk is elevated and the child assumes a quadrupedal stance. Forward motion occurs on the hands and knees in a smooth, coordinated, and perfect cross pattern. The extension of the right hand and the lift of the left knee, or the left hand and right knee, should be activated in a simultaneous action of forward movement.

Crawl

Creep

The hands, providing direction, should be placed flat on the floor, with fingers pointed straight ahead. The knees should be balanced under the pelvis, with the feet relaxed and the toes in contact with the floor. Minimum body rotation and smooth action of the limbs should occur. Eyes should be either focused on the back of the forward hand or kept up to guide the direction of locomotion.

When teaching children the skills of crawling and creeping, a good demonstration should precede the trials by the child. Frequently it may be necessary to guide the child's body parts through the correct crawling and creeping movements, especially the first few times the skills are attempted.

Variety in practicing the skills of crawling and creeping can be obtained by using a crawling tunnel or having the child travel a winding path, circumventing obstacles or following geometric forms. The child can follow a path of colored markers for his hands and feet or travel over and under obstacles. An obstacle course can be set up to include these and many other unique and varied patterns for the practice of crawling and creeping skills.

Walking

Walking is perhaps the most often used basic locomotor skill. It is incorporated in daily living to such an extent that the quality of one's walk is often taken for granted. Physically and mechanically, walking is the least demanding of bipedal locomotor skills. This is evidenced by the fact that walking is the first of the bipedal locomotor skills to appear in young children. Should the skills of walking never be mastered sufficiently, the child may not experience sufficient motivation to pursue the development of subsequent bipedal skills.

Mechanically correct walking begins with good posture. The description of good posture for any given individual entails an alignment of body segments resulting in minimum fatigue for that individual. Hence, good posture is to some degree an individual matter. The body alignment which constitutes good posture for any one individual may not necessarily constitute good posture for another. There are, however, certain key body alignment characteristics which generally are indicative of effective posture for all.

Good posture whether standing or walking is not necessarily a posture characterized by ramrod straightness. The spine naturally has two curves; a thoracic curve (upper spine) and a lumbar curve (lower spine). These curves should be moderate. The thoracic curve should not be such that it invokes a forward protrusion of the head and neck. In good thoracic curve posture the ear is generally aligned directly over the top of the shoulder. In good lumbar curve posture, the child should be able to stand with his back, hips, and heels against the wall and snugly fit his hand (palm flat against the wall) between the lumbar region and the wall. If the hand fits loosely, the lumbar curve may be excessive.

An excessive lumbar curve often produces an excessive thoracic curve and vice versa. These excessive curves place undue stress upon the posture muscles and ligaments which endeavor to maintain the spinal column in an erect position. Also, undue stress may be placed upon the last lumbar vertebra which junctions with the pelvis.

An excessive lumbar curvature often is accompanied by a sagging abdomen. This is caused by the fact that the forward tilted pelvis has caused the stomach muscles to stretch and become flaccid. An excessive thoracic curvature often is accompanied by a sunken chest. The chest, if sufficiently sunken through poor posture, may actually cause some mechanical blockage of breathing.

One may also note the existence of lateral curves in the spine. Lateral curves may be most easily spotted when viewing the child from the rear. Look for an elevated shoulder or shoulder blade and/or a tilted hip accompanied by a lateral deviation of the spinal column itself.

The feet should be pointing directly forward in good posture.

This helps assure that the feet are in a mechanically advantageous position to bear weight and facilitate locomotion.

Deviations from what is normally considered good posture should be assessed by a physician, preferably a pediatrician or an orthopedist. His assessment will assist in determining the degree to which the child's posture problems are remediable. To the extent that they are remediable, he may suggest appropriate activities and exercises.

The characteristics of good posture are an integral part of mechanically efficient walking. In addition, when walking, the arms should swing in opposition to the legs. In walking, weight is transferred from the toe of the trailing foot to the heel of the lead foot. All movements of both the arms, legs, and feet should be in line with the direction of the walk.

Learning to walk normally and naturally is an extremely vital skill for many mentally retarded and/or emotionally disturbed individuals. The public has stereotyped the ways in which it believes handicapped individuals are supposed to look. Unfortunately, the more deviant one looks the less likely are one's chances of success among many normal peers who dominate the society. One such stereotype involves the manner in which the handicapped carry themselves when walking. The handicapped individual whose postural carriage and walking characteristics approximate society's stereotype may find himself encountering unwarranted discrimination and rejection.

Learning to walk and carry oneself well is certainly no panacea for society's acceptance of the handicapped. In fact, such an approach circumvents rather than solves the problem created by society. The handicapped, however, cannot wait for society's stereotypes to dissolve. In the meantime, such skills provide immediately effective tools by which inroads to society can be made.

Running

Running is man's most rapid form of bipedal locomotion and is an integral part of many physical education and recreation activities. The child who has learned to run well is potentially capable of enjoying a host of physical education and recreation activities. Running well is an especially important skill among mentally retarded and/or emotionally disturbed children for whom success experiences are oftentimes quite limited. The inability to run well virtually assures failure in many activities. Such failure, particularly among mentally retarded and/or emotionally disturbed children, may prove sufficiently frustrating to invoke an avoidance reaction to those very activities which conceivably could bring years of enjoyment.

Running is an equally important skill in daily living. Often one must run to arrive at a given destination on time, or one may be required to run in an emergency. When speed is the major objective, there is no effective alternative to running.

The major difference between a run and a walk is that no matter how rapidly one walks, both feet are never off the ground at the same time. In walking, the heel of the lead foot contacts the ground before the toes of the trailing foot leave the ground. A walk becomes a run when the trailing foot breaks contact with the ground before the lead foot makes contact with the ground. Therefore, it is conceivable that a fast walk can be faster than a slow run. Frequently, in fast running, the heel never comes into contact with the ground.

Skilled running is characterized by the ability to run in a straight line. This is logical since stepping in any direction other than straight ahead would be counterproductive in terms of speed. The child may be assisted in visualizing correct foot placement if a long straight line is drawn upon the running surface. A line approximately two inches in width extending the full length of the distance to be run provides a concrete means of seeing proper foot placement the moment it occurs. To avoid failure among children whose feet seldom hit the line, lanes may be provided to direct proper foot contact. The lane may be twelve inches wide to begin with and gradually be made narrower as the child's skill level improves.

The feet should point straight ahead in running or perhaps be slightly pigeon-toed. This angle of foot placement maximizes the foot's leverage and thrust. Positioning of the feet may be seen if the child runs along a straight line in loose dirt. The angle of foot placement may then be viewed in relation to the straight line. Foot placement should be parallel to and preferably superimposed upon the line. The most commonly noted error in angle of foot placement is the toes-out position. Note that this angle of foot placement greatly reduces the foot's potential for leverage and thrust, hence substantial speed is lost. If the child is running on a hard surface, powdered chalk liberally dusted on the bottoms of the shoes, will record the child's foot placement.

In running, the arm swing should naturally oppose the feet. Arm swing should be in a forward-backward plane. Arm swing in any other direction is counterproductive to the development of thrust in the intended direction.

The head should remain stable, pointing in the intended direction of travel. Rotating one's head to the left and right as one runs can be uncomfortable and to some extent make it difficult to stay on course. Rotating the head back and forth is especially evident when children endeavor to run as fast as possible.

Running requires forward lean in order to maintain forward momentum. Generally, the faster one wishes to run, the greater should be the forward lean. When one is comfortably jogging, forward lean

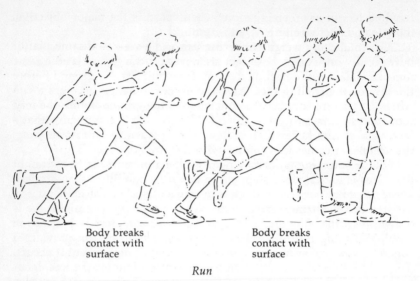

Body breaks   Body breaks
contact with   contact with
surface   surface

Run

may be hardly discernible. Yet, when one sprints forward, lean may be pronounced.

In all running, one should endeavor to relax. Relaxation while running facilitates coordination and helps minimize fatigue resulting from extraneous effort. Two indicators of relaxation occur when the jaw, hands, and fingers loosely wabble as one runs.

Note that there are occasions in physical education or recreation activities when one might be required to run backwards. This warrants at least minimal attention to the development of backward-running abilities.

Hopping

Hopping is defined as taking off on one foot and landing on the same foot. One should be able to hop on either foot and in any direction.

The leg which is not used for hopping is kept off the floor by bending it at the knee. The nonhopping leg and arms aid the body in balance. If the arms are not needed exclusively for balance, they can aid in lifting the body into the hopping movement.

Hopping is an extremely important basic motor skill in terms of safety. When one is pushed or falls off balance in any direction other than directly forward or backward, one hops to regain balance. The push or fall transfers weight solely onto one foot. Before balance is completely lost, the weighted foot and leg momentarily thrust the body into the air. While airborne, the same leg is aligned with the child's direction of travel. Thus, upon landing, balance is regained.

Hopping tends to be the most demanding of the basic locomotor skills in terms of strength requirements. This is true because hopping requires total body weight to be carried on one leg (the same leg) in each phase of the activity. For this same reason, hopping is also most demanding in terms of balance.

Children should be encouraged to hop in hopscotch type games or in relays. Colorful marks (e.g. footprints) should be drawn randomly upon the playing surface; the children should be encouraged to hop from mark to mark. In the initial stages of learning to hop, marks on the playing surface should be placed relatively close together. As hopping skill improves, marks may be placed increasingly farther apart.

Hopping from spot to spot may provoke timidity among children who fear the possibility of lost balance and a subsequent fall. If the child cannot hop from spot to spot, begin by having the child take off vertically and land in the same spot. The teacher may wish to hold the child's hand as an additional means of inspiring confidence. Should difficulty still be encountered, an assistant may be called upon to hold the child's other hand. If the child's hand is to be held, support the child no more than necessary to assure success. This approach enables the child to get a more true feel of the skill as soon as possible.

Hop

In teaching children to hop, one notices that they naturally tend to hop forward and on the preferred foot. To ensure that hopping becomes a truly versatile skill, be sure to provide learning opportunities which encourage the child to hop on the nonpreferred foot as well as the preferred foot and in a variety of directions.

Skipping

Skipping is perhaps the most complex of all basic locomotor skills for the mentally retarded and/or emotionally disturbed to learn. It involves not only an alternation of feet, but a combination of one walking step followed by an immediate hop on the same foot.

Mentally retarded and/or emotionally disturbed children should have mastered both walking and hopping before attempting the skip. The pattern for skipping is: left foot — step, hop; right foot — step, hop. In fact, the verbal command *"step—hop, step—hop, step—hop"* provides not only a verbal cue of the appropriate action, but also the correct rhythm.

The arm swing in skipping is similar to the alternate arm swing used in walking and running. The arms aid in maintaining body balance and assist in obtaining height. To obtain the desirable springy, joyful, carefree quality in skipping, movements should be performed on the balls of the feet.

Because skipping is a relatively complex basic motor skill, the teacher may need to employ relatively more concrete modes of instruc-

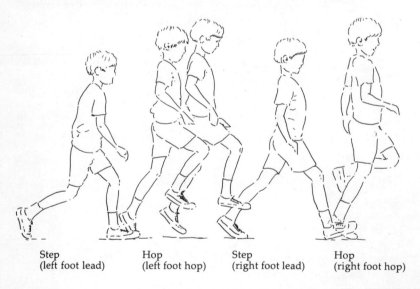

Step   Hop   Step   Hop
(left foot lead)   (left foot hop)   (right foot lead)   (right foot hop)

Skip

tion. One such mode involves the use of a full-length mirror. Both teacher and student hold hands and stand side by side approximately fifteen feet in front of (facing) the mirror. The child is instructed to perform simultaneously with the teacher. In addition, the teacher may verbally cue the child with *"step—hop, step—hop."* The combination of visual cues from the mirror and verbal cues from the teacher greatly facilitates the learning of this relatively complex skill. As the child progresses, the mirror no longer need be employed. Teacher and student still hold hands and skip to the teacher's *"step—hop"* verbal cue. Eventually, the *"step—hop"* verbal cue is sufficient, and the child skips by himself. Finally, the child may skip alone with no cues whatsoever from the teacher.

Because skipping is a highly rhythmic motor skill, the teacher may wish to incorporate records as a teaching aid. Any 2/4, 4/4, 3/4, or 6/8 time recording in which the beat is heavily emphasized and/or staccato would be appropriate. Initially, the teacher should verbally cue the children with *"step—hop"* until they naturally begin to pick up the rhythm from the music. Variety can be added by skipping for height, distance, or following patterns on the floor. See Chapter VII, Music, Rhythms, and Dance.

Sliding

Sliding is the most effective basic locomotor skill for rapid lateral movement. It permits not only quick movement to one side, but facilitates a rapid stop and the commencement of a slide back in the opposite direction.

Many of the games and activities enjoyed by mentally retarded and/or emotionally disturbed children require sliding as the most appropriate motor skill. Such games involve situations where one child is IT and another child attempts to run past IT to reach a goal or a safety zone. As the runner begins to weave and switch directions in an effort to get past, IT shadows the runner by sliding from side to side until the runner commits himself to running in one direction. If IT would prematurely break into a run and thus commit himself to one direction, the runner might easily take off in the opposite direction and reach his goal unimpeded.

Sliding is also an important skill to be incorporated in catching a ball which has been thrown or hit to one side of the catcher. If the ball is obviously to one side, the child may run to catch the ball. However, if the child is nearer the ball, one or two slide steps in the appropriate direction most quickly place the child in position to catch the ball.

The movement pattern for the slide is step—close step. In sliding to the left, the left foot would step to the side followed by an immediate slide of the right foot into position next to the left foot. This sequence would continue as long as a slide to the left was the objec-

| Step | Close step | Step | Close step |

Slide

tive. In sliding to the right, the right foot would step sideways first, followed by an immediate slide of the left foot into position next to the right foot.

Sliding may be taught most easily to mentally retarded and/or emotionally disturbed children if teacher and student face each other and hold hands. The child is instructed to do as the teacher does. Holding the child's hands, the teacher slowly begins to step—close step. As the child begins to move effectively with the teacher, the tempo may gradually increase. As the child's skill improves, teacher and student may work parallel to each other, but need not hold hands. Sliding may be taught using a full-length mirror with teacher and student performing side by side.

The slide may be performed to music in 2/4, 4/4, 3/4, or 6/8 time. Music selected should exhibit a staccato, well-accented quality. For rhythmic application of sliding see Chapter VII, Music, Rhythms, and Dance.

Galloping

Galloping is a modification of sliding. It involves the same step—close step foot pattern but is used for movements in a straight forward-backward plane or in a diagonal plane.

Galloping is used in situations similar to those in which sliding is used. The determination of whether one slides or gallops depends solely upon the direction of movement. Step—close step sideways or laterally is a slide. Step—close step in any other plane becomes a gallop.

When galloping diagonally to the right, the right leg leads in the step—close step pattern. When galloping diagonally to the left, the left leg leads in the step—close step pattern. When galloping either in a straight forward or backward direction either foot may take the lead depending upon the child's preference.

Galloping is most easily taught to mentally retarded and/or emotionally disturbed children through use of a full-length mirror. The child works beside the teacher and is instructed to parallel the teacher's movements.

To assure versatility in galloping, be sure to provide galloping experiences in all directions. Being able to slide in either direction sideways and to gallop in all remaining directions enables the child to move quickly in all directions without having to commit himself to any one direction. When a direction commitment is decided upon, the child merely ceases to gallop or slide and breaks into a run.

Creativity in galloping may be added by having the child imitate his interpretation of a farmer's horse, a parade horse, a frisky horse, or a race horse. In addition, the gallop may be performed to a moderate

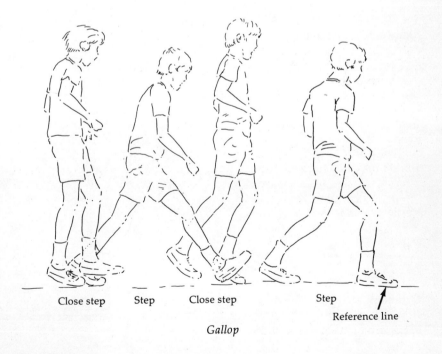

Close step   Step   Close step   Step

Reference line

Gallop

tempo of uneven rhythm in 2/4, 4/4, 3/4, or 6/8 time. The music should be of a staccato and well-accentuated quality. For rhythmic applications of galloping, see Chapter VII, Music, Rhythms, and Dance.

Leaping

Leaping is similar to running and is often used in conjunction with running. Where running accentuates forward motion, leaping accentuates upward motion. In leaping, as in running, the child takes off on one foot and lands on the other foot. Though there is no set rule regarding when a run becomes a leap, suffice it to say that a run becomes a leap when more effort is expended going upward than going forward.

In the takeoff phase of the leap as in the landing, weight should be concentrated on the ball of the foot. This provides maximum spring on takeoff and maximum cushion on landing. The knee bearing the weight upon landing should be slightly flexed to avoid jarring upon impact.

A leap may be used as the means of surmounting small obstacles. For example, one might leap across a small puddle or over a fallen log.

Leap

Leaping may be used in conjunction with a run to surmount greater obstacles. One may leap in conjunction with a run to catch a ball in flight.

In teaching children to leap, be sure to encourage the use of both the left foot and right foot as the takeoff foot. If the child can leap with equal ease off of either foot the skill naturally becomes more versatile.

Lengths of rope may be used in teaching the child to leap. Two ropes may be stretched and placed parallel to each other. The distance between the ropes may vary in accordance with the child's physical size and capabilities. The area between the ropes may be referred to as a river, and the child's objective is to leap across the river. Initially, the child may leap from a stationary position. As the child's skill improves, the leap may be preceded by a walk or run. To make the obstacle more challenging, the ropes may be placed farther apart and/or assistants may hold the ropes off the ground. If ropes are to be held above ground by assistants, be sure that the ropes are held in such a way that they may be easily released should the child catch his foot on a rope.

Colorful marks placed on the floor may be used as targets in leaping. Random placement of the marks may stimulate the child to leap for height, distance, and in various directions. For rhythmic applications of leaping see Chapter VII, Music, Rhythms, and Dance.

Jumping

Jumping is defined as taking off on either one or two feet, but landing on two feet. One may jump from a stationary position or from a run. Although one may jump in any direction, most jumping tends to occur vertically, straight ahead, or very nearly straight ahead.

The power necessary for a successful jump results from a vigorous extension of the hips, knees, and plantar flexion of the feet. The arms assist in lifting the body by swinging upward or forward in the desired direction of the movement. When landing from a jump the body should be relaxed. The balls of the feet contact the ground first while the knees and ankles bend to absorb the force. The arms may assist in balancing the body as the legs are extended and the child returns to a standing position.

In teaching the mentally retarded and/or emotionally disturbed child to jump vertically, encircle a piece of rope on the ground. The child's objective is to stand in the circle, jump vertically, and land back inside the circle. In order to motivate the child to jump straight up, the teacher may suspend a brightly colored ball or familiar toy directly above the circle. The object should be suspended with elastic to prevent its being detached when caught. If the elastic is suspended through an eyelet in the ceiling, the height of the ball or toy can be easily varied according to each child's vertical jumping capabilities.

One-foot
takeoff

Two-foot
takeoff

Jump

In teaching the mentally retarded and/or emotionally disturbed child to jump forward, two lengths of rope placed parallel to each other may be used identically to the way used when teaching the child to leap. In jumping the distance spanned by the two ropes, the child may take off from one or both feet. If the takeoff is on one foot, the takeoff may be preceded by a walking or running start.

Jumping off a low step while the teacher holds the child's hand may also facilitate the development of skill in jumping. Variety and motivation can be added to step jumping by painting colorful circles on the floor for the child to use as a landing target, and by increasing the number of steps from which he can jump into this target. If more than one step is used the child should jump from the side rather than forward over the obstacle of the lower step.

Kicking

One may note that kicking is a somewhat different type of motor skill than those previously discussed. All previous skills might be termed body projection skills. Each of the previous bipedal locomotor skills represents a means of projecting or moving one's body through space. Conversely, kicking is an object projection skill. The purpose of any object projection skill is to impart velocity to a projectile (e.g. a ball). Though one may well project one's body through space in an object projection skill, the basic purpose of such movement is to control the projectile's velocity and accuracy.

Kicking requires foot-eye coordination. Most American children never come close to realizing foot-eye coordination potential because foot-eye coordination activities tend not to be emphasized in American physical education and recreation. For mentally retarded and/or emotionally disturbed children whose formal physical education experiences often are nondirected and sometimes nonexistent, kicking skills seldom develop to the point of versatility and enjoyment. The lower extremities tend not to approach their potential for dexterity, and interest in kicking activities unfortunately wanes at an early age.

A ball may be kicked from a walk or run or it may be kicked from a stationary position. In either instance the ball may be rolling or it may be standing still.

In all kicking, the eye should be kept on the ball. This facilitates the desired foot-eye contact with the ball, hence foot-eye coordination.

The ankle of the kicking foot may be turned outward so that the ball is contacted by the inside of the foot. The ankle may be turned inward so that the ball is contacted by the outside or outside-top of the foot. The foot may point straight ahead so that the toe contacts the ball.

Controlling the ball is most difficult when the toe contact is utilized. The relatively pointed and small contact surface of the toe makes the direction of the ball highly unpredictable among marginally skilled and beginning kickers.

The height of the ball when kicked is determined in large part by the placement of the nonkicking (supporting) foot. With the supporting foot placed beside the ball, the ball may be expected to soar upward as well as forward. This is true because the placement of the supporting foot is such that it allows the kicking foot to get well under (and scoop up) the ball. With the supporting foot placed well behind the ball, the ball may be expected to follow a relatively low trajectory. This occurs because placement of the supporting foot behind the ball does not permit the kicking foot to get too far under the ball.

A series of short kicks designed to get the ball from one part of the play area to another is termed dribbling. In dribbling the ball, the prime concern is to keep the ball relatively close to the feet, and thus under control at all times. Dribbling is first performed in conjunction with walking, then with running.

In teaching children to kick, a wall may be incorporated so that the rebounding ball comes back to the child. The direction of the rebound immediately tells the child whether or not the ball was kicked in the intended direction. In a similar activity, children form a circle and kick the ball back and forth to one another. Note that in either

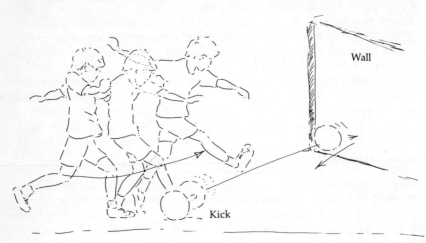

Wall

Kick

Kicking

Student running
or walking toward
ball to be kicked

Ball being
rolled to
student by teacher
or teacher's assistant

Kicking

Start-finish
line

Dribbling

activity, the ball may be kicked while it is moving or stopped and
kicked from a stationary position.

The children may walk or run to kick an oncoming ball which
has been rolled by the teacher or an assistant.

Dribbling may be taught by having the child maneuver the ball to
a given point and back again. This activity may become a relay with
more advanced children.

It is important that children learn to kick with either foot. The
child who kicks well with either foot is naturally a more versatile performer. In teaching mentally retarded and/or emotionally disturbed
children to kick with a specific foot, it might be desirable to tie a ribbon or similar colorful object to the kicking foot. This will help the
child remember which foot he is supposed to be using. It also enables
the teacher to immediately determine whether or not the child is using
the intended foot.

Ball Bouncing

Ball bouncing, also called dribbling, plays a major role in many physical education and recreation activities. It is a skill which requires concentration, visual tracking, and hand-eye coordination. The child may stand still while bouncing the ball or may walk, run, slide, or gallop.

In bouncing the ball, the child should be instructed to tap the ball, not slap it. A slapped ball soon bounces out of control. As the child becomes more highly skilled, he should be taught to bounce the ball off the thumb and fingertips. This affords greatest control over the ball.

Recordings in which the beat is heavily emphasized may be used as an aid in teaching children to dribble. The teacher should first practice with the record to be sure that the tempo is neither too fast nor too slow. When the record is used, the teacher should bounce the ball along with and in full view of the children. The teacher's participation plus the heavily accentuated beat of the recording gives the child both visual and auditory cues by which to conceptualize the rhythmic pattern which underlies dribbling.

In the initial stages of dribbling, the child may need to use both hands simultaneously. He may thrust the ball toward the ground with both hands and catch it with both hands following the rebound. As the child progresses in skill he may be soon capable of dribbling with one hand. At this stage, the child should be taught to dribble with either hand in order that dribbling might become a fully versatile skill.

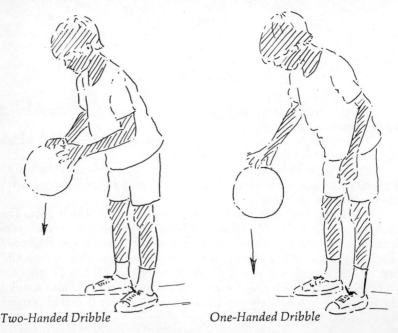

Two-Handed Dribble   One-Handed Dribble

Throwing

It is difficult to overemphasize the value of throwing skills in the mentally retarded and/or emotionally disturbed child's physical education and recreation experience. Throwing skills are of importance not only for their own sake, but are thought by some to be valuable lead-up skills in a variety of club, bat, and racket swinging activities. Throwing skills may be divided into three categories: underarm throws, sidearm throws, and overarm throws.

The underarm throw is perhaps the easiest throw of all to learn. In its initial stages, the underarm throw requires little more than a pendulumlike swing of the preferred arm. At a more advanced level, a step forward with the left foot preceeds the release of the ball, followed by a follow-through step with the right foot (right-handed throw). Learning to roll a bowling ball is an example of the kind of skill for which the underarm throw may be a lead-up.

Learning to throw sidearm is perhaps the least valuable skill for throwing's sake alone. In most throws where a sidearm throw might be used, an overarm throw is potentially more effective. Learning to throw sidearm, however, may be important as a lead-up skill in many racket, club, and batting activities. Swinging a baseball bat, table tennis paddle, or badminton racket is thought by some to be merely an extension of the sidearm pattern. Suffice it to say that proficiency in sidearm throwing might serve as a foundation for skills in which the length of the arm (and the margin for error) is increased through use of some implement for striking.

The overarm throw is generally the most effective of all throwing patterns in terms of velocity and distance potential. It may also serve as an important lead-up skill for swinging an implement overarm. One such example is casting a fishing rod.

Underarm Throw

Sidearm Throw

An extensive study of overarm throwing has been made by Wild (1947). Wild has found that four phases of overarm throwing evolve which are associated closely with chronological age. Though Wild's data were collected on normal children, the progression observed by Wild is applicable to the mentally retarded and/or emotionally disturbed. Also, the chronological age at which a particular pattern appears helps enable the teacher to assess the child's advancement or retardation in overarm-throwing ability relative to normal children.

Phase one (chronological age: two to three years). This throw involves only the arm. There appears to be no shift in body weight or rotation of the trunk. Both feet remain firmly planted on the ground.

Phase two (chronological age: 3½ to five years). This throw differs from the first in that body rotation has been added which increases the velocity of the projectile. Both feet, however, still maintain contact with the ground throughout the throw.

Phase three (chronological age: five to six years). This throw involves body rotation, but adds a step forward on the right foot as the ball is released (right-handed throw). Wild noted that many girls never progress beyond this phase.

Phase four (chronological age: 6½ years and older). In this phase, the left foot steps forward as the ball is being delivered. Weight is transferred from the right foot to the left foot. The right foot then steps forward in a follow-through motion as the ball is released.

In teaching children to throw, a wall may be used for hanging a target and to facilitate retrieving thrown balls. In teaching children to throw, utilize balls which they are able to handle and manipulate. A common tendency is to use balls too large for the child to handle.

Overarm Throw

Catching

In games and activities where throwing is of major importance, catching is often of equal importance. Catching is a skill which requires visual spatial awareness and hand-eye coordination. Because visual spatial awareness and hand-eye coordination are integral parts of skilled catching, learning to catch may be considered an effective means of enhancing those abilities.

A child learning to catch should keep his eye on the ball at all times. This may be difficult particularly for mentally retarded and/or emotionally disturbed children who have figure-ground discrimination problems. For such children, the background should be as plain as possible, and the ball should be of a contrasting color.

The child should first be taught to catch a rolling ball. As the child's skill progresses, he may be taught to catch a ball in flight and one which has rebounded from the surface.

The child should be taught to meet the ball with extended (but not stiff) arms and with fingers spread. Upon contact, the child should "give" with the ball. This maximizes the potential for simultaneously cushioning impact and grasping hold of the ball.

A ball caught below chest height should be caught with palms facing skyward. A ball being caught at chest height or above should be held in the palms away direction. Additional information on ball-handling skills may be found in Chapter VI, Movement Education.

Pushing, Pulling, Lifting, Carrying

Children often encounter situations requiring pushing, pulling, lifting, and carrying proficiencies. These proficiencies are not difficult to master, and, for most individuals, develop naturally. However, among many mentally retarded and/or emotionally disturbed persons such skills do not develop naturally. When called upon to execute the skills of pushing, pulling, lifting, and carrying such persons often become victims of inexperience and/or lack of comprehension. Their performance deficits, in turn, tend to result in wasted or misdirected effort, and increase the potential for unnecessary injury.

Significant efforts should be made to develop pushing, pulling, lifting, and carrying proficiencies among the mentally retarded and/or emotionally disturbed. In so doing, they will have been provided valuable skills to be used over the course of an entire lifetime.

Proper techniques in pushing, pulling, lifting, and carrying become increasingly important when the objects being manipulated are heavy or cumbersome. In the manipulation of such objects, body segments often must exert maximal or near maximal effort simultaneously to produce a summation of forces sufficient to move the object in question.

When pushing, the body moves forward, near forward, or sideward against resistance. Body lean relative to the ground should be in the direction of the object being pushed. One leg should be placed in near full extension well behind the object. This leg is a major force contributor during the push. The opposite leg is flexed to a somewhat greater degree than the driving leg and is placed ahead of the driving leg. It assists in the push, but also serves as a facilitator of balance.

During the push, the body should very nearly form a straight line from point of force application (foot to ground) to point of force application (hand to object). The straight body configuration pits bone against bone during the push, thus increasing the efficiency of the

Pushing

energy expenditure. In effective pushing, hip and knee extension are the major force contributors.

Objects with a high center of gravity coupled with a small base of support often tend to topple over when pushed (or pulled). When moving such objects, force should be applied relatively near the object's base to avoid its tipping.

In pulling activities, the body generally leans opposite the direction as in pushing, and grip strength is an important factor. When pulling, one leg should be almost fully extended and relatively near the object being pulled. The opposite leg assumes a somewhat greater degree of flexion. It assists both in the application of force and in the maintenance of balance. As in pushing, hip and knee extension are major force contributors. Additional pulling force results from simultaneous arm and shoulder action.

During a pull, the body should very nearly form a straight line from point of force application (driving foot against the ground) to point of force application (one's grip on the object). Often, heavy or cumbersome objects may be pulled with greater efficiency if a rope can be attached to the object. A top-heavy object should be pulled relatively near the object's base to avoid its toppling over.

Lifting is a common activity which becomes potentially danger-ous, especially when the object to be lifted is heavy or cumbersome. A typical injury resulting from improper lifting techniques is strain of the lower back.

Pulling

Whenever an object is to be lifted, it should be first manipulated so that one gains some insight as to the object's approximate weight. In preparing for the lift, one should be as near the object as possible. The knees and hips should be flexed with the back remaining perpendicular or very near perpendicular to the ground. The majority of force in lifting should come from hip and knee extension and NOT from the back. With the back erect and the majority of lifting force resulting from hip and knee extension, the potential for sustaining a back injury is greatly minimized. In lowering an object back to the ground, simply reverse the procedure for lifting. The brunt of the weight again should be carried by the lower extremities (i.e. hip and knee flexion).

Once an object has been lifted, it may be carried in a variety of ways depending upon the object's physical characteristics and weight. Objects with handles (e.g. suitcases) may require only one hand. Relatively small, lightweight objects may be carried under the arm. Larger, heavier objects may require the use of both hands with the object resting against the front of the body. Heavy or cumbersome objects may be carried on one shoulder with the hands being used to balance the object.

Whenever an object is too heavy or cumbersome for one person to handle, two or more persons should combine efforts. Lifting and carrying principles remain the same for each individual even though several individuals may be involved simultaneously. When more than one person participates in a lifting or carrying activity, it is especially

Lift with legs
NOT with back

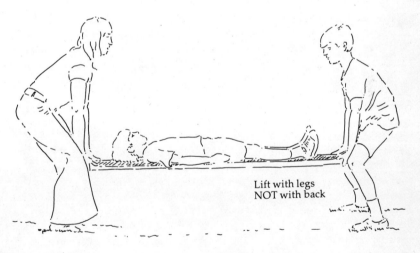

Lift with legs
NOT with back

Lifting

important to assure that efforts are coordinated. Signals should be given to inform each helper when to lift, carry, and lower the object. Such a procedure minimizes wasted or misdirected effort while reducing the possibility of injury to any one helper.

Ontogenetic Skills

Ontogenetic motor skills are those skills which are a part of one's cultural (as opposed to biological) heritage. Because ontogenetic skills are tied to cultural preference, they tend to be many and varied. Their extensive mention transcends the scope of this book. Some examples of ontogenetic skills include club, racket, and batting activities, casting a fishing rod, typing, dancing, riding a bicycle, and performing a cartwheel. Recall that while ontogenetic skills may be culture wide, phylogenetic skills tend to be species wide.

One's motoric repertoire is a conglomeration of both ontogenetic and phylogenetic skills. Phylogenetic skills and ontogenetic skills are related to the extent that skills which have their basis in phylogeny are often the foundational prerequisites for those having their basis in ontogeny.

SELECTED REFERENCE

Wild, Monica. The behavior pattern of throwing and some observations concerning its course of development, *Research Quarterly*, 1947, **18**, 246-259.

Chapter V

Play Therapy

Play can be defined as natural, overt, observable motor responses which are expressions of man's total personality. As one of the most commonplace of childhood phenomena, play constitutes much of the experimentation and emotional expression of the child. It reflects the serious business of youth and contains biological, psychological, and sociocultural influences. Play is an abstract, often vague, but essential element of human behavior that provides expression and challenge for the developing organism. It is selective, directed, persistent, and self-rewarding. Play is the purposeful activity of childhood that facilitates the acquisition of neuromuscular perceptual-motor, sensorimotor, and interpersonal skill development.

As voluntary activity pursued for its own sake, play is characterized by fun and designed to excite and amuse. It is living and need fulfilling. Through play the child builds up competence in dealing with his environment, learns about himself and his culture, develops his personality, and accepts his culture. Play, perhaps in its purest form, can be observed in a young child who runs about shouting and laughing, jumping and dancing, seeming to be completely dominated by an irrepressible desire for noise and movement, using play purely for its functional pleasure. All children, regardless of their race, religion, or social standing, engage in this natural phenomenon.

Theoretical Explanations

An understanding of play involves an attempt to understand human behavior. Educators, philosophers, sociologists, psychologists, and anthropologists have observed and studied play and its importance in man's development. Plato (380 B.C.) has been given credit for endorsing play.

> . . . in teaching children, train them by a kind of game and you will be able to see more clearly the natural bent of each.

Socrates (420 B.C.) has said of play:

> Therefore as I said before, our children from their earliest years must take part in all the more lawful forms of play, for if they are not surrounded with such an atmosphere they can never grow up to be well conducted and virtuous citizens.

Psychologist Karl Groos (1908) considered instinct to be the motivating factor in play. He believed that play is such an important element in the training of higher animals and man that nature provides a long period of immaturity to give an opportunity for it.

> Animals cannot be said to play because they are young and frolicsome, but rather they have a period of youth in order to play.

Groos described play as very important instincts which arise in each young individual before he has serious need of them. Play is preparation for adulthood, a time for exploring and developing the imagination, memory, and social self. It is a multidimensional process basic to the full development of man. Groos believed that play is necessary for the development of higher intelligence

> for if human beings were provided with perfect instincts, life would be automatic and there would be no such thing as education and no increase of ability or intelligence, either in the individual or the species.

In addition, he believed that play is the product of natural or hereditary impulses and is performed solely because of the pleasure it affords.

Friedrich Froebel (1912) was one of the earliest educators to write of the value of play as an educational process. He urged teachers to provide play activities for school children so they might release their energies and free their bodies, minds, and voices to search and explore, to frolic and question. Play, he wrote, is the highest phase of child development. Froebel's teachings are the cornerstone of the modern philosophy and methods of the kindergarten and play school.

Sigmund Freud and C. G. Jung were considered pioneers in the observations of play, including its symbolic, analytical implications. They were among the first psychologists to use play diagnostically. Freud has said of play (1953, p. 173-174):

We ought to look in the child for the first traces of imaginative activity. The child's best loved and most absorbing occupation is play. Perhaps we may say that every child at play behaves like an imaginative writer, in that he creates a world of his own or, more truly, he arranges the things of his world and orders it in a new way that pleases him better. It would be correct to say that he does not take his world seriously; on the contrary, he takes his play very seriously and expends a great deal of emotion on it. The opposite of play is not serious occupation, but reality. Notwithstanding the large affective catharsis of his play world, the child distinguishes it perfectly from reality; only he likes to borrow the objects and circumstances that he imagines from the tangible and real world. It is only this linking of it to reality that still distinguishes a child's "play" from "daydreaming."

Freud concludes that play activities in children are conditioned by repetitions in order to master inner and outer unpleasant experiences.

Erickson (1950) combines psychoanalysis and cultural anthropology in his approach to the study of play as an important part of the growing up process.

The play act is a function of the ego: an attempt to bring into synchronization the bodily and social process of which one is a part even while one is a self.

According to Huizinga (1950, p. 1), play has a significant function, there is some sense to it and it means something.

Play is older than culture, for culture, however inadequately defined, always presupposes human society, and animals have not waited for man to teach them their playing.

He goes on to state that nature gave children play with its tension, mirth, and fun, and that the fun element characterizes the very essence of play. He believes that play is irrational, voluntary activity characterized by freedom, enjoyment, pretending, repetition, order, and an air of secrecy.

Sociologist Caillois (1961) defines play as free, separate, uncertain, and unproductive, yet regulated and make-believe. Play patterns are conditioned by the culture and are, in turn, an index of culture. All societies play. Consequently, a study of play provides the cultural anthropologist with one means to be used in determining the status of a given culture development.

Piaget (1962, p. 52) states that play in its initial stages is behavior repeated for mere assimilation, purely for functional pleasure.

In so far as intelligence, imitation and play are concerned, all three, exclusively as sensory-motor, imitation is a continuation of accommodation, play a continuation of assimilation, and intelligence a harmonious combination of the two.

According to Piaget, play and games enable the ego to assimilate reality, allowing the child to integrate concepts from his social and objective worlds, reproducing what has struck him and evoking what has pleased him.

> . . . play is distinguishable by a modification varying in degree,
> of the conditions of equilibrium between reality and the ego.

The Piagetian scheme follows a sequential order containing three game categories, the progression of which is dependent upon the child's thoughts. From the ages of two months to two years, the child's play consists of practice games. These include the pleasureful exercise of physical skills, particularly within the sensorimotor phase. Symbolic games are played from the age of two years to seven years. These games are made up by individual children, played alone, and become characterized by make-believe and imitation. From the ages of seven years to eleven years, the child's play consists of games with rules. These are social games involving regulations imposed by the group and include the enforcement of sanctions for violations of rules.

Modern-day psychoanalysts have learned that by analyzing the play patterns of children they can diagnose some of their anxieties and troubles. Through the play process, sometimes referred to as play therapy or group psychotherapy, they have aided disturbed children in reaching an understanding of their problems and relationships to their environment.

Developmental Characteristics of Play

Babyhood

In all lands, play is the chief occupation of the young child during his waking hours. The child uses play to discover and learn about his body and the world around him. The free, spontaneous play of babies is more often solitary than social. This play, in which the child amuses himself, is classified as individual play.

By the end of babyhood (two to three years) the child engages in imitative play, which gives him an opportunity to practice adult skills without excessive censure or fear of failure. A child learns to understand his world by copying the acts of others. In the early forms of imitative play, the child imitates the parents, who have been imitating the child. An example of this would be a mother teasingly mimicking her child's handclapping. Soon the child reproduces the action voluntarily, pleasing both himself and his mother. As a child develops skill in imitation, he can imitate persons when they are no longer in his presence or imitate his own behavior in different environments. The child will begin to copy people in general and borrow from adults such routines as sweeping the floor or talking on the telephone.

Parallel play, in which a child plays beside rather than with other children, sharing the same physical environment but for the most part playing independently, is also common during babyhood. Through play the child gains developmental experience. It is the major business of life for him. The young child needs to be exposed to growth-giving activities to help build his confidence in dealing with his environment. These activities include grasping, visual exploration, exploring novel objects and places, manipulating the surroundings, crawling, creeping, climbing, walking, and running.

As early childhood approaches (two to four years), the child's sensorimotor play and kinesthetic activity, in terms of motions, gradually change to symbolic play and imaginative thinking. This play usually manifests itself in the form of mental images and symbols. In the second year of life the child engages in a great deal of large motor testing. He crawls or climbs over, under, and into things. He runs, pulls wagons, lifts objects, splashes water, and throws things. Much of this activity seems to occur for its own sake.

Early Childhood

Growth during early childhood (three to six years) proceeds at a slow rate as compared with the rapid rate of growth in babyhood. This is the ideal age to learn skills. The young child enjoys repetition and is willing to repeat an activity until he has acquired the ability to do it well. He is adventuresome and is not held back by fear of hurting himself or of the ridicule of his associates. Because his body is still pliable, with few conflicting skills to interfere with the acquisition of new ones, he learns quickly and easily.

Play in early childhood is influenced by sex and socioeconomic status. The child plays with toys as if they had the life qualities of talking, acting, and feeling of the people and animals they represent. Social play of the imitative sort involves group games using trucks, cars, houses, et cetera. Pantomine play begins to diminish. Dramatic play (ages two to three) takes the form of personification and make-believe use of the materials of play. The child uses toys and dolls as a substitute for the real thing, some of which may become fairly permanent imaginary companions or characters used as part of the play. These symbolic playmates aid in carrying out acts not permitted elsewhere. They extend the child's self into otherwise inaccessible domains. The ages between four and six are considered the expressive years for the maturing child.

During early childhood undefined group games are an important part of play. These games are simple, involve few rules, and are often invented on the spot. The children learn to play together, sharing things in a cooperative effort. Individual games that test skill are frequently employed. Climbing stairs gives way to jumping down steps three at a time or sliding down the stair rail. Associative play, where the child plays with children in similar or identical activities, is common. By the age of four, cooperative play begins to appear and the child plays as part of a group. Thus, the child begins the rudiments of team play as he begins to learn complex team situations and codified rules.

During childhood, testing occurs in play in the social form of games. The child validates himself by using others as his standard of competence, measuring his progress against competitors with similar talents. Games are frequently selected because they meet the child's emotional needs.

The play interests of young children conform more or less closely to a pattern which is markedly influenced by their natural readiness for certain forms of play and by the environment in which they are growing up. The most common play of preschoolers is toy play, dramatization, construction, and games. As the child grows older, other forms of activity make increasing demands on his time, energy, and attention. But the two dominant impulses of youth are toward activity and toward some kind of collective association. Both of these impulses find expression in forms of play.

Late Childhood

Late childhood (six to twelve years) is a period of slow and relatively uniform growth until the puberty changes begin. The ages between six and ten are considered aggressive years, and the ages from nine to twelve the rebellious years for the maturing child. When late childhood begins, the child has a remarkably large repertoire of skills learned during the preschool years. Play skills usually include throwing and catching balls, riding bicycles, skating, swimming, and constructing things from wood, clay, or other materials. Children's gangs develop during this period as play groups for having fun. Schools put restrictions on the amount of leisure time the child has for play, and the child's social class and school popularity will influence the channeling of his play activities.

During this period the child is capable of learning new skills. The new skills acquired by the child will depend upon his opportunity to learn, the guidance given by his superiors, his physical and social environment, and what is in vogue among his classmates. During this period, play becomes less active. Constructive play with wood and tools, drawing, painting, clay modeling, and collecting special items become increasingly popular. Other activities of play include games and sports, especially games of low organization. By the age of eleven or twelve, competitive games with emphasis on skill and excellence, rather than just fun, are included in the child's play activity.

Late childhood is a period in which the child engages in a wide variety of activities. It is a period of exploration and experimentation. Although imitating is still a major characteristic of play, tag games and games of hiding become popular and are then replaced by group games of low organization and activities of a self-testing and competitive nature. During late childhood boys prefer playing with boys and girls prefer playing with girls.

Values and Functions of Play

Play provides the child with meaningful, symbolic, and nonverbal activities through which he can express himself and learn. Thus, he has the opportunity to experience social, physical, intellectual, and emotional development.

Intellectually the child at play can be taught to listen. Eventually he will begin to grasp relationships between words and concepts, increasing his understanding of the world around him and verbalizing about these pleasurable play experiences. Through play activities the child can learn to perform mental tasks with greater facility, accuracy, and consistency. His conceptual and perceptual skills will develop in observation, memory, logic, deduction, and spacial relationships.

Physically, play activity gives the child an opportunity to learn and master fundamental motor patterns and skills, and to develop and improve his strength, cardiovascular endurance, muscular endurance, flexibility, skill, and general physical health. Through physical activity hand and eye coordination can be developed, precise body movements are learned, and sensory perception is refined. The child's self-esteem will be enhanced as his physical abilities improve.

Socially, the child develops interpersonal relationships as he learns to work, play, and share with others in a group. This creates an increased willingness and ability on his part to follow directions, to obey rules and regulations, and to accept decisions and discipline. Play provides socially acceptable channels and natural compensations for draining off excessive energy. Through play activities the child progresses in self-help skills, self-discipline, and self-direction. The play of mentally retarded or emotionally disturbed children provides opportunities to be with others, to establish identity, and to accept and contribute to group goals. Socialization occurs as the child learns to play by the rules and to conform to the group's expectations and controls. These play experiences are immediate and pleasurable. They are a part of his preparation for adult life. The cheering and laughter frequently accompanying play illustrate the fun aspects derived from play, contributing to its pleasurable effect. The attitudes and skills developed through play will determine the degree of the child's preparation for adult life.

Emotional growth in the form of increased emotional insight, stability, and strength can be by-products of play which result in a happier, more secure child (In play children bring feelings to the fore which they do not know they have or cannot put into words. Play is the safety valve for pent-up emotions.) Emotions of anger are aroused in the fighting play of children. This fighting play gives adequate opportunity for emotional expression, and through indulgence in it the emotions subside. Play can help a child become aware of both his own emotions and those of others. Through play the child can be helped to recognize and find solutions for the problems and conflicts in his life. Well-planned play activity can provide the child with socially acceptable methods of releasing aggressive and other violent emotional responses.

Play is a natural method of freeing a child from his inner frustrations, anxieties, tensions, and insecurities. One of the basic premises underlying play as therapy is that within the child there is a constant growing and striving for self-realization. Play offers the child an opportunity to experience development under the most favorable conditions. Since play is his natural medium for self-expression, the child is given the opportunity to play out his accumulated feelings of tension, frustration, insecurity, aggression, fear, bewilderment, and confusion. By playing out these feelings he brings them to the surface, gets them out in the open, faces them, learns to control them, and abandons them. When he has achieved emotional relaxation, he begins to realize the power within himself to be an individual in his own right, to think for himself, to make his own decisions, to become psychologically more mature, and, by so doing, to realize selfhood.

As a complex set of behaviors, play can include any combination of neuromuscular, sensory, and mental processes. Play actions usually follow a sequential, developmental progression which provides successful attainment and achievement of tasks in the biopsychosocial spheres. Play is repetition of experiences, exploration, experimentation, and imitation of one's surroundings. In addition, play is a preparation for life skills.

Play proceeds within its own time and place boundaries and is self-initiated, spontaneous behavior engaged in for fun. Play serves to function as an integrator of the child's internal world into the social world around him. Through play the child learns to cope with his environment and to extend his reaches into the world shared by others.

Because play is the most natural means of expression for a young child, its use as expressions of conflict and its therapeutic purposes are obvious. For the young child, learning takes place better through play and play situations than in structured environments.

Play behaviors include visual exploration, grasping objects, motor skills involving total body mobility, attention and perception, language and thinking, exploring novel objects and places, manipulating the surroundings, and producing effective changes in the environment. The child's play can center around animate play objects such as his parents, peers, animals, or his own body. Or, they can center around inanimate play objects. Play objects which change form or shape intrinsically when manipulated, such as paints, scissors, paste, pencils, crayons, paper, clay, sand, and water are considered creative or unstructured media. Constructional or pattern media include play objects which change form or shape only when combined with another like object or many dissimilar objects. These play objects include beads, blocks, tinker toys, and craft materials. Additional play objects which do not change form or shape when manipulated include toys for doll play, motor play, and mechanical play. Rattles, balls, guns, dolls, telephones, furniture, and other play equipment would be included in this group.

Stimuli such as novelty and related variables, opportunities for exploration, repetition, imitation of competent role models, and reward can facilitate play. Stresses such as hunger and anxiety and the association of play with isolation, fear, or pain can inhibit play.

The Mentally Retarded or Emotionally Disturbed Child at Play

The normal child at play moves rapidly, confidently, and skillfully from one activity to another and from one piece of equipment to another. His play is happy, enthusiastic, imaginative, and creative. He exhibits ease in forming personal relationships, delights in the use of play materials, has the ability to use substitute outlets for primitive drives, and has the ability to avoid the extremes of effect. This is not the case with the mentally retarded or emotionally disturbed child who is not as creative or imaginative as his normal counterpart. He cannot be turned loose and be expected to use equipment properly or to participate in normal activities with his contemporaries of the same chronological age.

The mentally retarded or emotionally disturbed child at play may be slow moving, clumsy and sedentary, or extremely hyperactive. Frequently his play patterns are random and unimaginative. He tends to follow set patterns of activity as prescribed by the play materials with which he is provided.

Research tends to indicate that the emotionally disturbed child is one who is unhappy and insecure within himself, has poor relationships with other individuals and his environment, and has excessive hostility. He exhibits fears or lives in a fantasy world, and may evidence too many nonorganic physical complaints or too little control over his bodily functions without organic cause. Nearly all of these children reflect learning disabilities and some exhibit clumsy and awkward movement patterns.

One of the most striking characteristics of the emotionally disturbed child is his excess of inhibition or aggression in play activity which is characterized by immaturity. There is frequently the absence of constructiveness and the presence of the impulse to destroy. His play may be marked by bizarre behavior, extreme self-insulation, language disturbance, aberrant reaction to physical pain, and relentless insistence on the perseveration of sameness. Destructive and aggressive play is likely to continue indefinitely in a certain type of emotionally disturbed child, but in the normal child there is a spontaneous and gradual transition to creative play. The destructiveness of the emotionally disturbed child differs from the destructive behavior of a normal child in both degree and quality. This destructiveness has a special meaning for the individual child himself. The emotionally disturbed child, if destructive, tends to destroy extensively and gets caught up in his urge to destroy, seemingly unable to stop or control it. Or, he may show no surface emotion in connection with his behavior, but underneath this apparent indifference there is evidence of strong feelings of guilt and fear expressed in tension, overexcitement, and sometimes rapid fatigue in play.

The mentally retarded child at play is able to perform at a level of complexity commensurate not with his chronological age but rather his mental age. The child's incapacity is reflected in both his play performance and social behavior. He lacks the ability to use toys appropriately, has little awareness of the function of each toy, and has no inventiveness or variety in its use. If the child's mental retardation is the result of brain damage, he may exhibit hyperactivity, perseveration, poor motor control, social ineptness, overreaction to minutiae, and a variety of speech difficulties. Some mentally retarded children are subject to excessive and useless movements, while others exhibit diminished mobility or muscular asthenia. The failure of these children to keep intellectual pace with their normal peers can contribute to personality maladjustment and the development of undesirable behavior patterns. A lack of emotional stability is frequently exhibited in competitive play and in circumstances in which more is expected of them than they are capable of delivering. Such instability usually manifests itself in expressions of fear and aggression. Aggression may also be an attempt to cover weakness, to demonstrate worth, to attract attention, or to relieve tension. Rebellious acts and other undesirable behavior can be similarly motivated. Occasionally, the mentally retarded child may use his handicap as a protective shield or as a means of obtaining sympathy to compensate for his lack of social acceptance.

A child who regresses to the level of play characteristic of a much younger child and remains for a long time at that level, a child who attacks or destroys persistently with concealed signs of emotion or with a display of real wildness in destruction, and a child who cannot play at all reveal by their behavior that something in their development is seriously askew. Play can become an effective therapeutic process for these children.

Most mentally retarded or emotionally disturbed children usually lack adequate play experience. They are frequently allowed little opportunity for successful achievement of play skills and show little interest in play. These children must be taught to play. They need to be taught the skills of individual play, parallel play, and especially group play. Since the form of play expression is determined somewhat by the environment and by the child's interaction with this environment, if suggestive toys are provided and proper guidance is given, these children can become more imaginative and creative in their play.

Many mentally retarded or emotionally disturbed children with higher grades of intelligence desire group activity. But, until they have been taught otherwise, they will usually play as very young normal children, as individuals within the group rather than as equally participating members of the group. These children are capable of learning relatively complex group games and team sports if proper instruction is given. The mentally retarded or emotionally disturbed child needs to be taught play skills progressively, allowing him to begin at his present elementary level and progressing at his own rate of development. Through play he can develop coordination, motor ability, and physical fitness. Social development and emotional growth can occur. Adherence to the rules of the game and to the sportsman's code of fair play can provide incentives for self-discipline and self-control. In addition, the child can develop respect for his own abilities and limitations and those of others as he cooperates and shares in a game situation.

The play patterns of the mentally retarded or emotionally disturbed child are conditioned by the severity of his disability, the presence of a physical handicap, and the degree of his emotional health. These children seek and receive the same benefits from play as normal children. As they experience success through play, they gain confidence in themselves and their abilities. This will result in more desire, drive, and motivation to take part in a variety of activities. Successful play experiences can make mentally retarded and emotionally disturbed children more likely to see a task through to its completion and less reluctant to try new activities. Eventually, these children will become less negative in their manner. Their self-esteem, feelings of individual worth, and sense of personal dignity will improve.

Successful play experiences are absolutely necessary for the development of the mentally retarded or emotionally disturbed child. Failure to have a variety of play experiences can lead to deterioration in other areas of development. According to Benoit (1955):

The play problem of the retarded is a problem which should be quickly and forcibly brought to the attention of all who have it in their power to contribute to its solution. Furthermore, it is mostly in play activities that they can obtain the beneficial stimulation they require for their development; it is mostly in play that they can learn the skills that lie at the root of social living . . . it follows that failure to provide play for them can only lead to deterioration. . . . They need frequent thrills of success in order to counteract the many frustrations they are likely to be subject to. It's in play that they work up a will to live, a will to do things, a will to grow.

Mentally retarded or emotionally disturbed children have greater success and more initial interest in activities that require physical movement and motor responses, although their motor responses may be less developed and potentially no greater than those of normal children. Solitary activities are not very successful with these children. They frequently do not respond well to competition, often becoming uninterested and aggressive if they lose, until they develop confidence and physical skill. Play activities dependent upon reasoning or involving complex use of language are generally unsuitable. Hyperkinetic, brain-damaged, and overactive children may evoke diffused hyperactivity if exposed to finger painting or running water. Hyperactivity may be reduced in children if they are presented with tasks which elicit sustained concentration and interest. They should be placed in a distraction-free environment filled with stimulating, attention-getting experiences. Movement experiences, if they are to be beneficial, should be neither too difficult or too easy, too threatening or too simple. They should meet the developmental readiness of the child.

The child who is only mildly retarded will prefer activities related to old experiences with goals that can be immediately reached. These children usually have a high index of social participation and like motor activities. They are, however, less versatile than the normal child and lack the ability to make complicated adjustment responses. The child with very low intelligence may be unable to catch objects as small as a ball or bean bag, catching with the arms and shoulders instead of the hands. These children lack cerebral motor ability and must be taught all skills separately. They do enjoy repetition in activity.

Teaching Techniques

Regardless of the cause or degree of their handicapping condition, most mentally retarded or emotionally disturbed children will experience positive development through play. An understanding of the developmental stages of play and the recognition of when the child is ready to move from one to the next are important considerations for working with these children. If play activities are to be successful, they should be selected to fit the needs and abilities of the child and be appropriate for his mental and emotional development. Because many of these children have low vitality and fatigue easily, new and complex activities should be planned for the first part of the lesson when the children are fresh and alert.

Mentally retarded or emotionally disturbed children should be provided with diverse programs that maximize physical achievement and produce immediate results. Free play and socially centered programing should be avoided until the acquisition of social, physical, and behavioral skills by the child are adequate for enjoyable participation in such activity. Goals should be set for individual accomplishment.

Skill instruction and participation should be provided at a variety of levels of proficiency. Play experiences should be highly structured so that they can contain the developmental activities the child needs, and at the same time extinguish those behaviors which interfere with academic learning. The child should be guided, encouraged, and motivated into activities that have meaning and importance to him. Novelty and frequent activity changes should be used to avoid boredom and/or inactivity, especially with emotionally disturbed children. This will aid in the prevention of disciplinary problems. Because of this frequent lack of sustained interest, a wide variety of play equipment should be available. This should include items on which the children can vent their aggressive tendencies in a socially acceptable manner. Large, inflatable plastic toys can be used for this purpose. There should be enough equipment for every child.

Any and all equipment and supplies necessary for the activity should be ready in advance. The activity should be kept snappy and lively. Most mentally retarded children will perform best the first few times they perform a skill. It is best to stop an activity at a high point of enthusiasm and before frustration or inability to perform occurs. Therefore, when signs of waning interest appear, the activity should be changed. Any necessary decisions which must be made concerning rules should be fair, impartial, and consistent for all children participating. The selection and arrangement of activities in the program can facilitate the development of desirable social skills. This is especially true if a genuinely warm and cordial environment is provided.

Whenever an element of hazard is involved in an activity, whether it is swimming, nature study, or working with tools, safety precautions should be very strictly observed at all times and infringements upon the safety rules should be punishable by temporary exclusion from the activity. Firm discipline which the child is capable of understanding must be established. The child should know at all times the limits on his activity and choice. For his own security he must always know exactly where he stands and what is expected of him.

The play activities selected should be designed to channel such behaviors as defiance and aggression and prevent conditions such as hyperactivity and boisterousness. Activities with a high probability of aggressive contact should be avoided. Rules and procedures should be used which will ensure the control of possible deviant behavior.

When selecting play activities the amount of body contact required, the difficulty and challenge of the activity itself, the complexity of the rules used, and the spread of winnership should be considered. If games and game-type activities are played, they should be well planned in all details and the teacher should possess a working, playing knowledge of the game.

When games are first introduced, they should be simple and require few participants. Explanations, verbal directions, and replies to questions should be brief, simple, and as direct as possible. Demonstrations are a most effective method of instruction and should be used whenever possible. They should be adapted to the intellectual abilities of the children. Game-type activities should be included for the spirit and enjoyment they provide. A wide variety of games should be avoided as this may be confusing to the children. Games selected should provide all children with an equal chance for participation, and games in which players are eliminated should be avoided. Lead-up and modified games should precede the introduction of highly organized and complex team activities. Complex skills can be learned by the mentally retarded or emotionally disturbed child if instruction is slow and careful and if the skills are broken down into their smallest component parts. A review of game skills may be necessary at the beginning of each class period to refresh the children's memories.

Stress should be placed on the cooperative rather than the competitive aspects of the games selected for inclusion in the program, giving the child a chance to compete against himself in attempting to attain a better score, greater height, faster time, or more distance rather than competing against others in the group. Games chosen should require little in the way of memorization of playing rules, strategy, or movement patterns. They should be selected and modified so that all can enjoy participation and experience a degree of success. Modifications might include substituting walking for running or skipping; using a bounce, roll, or underhand toss to replace throwing; hitting on the second or even third bounce; reducing the size of the playing field, court, or play area; restricting players to definite places or positions on the field; substituting lighter, smaller, and more easily controlled equipment; using plastic materials and supplies; using beach balls, balloons, and more than one ball where appropriate; allowing players to hit the ball any number of times or in any sequence; and permitting players to hold the ball for a longer period of time.

A developmental teaching approach which encompasses small, sequential, and concrete steps is ideal with most mentally retarded or emotionally disturbed children. The mental and emotional age of the child should be considered when toys and skills are selected for play.

If toys are too fragile or the skills too refined for the child's chronological age and developmental level, he may find it difficult to play successfully without injury to himself or his toys. It may, therefore, be necessary for the teacher to improvise sturdy equipment for the older children in the group.

The methodology employed is extremely important as a means of controlling the play environment. Mentally retarded or emotionally disturbed children can participate successfully if their interest is aroused and maintained, if they can grasp the nature of the activity, and if they are not required to remember too many directions. Teachers should not adhere to mechanically standardized approaches, but rather should focus on the uniqueness, complexity, and developmental diversity of each child. The teacher must be aware of the child's inner world, his emotional needs, and his environmental problems. Teaching methods should be simple and open-ended. They should reflect teacher sensitivity, flexibility, adaptability, innovativeness, and creativity. Methods used should have a highly personal, artistic quality combining sound judgment, good taste, and individual intuition.

Methods for arousing interest might include the use of visual aids such as simple, colorful pictures for the introduction of a new game. An appropriate short story related to the activity, or the use of a song or music to precede or accompany the activity may also be motivational. Praise should be offered generously for the child's efforts.

The teacher must possess patience, empathy, a sense of humor, and an appreciative commitment to the child as an individual of worth and dignity who can progress, achieve, and succeed. In addition, the teacher should use a minimum of reliance on verbalization in promoting behavior change, especially in the initial stages. If verbal commands are used, comprehension on the part of the child is essential. To ensure understanding it may be necessary to have the child repeat the command before he is expected to execute the movement. The results of such structured experiences will be wholesome, vigorous activity and its accompanying physical development and spirit of fun.

Developing the Skills of Play

Individual Play

The first developmental level of play is classified as individual play in which the child amuses himself. This play is usually free, spontaneous, and solitary. It may be necessary to teach the mentally retarded or emotionally disturbed child the simple skills of individual play involving visual exploration, grasping objects, manipulating objects, crawling, creeping, walking, and running.

Simple play toys such as five- and six-piece animal puzzles, five- and six-piece color and shape recognition puzzles, hammer peg sets,

Individual Play

creative building blocks, interlocking toys such as Krazee Klowns, screwing toys such as nuts and bolts or Kitty in the Kegs, and stack color and size sets can be used to teach the child the basic skills of visual exploration and grasping and manipulating objects. The child should be taught these skills on a one-to-one basis. Many mentally retarded or emotionally disturbed children may need more than a demonstration in how to complete these tasks. It may be necessary to guide their hands through the skills, at least the first few times they are attempted.

The skills of crawling, creeping, walking, and running are considered natural and alternate gross motor skills. They are used as transportation patterns by the child to mobilize his exploration of space as he searches and discovers his environment. These and other locomotor skills which can be used by the child as he participates in individual play are described in Chapter IV, Basic Motor Patterns and Skills.

Imitative Play

Frequently, the mentally retarded or emotionally disturbed child does not play as imaginatively as the normal child. Instead, his play is mechanical and repetitious. Through constructive play experiences, the child can gradually become freer and more imaginative in his play.

He will also learn, through play, how to handle his anxieties, using socially accepted methods for their release. If proper guidance is given, the child can learn to act out his conflicts in play. This will give him the strength and experience which life does not provide, but which he needs to mature socially.

Imaginative play is the precursor of creativity. It promotes, within the child, an effective interaction with his environment. Through the symbolic make-believe which imaginative play provides, the child is assisted in assimilating reality at his own level. Imaginative play is a healthful childhood approach for the mentally retarded or emotionally disturbed child to use in approaching life's various tasks and adult roles. These adult skills can be practiced in imaginative play without fear of failure or excessive censure.

The proper selection of toys and play objects is imperative if the ability to play imaginatively is to be developed in the mentally retarded or emotionally disturbed child. These children are great mimics. They can be encouraged to imitate good demonstrations, imitate actions of people, or pretend to be animals. Animal imitation can include waddling like a duck, hopping like a bunny, leaping like a frog, or imitating the actions of any other familiar animals.

The child may be given a baby doll and asked to pretend that he or she is the baby's mother or father. The child can be asked simple questions, such as: *"The baby is hungry, what should you do?"* It may be necessary, at first, to make suggestions to the child or even show him how to feed the baby doll with a bottle or spoon.

Much practice and repetition may be necessary before the mentally retarded or emotionally disturbed child learns to play imaginatively. If the child does not remember the play skills from day to day, they should be repeated. A new approach may possibly be necessary if the child is to understand the tasks he is asked to perform.

With patience, repetition, and practice, the mentally retarded or emotionally disturbed child will eventually learn to play imaginatively. The child's level of ability in this type of play will, however, be dependent upon the degree of his handicapping condition.

Fantasy Play

Fantasy play provides the child with a concrete method of expressing his fears, hopes, and needs. It is a form of wish fulfillment which provides the child with the means for satisfying the desires he cannot or dares not express in words. The playacting of fantasy play assists the child in overcoming the pain and fear experienced in his real world.

Children, especially those who are mentally retarded or emotionally disturbed, long for constancy in their lives. They need a safe, accepting, predictable environment. If anything changes this, the normal child will, in all probability, bring it back through play. This is not usually the case with the mentally retarded or emotionally disturbed child. They may lack the daring and energy to remake their world in play. They may be afraid of make-believe. To them, it may be a means of lowering their guard and leaving themselves vulnerable to the threats of the real world.

These children need to be taught the skills of fantasy play as a means of expressing the fears, hopes, and needs which are not satisfied in their everyday life. By developing the skills of fantasy play the mentally retarded or emotionally disturbed child will be better prepared to adjust to difficult life experiences.

The development of fantasy play, like imaginative play, depends upon the proper selection of toys and play objects. Paints, clay, sand, and water are useful media for fantasy play. These materials can be used by the child symbolically as a means of expressing his fears, hopes, and needs.

Before the child feels free enough to express himself fully in fantasy play, the teacher must be sensitive to the child and his feelings. He must accept the child's attitudes and convey to the child a consistent and sincere belief in him. The teacher must respect the child as he is.

At first, the mentally retarded or emotionally disturbed child may express diffused and undifferentiated emotions. His feelings may be negative. Frequently, he has lost contact with the people and situations which may have originally aroused his feelings of frustration, anger, fear, or guilt. The child's emotions are frequently magnified, generalized, and easily stimulated or evoked. They are no longer tied to reality.

The mentally retarded or emotionally disturbed child may see himself as an inferior person, unloved, inadequate, and afraid of the consequences of his behavior. He may be threatened by criticism and punishment. Reward and approval may be perceived as attempts to change or modify him. Punishment and disapproval may be reminders and reflections of his past inadequacies, reinforcing his feelings of insecurity or terrifying him. However inadequate his feelings may be, and in spite of all allurements, the mentally retarded or emotionally disturbed child may struggle to maintain his own picture of himself.

The teacher should not attempt to modify the child or pressure him to change. He should respect and accept the child entirely. If the child feels secure and unthreatened, he can begin to express himself fully without feeling ashamed or guilty. The child will eventually learn to make decisions and to act spontaneously and confidently. He will grow within himself and gain a more realistic impression of himself. Eventually, the process of depicting his imaginary and real life through fantasy play will enable the mentally retarded or emotionally disturbed child to resolve his emotional problems and interpersonal conflicts. He will have a socially acceptable method for the release of his emotional tensions.

Creative Play

Creative play is thoughtful, exploratory play with materials, objects, feelings, and ideas. As the child manipulates these materials and objects with meaning and purpose to convey or fulfill his intent, he engages in the creative process. Creative play increases the child's insight and sensitivity. It encourages learning through exploration, experimentation, manipulation, and transformation. The creative process expands the human potential as it develops curiosity, flexibility, improvisation, commitment, and the courage to risk.

All children, including the mentally retarded and emotionally disturbed, have creative potential. Creative play behavior can be nurtured in these children. Rich and varied sensory inputs, sensory stimuli, and kinesthetic experiences form the necessary basis for symbol formation and perceptual and cognitive development. Such experiences will provide the child with enriching cues about reality and discriminations about the self and the real world.

The child's environment should contain sensory-cultural enrichment. He should be provided with stimulating and varied play milieus which include easily accessible toys, raw materials, and physical objects which engage the senses. This type of environment encourages initiative and provides the child with opportunities for exploratory play behavior. Creative play can be further increased by providing the child with meaningful contacts with accepting adults and then allowing the child time to privately assimilate these experiences in his solitary play activity.

According to Michelman (1971), there are three stages of development in the creative process. The first is a manipulative stage that satisfies the child's tactile and emotional impulses. This is followed by an exploratory stage during which the child experiments and plays with the materials in his environment to discover their potential. The final level of development in the creative process is a stage of form consciousness where the child employs the materials in his environment to fulfill his intent and desire for expression.

The mentally retarded or emotionally disturbed child should be allowed to discover for himself, partly through his own spontaneous activity and partly through the materials set up for him. He should perceive the world he lives in and be allowed to react to what he sees and feels, selecting, interpreting, and reforming the elements in his environment and communicating his emotions and insights through his play materials. The resulting creative expression of the child will mirror how he feels, thinks, sees, and imagines.

Shapes, colors, textures, and three-dimensional forms should be available for the child to use in exploration and experimentation. Mentally retarded and emotionally disturbed children need the self-confidence, independence, and satisfaction they will derive from their own creative achievement. This will facilitate their development and adjustment into the adult world around them.

Parallel Play

Parallel play is activity in which the child plays beside rather than with other children, sharing the same physical environment, but for the most part, playing independently. This form of play can easily be developed in the mentally retarded or emotionally disturbed child by utilizing the skills developed in individual play, but having two or more children share the same play environment. The children can participate in similar or identical tasks, individual games, crafts, musical activities, informal and imaginative play, or apparatus play.

The skills of parallel play are necessary in the child's developmental process. They serve as a forerunner of group play skills.

The first experience at parallel play should involve mentally retarded or emotionally disturbed children who are at the same developmental level mentally, physically, emotionally, and socially. Later experiences can mix children of differing ability levels. Care should be taken, however, to ensure that the children can share the same physical play environment successfully. This would infer that a very strong

Parallel Play

child should not be placed with a very weak child unless the experience can be successful for both children, contributing to their physical, mental, social, and/or emotional development.

Additional skills which can be used in parallel play are described in Chapter VI, Movement Education and Chapter IX, Developmental Gymnastics.

Group Play

Group play with mentally retarded or emotionally disturbed children should begin as partner play. Two children of approximately the same developmental level mentally, physically, emotionally, and socially should be taught to play together, sharing things in a cooperative effort.

Activities for Cooperative Partner Play

Thread the Needle. The children stand facing each other with both hands clasped together. They step through the loop made by their hands and arms without breaking their clasp. Next, they unthread the needle by stepping back to the starting position.

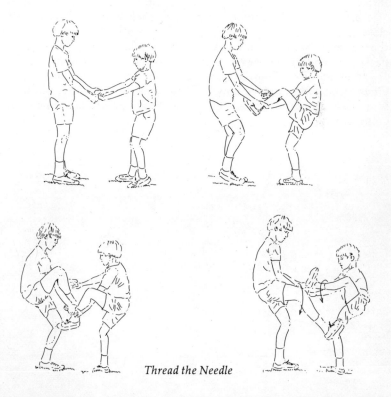

Thread the Needle

Sit and Stand

    Sit and Stand. Partners sit back to back with the feet drawn up close to the body. By pressing against each other's back, they stretch the legs and rise to a standing position. By relaxing the pressure on the back and bending the legs, they return to a sitting position.

    See-Saw. Two children stand facing each other with hands grasped. One of the children goes down to the squat position. By mutual consent they change — the squatter standing up, the standing partner going down.

See-Saw

Spinning Tops

Spinning Tops. Partners link hands and, with one foot to the center, spin around with each other.

Sawing Wood. Partners grasp hands and stand facing each other with one foot forward. The sawing effect is obtained by a big turning movement to the left, and then to the right. The turning movement is combined with a stretching of the arms on the forward-turning side.

Sawing Wood

The tossing of gayly colored balls would be another excellent means of teaching the rudiments of cooperative play. This can be done as partner play or in small groups. Throwing and catching skills are described in Chapter VI, Movement Education.

Partner play can also be used to develop the competitive aspects of play.

Activities for Competitive Partner Play

One-Hand Tug-of-War. Opponents, standing sideways to each other, take a wrist grasp. They take the strain, and then pull. This can also be done as a two-hand tug-of-war.

Inner Tube Tug-of-War. One of a pair is standing inside an inner tube which is held at about waist height. The opponent holds the inner tube from a standing position outside. His face is toward the back of the person in the tube. The opponent tries to pull the person in the tube backward as he offers resistance.

Dodger and Marker. One of a pair acts as the dodger, the other as the marker. On the signal the dodger tries to get as far away from the marker as possible by dodging, changing directions, et cetera. The marker tries to keep within arm's length at all times. On the signal, all

Inner Tube Tug-of-War

stop as quickly as possible to see which is the successful one — the dodger or the marker.

Touch Hands and Run. One of a pair holds out his hands, palms up. The opponent stands facing him and tries to touch his hands and run away to a given mark without being caught. The chaser can only chase after his hands have been touched.

After two children have learned to play together cooperatively and competitively, the group can be enlarged to three, then four, and so on. The type of activity chosen and the cooperative or competitive skill of the children should determine the size of the group used in play. Large group activity should be avoided, at least until the children have developed all of the skills necessary for success in such a play environment.

Rhythmic experiences are one of the best activities to use for organizing and unifying a group of mentally retarded or emotionally disturbed children at the beginning of a play period. Simple rhythmic activities which can be used for this purpose are described in Chapter VII, Music, Rhythms, and Dance.

Group play with mentally retarded or emotionally disturbed children can include undefined simple group games which involve few rules, group games of low organization, tag games, and games of hiding. Later, the children can begin to learn the rudiments of team play, including simple team situations and rules. Care should be taken in the selection of all group play, ensuring that the activity provides maximum physical achievement in which the child can experience success.

If games of hiding are used, they should be confined to a controlled area. They should not be used with a large group of children. The use of undesirable hiding places should be forbidden. The best

Small Group of Three Children Playing   *Group Playing Steal the Bacon*

play area for hiding games would be indoors in a controlled area. A whistle or similar signal should be used to call the children in who have not been found. To ensure the return of the children, a reward could be given to those returning when the whistle is used.

When selecting simple group games for use with mentally retarded and emotionally disturbed children, the following criteria should be used as a guide. A relatively small, but adequate play space should be used. All of the children should participate in the same or similar manner. Any choices which the children are required to make should be few in number. The activity should use a limited number of motor skills in relatively fixed or standard playing positions with definite restrictions on the possible directions of movement involved. No penalties or privileges should be associated with the child's quality of performance. Administrative personnel involved in the game should remain the same throughout.

All precautions necessary for the safety of the children should be followed when group play is used. Rules should be kept simple enough for the children to understand. Usually, a simple demonstration preceding the activity will assist the children in their understanding of the game. Repetition of the demonstration and explanation may be necessary.

Simple Group Ball Games

Toss Ball. Toss ball is a simple game of tossing and catching. The children are in a circle, with one player in the center. The child in the center tosses the ball to any child in the circle, who tosses it back to him. When this game is first played, the teacher can be the player in the center. For variation, the game can be played with no one in the center. The ball is tossed from one player to another across and around the circle. A soft, large ball or bean bag should be used for toss ball. A maximum of eight children should be in the circle. The child who is in the center should have good throwing and catching skills.

Circle Stride Ball. A soft, large ball is used. From eight to ten children are in a circle. Each player stands in a stride position with his feet touching a foot of the player on each side of him. The child who is IT stands in the center of the circle with the ball. He rolls the ball, attempting to roll it out of the circle between the feet of one of the players. If he is successful, the person who allows the ball to pass out of the circle between his feet becomes IT, and the center player takes his place in the circle. The players must use their hands to stop the ball, and they must not move their feet. A ball which goes out of the circle between two players is recovered by a nearby player who tosses the ball to the player in the center. He then takes his place in the circle and play is resumed. The child who is IT should roll the ball with an underhand throw. The ball should be kept on the ground. For variation, the children can keep their hands on their knees when not hitting the ball. If

Circle Stride Ball

the children try to be IT by letting the ball go through their legs, the rules can be changed. The player who lets the ball go through his legs must get it and stay outside the circle until he is successful in catching another ball which goes through someone else's legs.

Touch Ball. Eight to ten children are in a circle. One child, who is IT, stands in the center of the circle. A large, soft ball is passed from player to player around and across the circle. The child who is IT must try to tag the ball. When he does, the child who threw the ball or touched it last becomes IT.

Teacher Ball. The children are in groups of six to eight players with one child in each group as the leader or "teacher." The "teacher" faces the other children, who are in a line about eight feet from him. He tosses the ball to each player in turn, starting at the head of the line and continuing through the foot of the line. Each child, upon receiving the ball, tosses it back to the "teacher." Anyone who misses the ball goes to the foot of the line. If the "teacher" misses, he goes to the foot, the child at the head of the line becomes the "teacher," and play continues. The children should be encouraged to throw and catch the ball correctly. If the ball was not caught because it was not thrown properly, no penalty should be given. A large, soft ball or bean bag should be used.

8'

"Teacher"

Teacher Ball

Simple Group Games

Busy Bee. The players are divided in partners. The teacher calls out commands that the partners obey. *"Back-to-back, side-to-side, toes-to-toes,"* et cetera. The couples do as commanded. When the teacher calls out *"busy bee"* each child must find a new partner.

Poison. Play in groups of four. All link hands to form a circle around some object, such as a medicine ball, towel, or bean bag. On the signal all pull and try to make one of the group touch the object in the middle.

Witch's Carpet. Two or three rugs or similar objects are laid or marked on the floor and are called the witch's carpet. The children form in line and march around the room, following a leader who takes them across the witch's carpet. The leader should be skillful enough to lead the children in a variety of movement patterns such as marching, skipping, hopping, et cetera, to music or the clapping of hands. When the music stops with a loud bang or with one loud clap of the hands, the children must stop immediately. Any child having any part of his feet on the witch's carpet when the music stops must leave the line. When the leader is caught, the next child in line becomes the new leader. The game continues until all children have been caught or a designated time has lapsed.

Posture Tag. The children are in a circle. One child is a chaser and another a runner. Each of these children puts a bean bag on his head and keeps it there, without using his hands, while running. These two players run around the circle. When the runner wishes to stop running or shows evidence of being tired, he puts his bean bag on the head of someone else, who then becomes the new runner. The chaser follows the same procedure. Whenever the chaser tags the runner, they both select someone to replace them. If the bean bag falls off the child's head, he must stop to pick it up, even at the chance of being tagged.

Cherry Pie. All the children have joined hands in a circle except one child who is on the outside. With his hands and arms held straight out in front of him as if they were a big knife, he "cuts" the joined hands of any two players in the circle, saying "cut the pie." The two players in the circle whose hands were separated run around the circle in opposite directions. The one who was IT takes the vacancy left by one of the runners. The runner who first completes the circle and runs through the other vacancy to the center of the circle says, "cherry pie, here am I!" He becomes the next IT, while the other player rejoins the circle. When teaching this game, the children should be taught how to pass each other safely when running around the circle. The child who is IT should not use a great deal of force when bringing his arms down across the arms of other players. The "knife" should leave an opening in the circle so the runners can locate the vacant spot.

Knife

Cherry Pie

Tag Games

Run, Old Bear. A base line is marked off at one end of the playground or gym. One player is chosen to be the Old Bear. He stands with his eyes closed and his back to the other children at the opposite end of the playing area. The others are children out playing. The Old Bear must hide his eyes until the teacher calls, *"Run, Old Bear."* The children run and try to reach the base line before they are tagged. If any are tagged, they must be Old Bear. If the children do not come near enough to Old Bear, dare them to touch a certain place with their feet.

Partner Tag. Each player links one elbow with a partner. Two children are without partners. One is the chaser and he tries to tag the other, who is the runner. The runner is safe when he links elbows with any player. The partner of the player with whom he links elbows immediately becomes the runner and is chased. When a chaser tags a runner, the runner becomes the chaser and the chaser becomes the runner.

Nose and Toes Tag. This game is played as a simple tag game, except that the runner may escape being tagged by grasping his nose with one hand and his foot with the other hand. A player who is tagged becomes IT and the game continues.

Catch of Fish. Players are divided into two equal groups, the fish and the net. Each group stands behind goal lines drawn parallel to one

Net

Fish

50′

Goal line

Catch of Fish

another about fifty feet apart. The players of one group join hands to form a fish net. The players of the other group represent fish. At a signal, both groups advance toward one another. The fish attempt to reach the opposite goal, while the net attempts to stop them by closing around them. The fish may escape around the ends of the net, but they may not run through or under the net. If the net breaks, the fish escape. Those who are caught remain out of the game until all have been caught. The two groups alternate playing net and fish.

Games of Hiding

Hide and Seek. One player is IT and stands at a goal such as a post. The other players hide. The player who is IT counts slowly to ten. Teacher assistance may be necessary in counting. IT then calls that he is coming to look for the other players. The first one whom he finds is IT the next time the game is played. IT continues the search until all players are found or a whistle is blown. For variation, a hider may save himself by reaching and tagging the goal before the seeker does. He is not considered "caught" if he tags the goal before IT does. Then, the first player found and "caught" is IT the next time the game is played.

Sardine. This hide-and-seek game differs from the usual in that the player who is IT hides and all of the others try to find him. IT is given time to hide and then, after an established period of time, the others start to hunt for him. Any player finding him must hide with him. The last one finding the hiding place is IT for the next game. If there is not room for all players to hide in the hiding place, they must wait within sight of the hiding place until all have found the original hider.

Relay Races

Bean Bag Toss Relay. The players stand in line formation, with an equal number on each team. A large circle is drawn on the floor or ground approximately ten feet in front of each line. The first player of

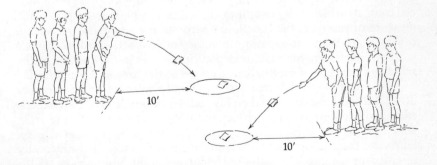

Bean Bag Toss Relay

each team has three bean bags. At the starting signal the two players try to toss the bean bags, one after the other, into the circle. One or more points may be given for each bag resting in the circle or on the line. After the last bag is thrown, the player picks up the bean bags and gives them to the second player in line. He then goes to the end of the line. After all players have had a turn at throwing the bean bags, the winning team is declared by the highest score. Extra points may be given for the team that finishes first.

Over-Under Relay. The players stand in line formation, with an equal number on each team. The players are about a foot apart. The first player of each team holds a ball and on the starting signal, passes the ball over his head to the next player, who passes it between his legs to the next player, and so on until the ball reaches the last person in line. When the player at the end of the line receives the ball, he carries it to the head of the line. The procedure is repeated until everyone is back in his original starting position. If the ball is dropped, the player losing it must recover it and return to his position in line before passing it on to the next player. The team finishing the relay first is the winner.

These games are a small sample of the many group play activities that can be taught to mentally retarded or emotionally disturbed children. Most elementary physical education textbooks contain additional games which can be selected to meet the developmental level of the mentally retarded or emotionally disturbed children for which they will be used. Care should be taken in the selection of these activities so that they are appropriate for the physical status, mental readiness, social interests and emotional needs of the children. In addition, all necessary safety precautions should be followed.

Play and Recreation

Play and recreation are frequently considered synonymous. They both can provide a balanced diversion to the routine activities of everyday life. These experiences can provide the child with pleasurable social contacts which carry over into adult life. The pleasure in play is the pleasure of mastery; the functional becomes fun. Play and recreation can be more than participation in some form of activity during one's leisure. The determining factor in playfulness lies in the attitude of the mind and the type of motivation involved at the time of the activity.

Any activity which meets the mentally retarded or emotionally disturbed child's needs, based on his abilities, interests, and past experiences, which permits him to function, achieve, and succeed, and from which he derives enjoyment and satisfaction can be considered play. Likewise, these activities can be considered recreation. If the mentally retarded or emotionally disturbed child is taught how to play, if his play activities are satisfying and rewarding, if he is provided with an opportunity to learn games that can be played during his leisure hours, and if play as a recreational pursuit is encouraged, play will become part of his recreation. It will be selected as his choice of activity during his leisure time.

SELECTED REFERENCES

Benoit, E. Paul. The play problems of retarded children. *American Journal of Mental Deficiency*, July 1955, **60**, 41-55.

Caillois, Roger. *Man, play and games*. New York: Free Press of Glencoe, 1961.

Carpenter, John R. Role reversal in the classroom. *Group Psychotherapy*, 1968, **21**, 155-167.

Davis, John Eisele. *Clinical applications of recreational therapy*. Springfield, Ill.: Charles C. Thomas, Publisher, 1952.

Erikson, E. H. *Childhood and society*. New York: W. W. Norton and Co., 1950.

Florey, Linda. An approach to play and play development. *American Journal of Occupational Therapy*, 1971, **24** (6), 275-280.

Freud, Sigmund. The relationship of the poet to daydreaming. *Collected Papers*, Vol. 4. London: Hogarth Press, 1953, pp. 173-174.

Froebel, Friedrich. *The education of man*. New York: D. Appleton and Co., 1912.

Ginott, Haim G. *Group psychotherapy with children*. New York: McGraw-Hill Book Co., 1961.

Groos, Karl. *The play of man*. New York: D. Appleton and Co., 1908.

Haun, Paul, *Recreation: A medical viewpoint*. New York: Columbia University, Bureau of Publications, 1965.

Hejna, Robert F. *Speech disorders and nondirective therapy; Client-centered counseling and play therapy*. New York: Ronald Press Co., 1960.

Huizinga, Johan. *Homo Ludens* (Man the player). Boston: Beacon Press, 1950.

Jackson, Lydia and Kathleen Todd. *Child treatment and the therapy of play*. New York: Ronald Press Co., 1950.

Leland, Henry and Daniel Smith. *Play therapy with mentally subnormal children*. New York: Grune and Stratton, 1965.

Michelman, Shirley. The importance of creative play. *American Journal of Occupational Therapy*. 1971, **25** (6), 285-290.

Mitchell, Elmer D. and Bernard S. Mason. *The theory of play*. New York: A. S. Barnes and Co., 1948.

Moustakas, Clark E. *Children in play therapy: A key to understanding normal and disturbed emotions*. New York: McGraw-Hill Book Co., 1953.

Piaget, Jean. *Play, dreams and imitation in childhood*. London: Routledge and Kegan Paul, 1962.

Poindexter, Hally B. W. Motor development and performance of emotionally disturbed children. *Journal of Health, Physical Education and Recreation*, June 1969, **40**, 69-71.

Rhinard, Larry D. A comparison of the effectiveness of nondirective play therapy and behavior modification approaches. Unpublished doctoral dissertation, Florida State University, 1970.

Robertson, Mary and Frances Barford. Story-making in psychotherapy with a chronically ill child. *Psychotherapy: Theory, Research and Practice,* 1970, 7, 104-107.

Schrut, Albert. What play reveals about your child. *Parent's Magazine,* 1969, 44, 54+.

Sessoms, H. Douglas. The mentally handicapped child grows at play. *Mental Retardation,* August 1965, 12-14.

Sutton-Smith, Brian. Child's play — very serious business. *Psychology Today,* December 1971, 5 (7), 67-69, 87.

Oliver, James N. Add challenge with variety in activities. *Journal of Health, Physical Education and Recreation,* April 1966, 37, 30-32.

Takata, Nancy. The play history. *American Journal of Occupational Therapy,* 1969, 23 (4), 314-318.

Takata, Nancy. The play milieu — a preliminary appraisal. *American Journal of Occupational Therapy,* 1971, 25 (6), 281-284.

Tisza, Veronica B., Irving Hurwitz and Kristine Angoff. The use of a play program by hospitalized children. *Journal of The American Academy of Child Psychiatry,* 1970, 9, 515-531.

Chapter VI

Movement Education

Basic movement, movement exploration, and movement education are terms associated with the "new look" in elementary school physical education. Although these terms are frequently used interchangeably, they refer to three completely different approaches to physical education, each of which should be used to complement existing programs.

Basic movement is used to identify the core content of an activity program and includes those skills which enable the child to handle himself well in a variety of movement situations. It is the foundation upon which the complex movements for all activity areas of physical education are built. Basic movement skills are described in Chapter IV, Basic Motor Patterns and Skills.

Movement exploration refers to the problem-solving approach to the teaching of physical education. It is child centered, informal, noncompetitive, and carefully planned to provide total involvement, progressive development, and successful experiences for each child in the class. The child is required to think out new ways of performing a task which have not previously occurred to him. He is not told how to do a task, but is told what to do. The child, therefore, becomes more perceptive about his own ability. Emphasis is placed on the development of a generalized ability to handle one's body efficiently. The challenge or question asked is the medium through which movement exploration is conducted. The teacher does not demonstrate but should have a preconceived idea of the general kind of response the child will make and be able to recognize correct and incorrect responses to the questions asked. Questions usually begin with the words: *"Who can . . . ?"* *"Can you . . . ?"* *"What can . . . ?"* *"How can . . . ?"* *"Show me . . . !"*

Movement education refers to activity programs which include the basic movement content and the problem-solving approach of movement exploration. The intent of the program is to help the child become aware of his own potentials for moving efficiently and effectively in all aspects of living, including motor tasks involved in daily activities for play, work, and creative expression. Through movement education the child develops his general capacity for movement and learns the fundamentals necessary to facilitate his subsequent skill development.

Movement education incorporates the child's natural inclination to move freely, to be creative, and to test his own abilities. The goal is easy, fluent, efficient performance. The child learns to solve problems dealing with gravity (balance and posture), direction, the control of objects (manipulative skills), and strength and endurance. The fundamentals of movement are explored and built upon so that the child develops an awareness, understanding, appreciation, and control of the many ways in which his body can move through space, with variations in time and force or power and economy of movement. The child becomes better able to direct the actions of his body, understand his capabilities for movement, and develop confidence in his movement activity. Freedom of movement and creativity are encouraged because there is no single response to the problem presented. This true creative freedom enables the child to move more and to move more easily. Movement patterns are developed in anticipation for later use in specific game activities. Movement education can be used to teach the fundamentals of dance, gymnastics, ball skills, swimming, basic movement patterns, and numerous miscellaneous skills.

As an individualized method of instruction, the movement education approach eliminates inactivity and waiting for turns. Every child is totally involved intellectually and physically, solving a common problem at his own level of development and structuring his own movements within the restrictions of the problem. This child-centered approach allows for more teacher-student interaction on a personal basis. It provides a built-in safety factor because the child will usually not attempt skills beyond his capacity for success. When the children are kept interested and deeply involved in personal movement problems, discipline problems are usually nonexistent. The continuous movement and vigorous activity, which are by-products of movement education, contribute to physical fitness and exercise the muscular and organic systems of the body in a natural and functional way. Because goals are personal, every child's level of motor skill will be increased according to his own ability, readiness, and interest. Success will be experienced, satisfaction and fun will result.

The movement education environment, which is natural, informal, and noncompetitive, facilitates self-expression and the development of social awareness as the child learns to work as a member of the group and individually within the group. The open-ended challenge of the questions asked encourages maximum involvement. The child is given freedom to create, to express himself, and to try out his own solutions to problems without the fear of failure. As personal success in movement skills enhances the child's confidence, his self-image improves and he frequently performs better in his academic environment.

The movement education teacher is a guide, not a director. He must possess a knowledge of the characteristics of young children and an awareness of basic body movements and their proper performance if he is to provide suitable tasks and problems for the children to solve. If movement education lessons are to be effective, the teacher's job of planning is greater than that of the teacher using a typical physical education approach. Although the teacher does not demonstrate skills, it is frequently valuable for the child to see and try other children's solutions to the problems presented. This is especially true when working with the mentally retarded or emotionally disturbed child.

The instructional program in movement education should be planned according to the developmental level of the children. It should include a systematic progression from simple to more complex skills which are arranged in units of instruction. The child should be given ample opportunity to explore, select, repeat, and polish his skill performance.

The framework for a movement education curriculum consists of three basic concepts. Units of instruction for these concepts are built around movement themes.

1. *Use of the body* refers to all of the ways in which the body and its parts can move and the changing relationships of body parts to each other and to objects in space. Themes for the development of body awareness would include transfer of weight, reception of weight, loss and recovery of balance, and shaping movements such as curling, stretching, or twisting. Body awareness activities can be developed through individual work problems or partner and group work problems involving matching movements, contrasting movements, meeting and parting and passing around, over, or under other children or equipment.

2. *Use of space* refers to where the body can move within self-space and into general space. Spatial awareness concepts include all of the variety of directions (forward, backward, sideward, diagonal), levels (high, medium, low), in-flight movements, and ranges and shapes the body has the ability to use.

Movements can be locomotor or nonlocomotor, performed alone, with others, or in relationship to static and moving objects.

3. *Quality of the movement* refers to how the body can move. Qualities include the strength or force of the movement (the contrast between strong, vigorous, heavy movements and light, almost weightless movements), the time of the movement (its quick, slow, accelerated, or decelerated character) and the flow of the movement (its continuous, broken, successive, or simultaneous pattern).

When working with mentally retarded or emotionally disturbed children the problem emphasis should be on a single concept and a simple theme. Instruction should begin at the base level, with content that is simpler than skills. Approaches should be used which progress from general to specific movement problems. The problem-solving situation should be carefully structured to develop the intended skills. Begin by having the children arranged in an informal, scattered formation and limit the choice of activity or movement in some way. An example would be: *"How can you travel from one end of the line to the other, using one foot and both hands?"* The degree of freedom permitted the children will depend on their ability to function in the informal atmosphere. Some mentally retarded or emotionally disturbed children will need more direction and structure than others.

Although there is no research available to indicate the value of movement education for the mentally retarded or emotionally disturbed child, this approach has been used successfully in both England and the United States with these children. The raw data of limited personal observations tend to indicate that this is an effective method of teaching base level content simpler than skills to the mentally retarded or emotionally disturbed child.

Fundamental Skills

Fundamental locomotor and nonlocomotor skills are discussed in Chapter IV, Basic Motor Patterns and Skills, and Chapter VII, Music, Rhythms, and Dance. The movement education approach can be applied to the teaching of these skills by using questions, similar to those included in the remainder of this chapter, which develop the desired skills in a systematic progression from simple to more complex.

Manipulative Skills

When developing manipulative skills with mentally retarded or emotionally disturbed children each child should have his own piece of equipment. Practice should begin with nonlocomotor activity in self-space and gradually progress to locomotor activity in general space.

The terms used in the questions asked should be within the child's level of comprehension. It may be necessary to demonstrate the meaning of the words used in the questions, but not how to solve the problems. Repetition as a reinforcement should be used frequently. A slow, sequential progression with much repetition should be used to develop desirable skills.

Balloons, Bean Bags, Balls

The use of balloons, bean bags, and balls in programs for the mentally retarded or emotionally disturbed child contributes to the development of the child by increasing attention span, gross motor coordination, hand-eye coordination, foot-eye coordination, and self-confidence. In addition, these skills can stimulate and improve body balance, spacial concepts, body rhythm, body relaxation, socialization, and vocalization. Many severely handicapped children will respond favorably to balloon, bean bag, and ball activity in individual, parallel, and group play situations.

With many mentally retarded or emotionally disturbed children it may be necessary to begin manipulative skills by throwing and catching balloons. As arm strength is developed the children can progress to bean bags and then large beach or rubber balls.

Balloons

Questions for developing balloon activities might include: *"Can you tap the balloon into the air with one hand? . . . the other hand? . . . both hands together? . . . with a body part other than the hands? . . . using the feet?"* These same skills can be performed as the child is sitting on the floor with both feet in the air. The same questions can be asked, substituting feet for hands and encouraging the children to tap the balloon with the feet.

Running or other locomotor skills can be combined with balloon handling. Such questions as: *"Can you run (skip, slide, gallop, et cetera) as you tap the balloon into the air? . . . with one hand? . . . the other hand? . . . both hands?"*

A partner can be added and, using only one balloon, the children can be asked if they can tap the balloon back and forth. Next, the children can be asked if they can press the balloon between different parts of their bodies and change body positions and levels. Additional questions can be asked to encourage the children to pass, hit, kick, and catch the balloon from various stationary or moving positions.

Bean Bags

Activity with bean bags can include questions designed to encourage tossing them up in the air and catching them with both hands or one hand. The children can throw the bean bag very high and catch it high in the air or low near the floor. They can toss the bean bag at a distant target on the floor, run to pick it up, and return to their original starting position. Additional questions might include:

> *Can you toss the bean bag across the body from hand to hand in a rhythmical swing? . . . with the palms down (up)? . . . the eyes open (closed)? Can you walk (run, skip, slide, gallop) with the bean bag on your head? Can you sit down, keeping the bean bag on your head? . . . stand up? Can you place the bean bag between your feet and hop forward (backward)? Can you lift the bean bag off the floor with your toes? . . . place it on the line (circle, et cetera)? Standing, can you throw the bean bag high into the air, lie down quickly, and catch it? Lying down, can you throw the bean bag high in the air, stand quickly, and catch it?*

Using partners, the children can be asked to toss underhand or overhand and catch, throw high or low and catch high or low, throw to unexpected positions and catch, throw and catch two bean bags, or throw two bean bags from the same hand. *"Can you toss the bean bag through your legs to your partner?" "Can you toss the bean bag high to your partner who slides it along the floor back to you?"* The children can create their own variations using the bean bag.

Clown Target

More difficult activities with one bean bag would include tossing it overhead out of reach and running sideways to catch the bean bag, throwing it forward and running to catch it, starting to throw it forward but making a quick turn and throwing it to a partner, walking with the bean bag placed on the instep, swinging the leg forward and backward with the bean bag on the instep, circling the leg with a bean bag on the foot, swinging the leg to toss the bean bag off the foot and away from the body, swinging the bean bag up from the foot and catching it, placing the bean bag between the feet and springing forward, placing the bean bag between the feet and jumping upward to release and catch the bean bag, tossing the bean bag into a hoop or other object, and kicking the bean bag from the foot to a partner.

The mentally retarded or emotionally disturbed child will enjoy tossing the bean bag at a target such as a clown's face. Large openings can be made for the eyes and mouth. The children can be asked: *"Can you toss the bean bag into the clown's mouth? . . . right eye? . . . left eye?" "How many times can you throw the bean bag into the clown's mouth (right eye, left eye)?"*

Balls

The traditional method of teaching ball-handling skills is described in Chapter IV, Basic Motor Patterns and Skills. When the movement education approach is used the environment and questions are structured to develop desirable ball-handling techniques. Each child has his own ball. The following progressions are arranged by categories. They should be used only as a guide in the development of the desirable skills.

1. *How many things can you do with the ball while standing in your self-space?*
   a. *Can you bounce the ball with control? Can you bounce the ball and catch it? . . . with two hands? . . . with one hand? . . . with the opposite hand? Can you bounce the ball head high? . . . knee high? . . . waist high? . . . shoulder high? . . . ankle high?* (Identification of body parts is learned in this activity.) *Can you bounce the ball continuously? Can you find a square (triangle, circle) and bounce the ball in it? Can you bounce the ball hard so that it goes high into the air? While the ball is in the air, what can you do under it? Bounce the ball as quickly as you can. Sitting on the floor with the knees bent (straight), can you bounce the ball over your legs?*
   b. *Can you toss the ball into the air with control and catch it? . . . higher? Can you toss the ball high and catch it on the way down? Can you count the number of times you can toss and catch the ball without missing? Can you toss the ball into a square (triangle, circle) on the floor? . . . into a*

Ball Handling in Self-Space

box? (Colorful objects such as clown faces can be used for targets with the children aiming at an open mouth.) *Can you toss the ball over a rope and catch it yourself on the other side? Can you toss the ball against the wall and catch it? Can you throw it forcefully against the wall?* (Yarn or paper balls are excellent for practice of this skill.)

2. *Move into general space and see how many ways you can control the ball while moving. Can you bounce the ball as you walk? Can you bounce the ball as you jump up and down? Can you bounce the ball, keeping it low, as you move? Can you bounce the ball in a curved path on the floor? How many ways can you control the ball at a low level taking a curved path? Can you kick the ball with your foot? How many ways can you control the ball with your feet? Can you control the ball with your head? Can you throw the ball and hit a spot high on the wall?*

3. *With partners and one ball between you, how many ways can you control the ball? Can you increase the distance between you and your partner? While moving can you toss (roll,*

1
2

Ball Handling in General Space

    bounce) the ball to your partner and catch it? Can you alter-
nate one roll and one toss? Sitting on the floor can you roll the
ball to your partner?
4. Miscellaneous ball skills might include pushing the ball with
various parts of the body, pushing the ball with the feet
around obstacles, passing the ball in a circle (finger dexterity),
and holding the ball with two parts of the body as you change
levels.
5. Music can be used to add interest and variety to ball-handling
activity. The music used should be strongly accented and the
melody not too distracting. Begin with a simple drum beat.
When the children can handle balls in rhythm with the drum,
add music. Because of its swinging character, waltz music is
excellent for this purpose. The children can be asked: *"See
how many ways you can keep the beat of the music with the
ball."* Questions can encourage them to add patterns to their
ball handling. They can be asked to bounce, roll, or toss the
ball in rhythm and alone or with a partner. Specific suggestions might include: *"Can you pass the ball in a circle in*

rhythm to the music?" "Can you bounce the ball on the first note and hold it through the measure?" "Can you toss the ball into the air and catch it in rhythm with the music?" "Can you toss the ball, bounce it, and then catch it in rhythm with the music?" "Can you roll the ball to a partner in rhythm with the music?" "Who can bounce the ball to a partner who will hold it for a measure before bouncing it back?" "Who can bounce the ball, clap his hands, and then catch the ball?" "Who can bounce the ball, turn around, and then catch the ball?" "Can you tap the ball into the air in rhythm with the music?" Using polka music the children can bounce the ball continuously in rhythm, dribble in place, dribble under one leg, dribble behind, dribble and move into a circle (triangle, square, forward, backward, or sideward), stop and go while dribbling, or dribble the ball as they hop (skip, slide, jump). In addition the children can create their own ball combinations and routines to music, alone or with a partner.

6. Large, thirty-inch cage balls can be used in small group or team activities for pushing, throwing, or kicking. The best method to use in kicking the ball would be for the children to sit on the floor in a large circle and kick the ball across and back and forth. With the children in teams, the ball can be thrown over a low net. This activity should permit the children to volley, throw, or catch the ball in the air or after one or more bounces. The children should also be permitted to run short distances with the ball in their hands. They should NOT, however, be permitted to kick the ball, step or throw the ball out of bounds, or let the ball rest on the floor.

Ropes and Rope Jumping

The movement education approach to the use of ropes and rope-jumping skills in programs for the mentally retarded or emotionally disturbed child contributes to the development of body control, improved posture, poise, balance, fitness, and creativity. Rope activity can provide skill challenge and fun. In addition, activities selected can aid in developing laterality, directionality, and other perceptual-motor skills.

Ropes

Each child has his own rope, which is placed on the floor to form a straight line. The child is asked:

Can you walk on your rope as if it were a tightrope? How can your arms aid in balance as you walk on the rope? Can you walk on the rope touching your heel against your toe?

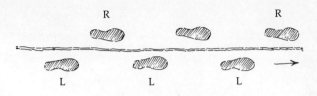

R R

L L L

Crisscross Foot Pattern

Can you count the number of steps you can take along the rope? (This is especially good with the emotionally disturbed child.) *Can you walk backward on your rope? Who can crisscross, going from side to side without touching the rope? Can you crisscross using your hands and feet, without touching the rope, and moving forward (backward)? Who can hop from side to side without touching the rope? Who can jump back and forth over the rope? Who can hop on one foot on the rope? . . . change and hop on the opposite foot? Can you make the rope into a circle (triangle, square) and stand inside without touching it? How much floor space can you cover in the circle (triangle, square) without touching the rope? Can you touch the floor space inside the circle (triangle, square) with three (four, five) different body parts? Can you jump (walk, hop, skip, et cetera) around the outside of (on) your circle (triangle, square)? Can you make your body into the shape of your rope?*

Using two ropes, the children can practice hopping, leaping, et cetera. With two ropes per child, crossed +, the child can hop or skip around the ropes and put one movement into each quarter of the rope pattern.

With the rope held in the hands, the children can pull hard on both ends of the rope. *"How many places can you take your stretched rope?"* This activity can be practiced until the children can make continuous, smooth, flowing movements as they hold the stretched rope.

Rope Jumping

Many mentally retarded or emotionally disturbed children will have difficulty learning the skill of rope jumping. A slow, sequential progression should be used in teaching this skill. Rope length is important for success in rope jumping. The proper length can be determined by having the child stand on the rope with both feet. With his arms held close to the body, the rope should reach shoulder level (armpits).

Rope Jumping

Correct form in rope jumping includes keeping the body erect with the eyes looking straight forward, keeping the legs and feet together with the knees slightly bent, gripping the rope loosely with the hands, and holding the arms close to the body as the rope is turned. The jumping motion should be entirely on the balls of the feet. The arms and shoulders begin the rope swing. After the first rope revolution, all turning action comes from the wrists. A double-time jump, in which the child takes two steps or a hop and a step between rope swings, should be taught. The mentally retarded or emotionally disturbed child should have mastered the skill of jumping, as described in Chapter IV, Basic Motor Patterns and Skills, before learning the skill of rope jumping.

Begin the development of rope-jumping skill by having the mentally retarded or emotionally disturbed child practice a double-time jump without the rope. Holding the rope behind the feet, the child should next practice swinging the rope up and over the head. The child may only be able to get the rope up to his shoulders on the first attempt. Practice should continue until he can swing the rope over the head. Next, have the child practice jumping over the rope as he holds it in front of his feet. When the child can swing the rope over his head and jump over it with both feet, he is ready to try rope jumping. Begin with one complete rope revolution and one jump. When this can be performed successfully, have the child try two, then three jumps, and then continuous jumping.

If the movement education approach is used to teach the skill of rope jumping, appropriate questions, designed to develop the afore-mentioned skills, should be used by the teacher.

Music can be added to the skill of rope jumping. Any good polka, fast march, or fox trot music with a strong beat is appropriate. The children can be asked to perform what they "feel" can be done to the music. Later, special steps can be added, and the children can create rope-jumping routines to the music.

Batons

Batons, wands, or lumi sticks can be used in a movement education program to increase finger dexterity, hand-eye coordination, agility, and balance. The following questions are suggested as a guide in de-veloping skill with this type of manipulative equipment:

> *Can you move the baton in a circular motion with your fingers? . . . with the other hand? Can you move your fingers up and then down the baton as if they were a worm crawling up a tree? . . . with the other hand? Can you toss the baton from hand to hand? Can you pass the baton around your body? . . . in the opposite direction? Can you pass the baton around and in and out of your legs? . . . in the opposite direction? Can you toss the baton in the air and catch it? Can you bounce the baton on the floor and catch it? Can you roll the baton back and forth on the floor? Can you balance the baton on the floor? . . . clap your hands once and catch it before it falls? . . . move around it without knocking it over? Can you balance the baton on the palm of your hand? . . . on two fingers? . . . on one finger? . . . with the opposite hand? What different way can you balance the baton? Can you turn around while balancing the baton on your hand? Can you move your body down low and then come back up while balancing the baton? Can you hold both ends of the baton and step over it? Can you balance the baton on one foot? . . . the other foot?*

Hula Hoops

Hula hoops can be beneficial in helping the mentally retarded and/or emotionally disturbed child develop agility and coordination. They can be used in either a traditional or movement education program. Questions might include:

> *Can you make the hoop turn circles (spin) while it is on*

one arm? . . . neck? . . . ankle? . . . wrist? . . . elbow?
How close to the floor can you spin the hoop? How high off
the floor can you spin the hoop? Can you spin the hoop as
you move around the room? Can you roll the hoop along the
floor? How many ways can you twist (bend) while holding
the hoop? What can you do with a foot and two hands hold-
ing the hoop? With one edge of the hoop on the ground, can
you step in and out (through, around, over) the hoop? Can
you sit in the hoop without touching it? Can you jump with
the hoop as if it were a jump rope?

With a partner holding the hoop on edge (or parallel to
the floor), how can you move in (around, over, through) it?

With a partner holding two hoops, how can you go
through them?

Hoops can be placed on the floor in various patterns. Using a
color code, the children can be asked to progress through the hoops
using a variety of locomotor skills (walk, run, jump, hop, skip, leap).
The children can be asked to place the right foot into the red hoops,

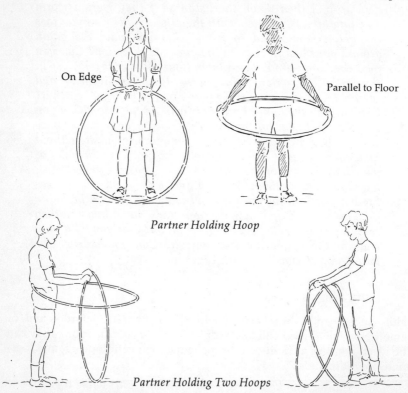

On Edge

Parallel to Floor

Partner Holding Hoop

Partner Holding Two Hoops

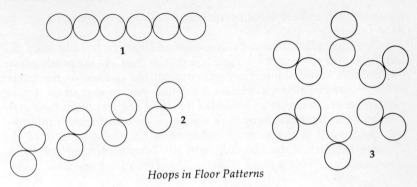

Hoops in Floor Patterns

the left foot into the yellow hoops, and both feet into the blue hoops. If some of the mentally retarded or emotionally disturbed children are having difficulty identifying the right or.left leg, red ribbon or crepe paper can be tied around the right leg and yellow ribbon or crepe paper around the left leg.

Hula hoops can be used with bean bags. The children can toss the bean bags into a hoop placed flat on the floor or throw it through

Tossing Bean Bag into Hoop

Tossing Bean Bag through Hoop

a hoop which is held by a partner and with one end resting on the floor.

A game called *Musical Hoops* can add variety to hula hoop activity. Place the hoops in a large circle on the floor. As the music plays, the children walk counterclockwise around the outside of the circle. When the music stops, everyone must find a hoop and sit in it. The element of elimination can be added by using one less hoop than children and removing one hoop each time a child is eliminated, until only one child is left in the game. Another variation would be to have the children perform a specific skill with the hoop each time the music stops, such as: *"Find a hoop, pick it up, and spin it on one arm."*

Musical Hoops

Poison Hoop

Poison Hoop can be enjoyed by most mentally retarded or emotionally disturbed children. The children join hands in a circle. One or two hoops can be used. The children pass the hoops around the circle by climbing through them. Music is used. When the music stops, whoever is caught with the hoop receives a point against him. When the children tire of the activity, the child with the fewest points against him is the winner.

Balance Skills

Many mentally retarded and/or emotionally disturbed children exhibit difficulty when performing activities which require balance. Because balance is a foundation for more complex movement skills, balance activities should be included in all skills programs for these children. Program variety and the use of motivational techniques are essential. In many cases it may be necessary for the mentally retarded or emotionally disturbed child to try the movements on the floor before attempting them on a balance board or balance beam.

Balance boards and balance beams can be used to develop balance, agility, coordination, laterality, directionality, posture, and self-confidence. A description of this balance equipment can be found in Chapter XII, Innovative Equipment. Each child should have his own balance board. Approximately six children can work on one balance beam, but only one child should be on the beam at a time.

Balance Boards

If the movement education approach is used with balance board activity, questions might include: *"Can you tilt the board back and forth without falling off?"* Some children may need teacher assistance the first time they try balancing on the board. The teacher should stand facing the child and hold both hands. When the child can balance with a two-hand assist, hold only one hand, then remove all support but be ready to offer assistance if necessary.

Can you bounce and catch a ball in front of you as you balance on the board? Can you throw the ball at a target as you balance on the board? Can you bend over and touch your feet, then stand back up without losing your balance? While balancing can you touch your shoulders (knees, toes, head, hips)? Can you change your body level as you balance? Can you balance on one foot? . . . the other foot?

Balance Beams

The traditional approach to the use of a balance beam is included in Chapter IX, Developmental Gymnastics. The activities described here should be performed on a balance beam which is approximately six to ten inches off the floor. The movement education approach can be built around the following questions:

How can you move from one end of the beam to the other? Can you find a different way to move along it? Can you place the heel of one foot against the toes of the other foot on each step? What can you do with the other parts of your body as you move? How can you use your arms to help you balance? Can you take long (short) steps as you move forward (backward) along the beam? Can you keep one foot in front of the other at all times? Can you make your feet meet and part as you step sideward along the beam? Can you walk forward (backward, sideward), touch the beam in the center with one (two) hand(s) and walk to the end of the beam? Can you walk forward (backward, sideward), turn in the middle of the beam and walk backward (forward, sideward) to the end? Can you change body levels as you move along the beam? Can you pick up this cup (or other object) halfway across and carry it to the end? Can you pick up the cup with the hand away from it (crossing midline of body)? Can you reach behind you to pick up the cup? Can you play "catch" with me (teacher) as you walk along the beam? Can you bounce a ball as you walk along the beam? How many different ways can you get off the beam? Can you lift one foot high in the air before you step on it? Can you touch your

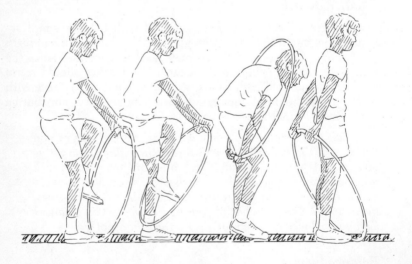

Balance Beam and Hoops

knee to the beam after each step? Can you lift the knee high after each step? Can you carry a ping pong ball in a spoon as you cross the beam? Can you walk the beam going over (through) hoops?

Balance beams can be used in obstacle courses. Footprints and/or handprints can be placed on the surface of the beam to assist the children in performing the desired movement patterns or the children can play "follow the leader" on the beam. Music can be used to encourage creativity in balance-beam activity.

Miscellaneous Skills

Tires

Old automobile or truck tires can be used for a variety of movement activities which contribute to the development of coordination, agility, and balance. Additional information on use of tires can be found in Chapter XII, Innovative Equipment. The movement education approach using tires can be built around the following questions:

One tire per child:

Who can run around his tire? Can you go the other way? What different way can you move around your tire? Can you put one foot in the middle of it as you jump over it? Can you carefully put both feet in the middle of the tire as you jump across? Can you bounce on the tire? Can you jump on the tire and bounce off? Can you stand on the tire and jump in the middle? Can you jump out in a different direction?

Several tires in sequence, flat on the ground:

Can you run quickly through all the tires without touching? Can you run through all the tires putting one foot in the middle of each? How quickly can you do this? Who can think of a new way to use the tires? Can you put two feet in each tire? How quickly? Can you walk along the tires without touching the ground? Can you jump along the tops of the tires? How can you go along the tops using your hands and feet? Can you jump (hop) in and out of each tire?

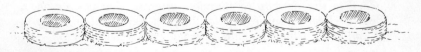

Tires Flat on Ground

Tires Standing on End

Several tires in sequence, secure in the ground and standing on end, level or uneven:

> *Can you go along the tires without touching the ground? Can you use your hands and feet to move along the top of the tires? Can you skip a tire? How few tires can you use?*

Parachutes

Parachutes for use in parachute play can be purchased at a nominal cost from most Army-Navy surplus stores. Inclusion of this kind of activity as part of the mentally retarded or emotionally disturbed child's movement experiences contributes to the development of the big muscles of the entire body, increases strength and endurance, helps develop the team work which many mentally retarded or emotionally disturbed children lack, improves rhythm and coordination, and is exciting and fun.

The children will usually be fascinated by the color, size, and texture of the parachute. Most of the mentally retarded and/or emotionally disturbed children in the class will enjoy a brief explanation of the parachute and the principles involved in its use.

A traditional or movement education approach can be used in teaching parachute play. Begin by having the children sit around the edge of the parachute, which is spread out on the floor. Ask them to grasp the rim of the canopy, preferably with palms down.

> *Can you stand up without letting go of the parachute? While holding onto the parachute, how far back can you step? If you pull hard can you step back even farther? How far overhead can you hold the parachute? How low to the ground? Can you walk (run, hop, skip, gallop) to the right as you hold the parachute? Can you go to the left? Music can be added to this activity to stimulate interest. Can you lie on your back with your legs under the parachute? Holding onto it, can you lift the parachute over your head? How high?*
>
> *Can you shake the parachute and make it look like the waving motion of water? Try to shake the parachute slowly*

so that everyone is going up and down at the same time. Can you keep your arms straight and shake vigorously? Can you shake slowly and when I blow the whistle run to the center without dropping the parachute? Now, shake until it really fills with air, then push the edge of the parachute to the ground.

Starting with the parachute spread on the ground, when I blow the whistle can you stand up straight and fast, pulling the parachute up and over your heads? (Everyone must rise and stretch simultaneously if this skill is to be successful.) *Can you return the parachute quickly to the ground and lift it high again? This time, when the parachute is up high and I blow the whistle, let go of the edges and see how high it will continue by itself. This time when the parachute is up high, can you hold your arms high and let the parachute glide down?*

Starting with the parachute spread on the ground, when I blow the whistle can you stand up straight and fast, pulling the parachute up and over your heads? When the parachute is high enough for you to see the people on the other side (it may be helpful for the teacher to blow a whistle as a signal), *take three steps quickly forward, keeping your hands and arms raised over your head. When I blow the whistle* (when parachute reaches its peak) *move quickly back to your starting position. This time when I blow the whistle* (the parachute reaches its full height), *quickly bring your hands down to the floor.* This skill can be performed with some of the children inside and some outside of the parachute.

Let's stretch the parachute and hold it low. Who can crawl under it? Shake the parachute until it gets really high. When I blow the whistle let go of the edges and get inside. Shake the parachute until it gets really high. Who thinks that on the signal "go" he can run under the parachute from one side to the other without getting caught inside? (The teacher should say "go" when the parachute is filled with air and on its way up.)

Mouse Trap is a game which can be played with a parachute. Choose three or four children to be mice. The other children hold and shake the parachute, keeping it high. The mice run back and forth under the parachute. When the teacher blows a whistle the children holding the parachute bring it quickly to the floor, trying to trap the mice inside. Note: A severely disturbed child should NOT be chosen as a mouse.

Another fun activity with a parachute is to give the children num-

Parachute Play

Team A   Team B

Team Parachute Play

bers. The children shake the parachute, keeping it high. The teacher calls a number and the children with that number exchange places by going under the parachute.

Beachballs can be used to add variety to parachute play. One ball is placed in the center of the parachute. *"Can you shake the parachute up and down, keeping the ball in the parachute? How high?"* This exercise can be repeated with several balls.

A game can be played with one ball in the parachute. The children are divided into two teams. Working together as a team, the children try to roll the ball off the opponent's half of the parachute. Team play should be emphasized. One point can be given each time the ball is sent off the parachute to the floor.

Scooters

Scooters can be a valuable addition to a mentally retarded or emotionally disturbed child's movement experiences. They are excellent for the development of arm and leg strength, coordination, balance, spatial relationships, and depth perception in relationship to the room. If scooters are used in the program, the children should NOT be permitted to stand on them or push them with their hands or feet. When scooters are used the children should sit, kneel, or lie on them in a prone or supine position. The child's body weight can be wholly or partially supported on the scooter. There should be one scooter for every child.

Can you sit on the scooter and push with your feet to move backward? . . . pull with your feet to move forward? Can you move in a circle? Can you follow this curved (zigzag) line?

Can you kneel on the scooter and use your arms to pull your body forward? . . . push your body backward? Can you move in a circle? Can you follow this curved (zigzag) line?

Can you lie on your stomach and use your hands to pull your body forward? . . . push your body backward? Can you move in a new direction? Some children may be more successful in this activity if their body weight is supported on two scooters.

Sitting on Scooter

Lying on Face on Scooter

"Can you lie on your back and use your hands and feet to move your body around the floor?" Some of the children may find the back lying position difficult to use. Practicing a crab walk without a scooter will facilitate the learning of this skill.

Relay races can be played with the children sitting, kneeling, or lying on their scooters. Obstacle courses can be set up for use in scooter play.

Aquatic Skills

The traditional method of teaching swimming is included in Chapter X, Swimming and Water-Related Activities. The movement education approach can be used in an aquatic environment to enhance the mentally retarded or emotionally disturbed child's self-identification and self-understanding. At the same time the child's need for better control of his body, vigorous activity, self-expression, confidence, and the joy of achievement can be satisfied.

The movement education approach can be used most effectively to develop a readiness for learning the coordinated movements of swimming. Concepts of breath control, buoyancy, balance, body image, spatial awareness, locomotion, and force in the aquatic medium can be explored and discovered. Hoops, wands, ropes, balls and other small manipulative equipment can be used to add variety to these experiences.

The following questions are just a few of the many possible examples which can be used in the aquatic environment to teach fundamental skills using the movement education approach.

Breath Control

Can you catch some water and hold it in both hands? Can you wash your face with the water in your hands? Try to blow all the water off your hands. Can you place your hands in the water and blow the water off them? Can you place your mouth under water and blow the water away? Can you put more of your face under water and still blow the water away? Can you put your face and head under water and hold your breath? How long? Can you pick up these buttons from the bottom? Can you blow water away from you, then raise your head for more air to blow away? How many times can you do this?

Balance and Buoyancy

Can you rest your arm on the water? Will it stay there if you don't try to hold it up? Try this with the other arm. Can you submerge your body up to the neck? . . . and balance on one foot? Can you submerge all of your body? What happens when you try to keep your body under water? Can you touch the bottom with one hand? . . . two hands? . . . two hands and only one foot? What other part of your body can you use to touch the bottom? Can you kneel (sit) on the bottom? Do you know why it's difficult to stay down? Can you bend forward at the waist and let your head and chest rest on the water? Hold your breath and try to fall down in the water. What happens to your body when you do this? Can you hold on the edge and lie flat on the water on your face? . . . back . . . can you curl your whole body and stand? . . . can you curl and then stretch out? Can you find a new position in which you can stay in the water without touching anything?

Body Image

Can you move your arm back and forth through the water? . . . the other arm? . . . your leg? Can you touch your right hand to your left knee? . . . left hand to right knee? Can you touch your foot with one hand? . . . the other hand (foot)? Can you put yourself in front of me? . . . behind me? . . . under me? . . . far away from me? . . . near me?

Simon Says can be played in the water with the mentally retarded or emotionally disturbed child to help him develop an awareness of the various parts of his body as they move independently or in relation to other body parts in the water. This game will also help the child discover how it feels to move a body part in or through the water.

Spatial Awareness, Locomotion, and Force

Can you walk around the pool keeping your feet on the bottom? Can you walk using very large (small) steps? How quickly can you do this? Can you lift one foot high off the pool bottom as you move? Can you find another way to move through the water? Can you run (jump, hop, et cetera)? Try moving backward through the water. Can you go sideward? Can you move without (with) splashing water? Can you use your hands and arms to push the water in front of you? Can you push the water from the front to the back of your body? Let your body do whatever it wants as you push the water. Can you float on your face and push the water backward with your hands? What other part of your body can you use to push the water backward? Can you make your body very small (large) and move through the water? Can you make your body small (large) underwater? . . . and move? Can you find a new way to move around the pool?

The children can experiment with pushing and pulling light and heavy objects around the pool. This will enhance their concepts of resistance and force in the water.

Recreational Aspects

Skills developed by the mentally retarded or emotionally disturbed child through a movement education teaching approach can be used in the pursuit of recreational activity. Balloons, bean bags, ropes, batons, hula hoops, tires, and parachutes can be used in game activity at parties for these children. Most of the skills included in this chapter can be used in individual play activity to fill the mentally retarded or emotionally disturbed child's many free hours.

The recreational aspects of swimming are numerous. These are discussed in Chapter X, Swimming and Water-Related Activities.

In a community recreation environment the mentally retarded or emotionally disturbed child can participate in parachute, tire, scooter, hula hoop, rope, baton, balance beam, balance board, balloon, bean bag, and ball play with "normal" children. These same activities can be used by the child with his family at home or while engaged in family outings.

Any skill which contributes to the development of the mentally retarded or emotionally disturbed child's self-concept and his ability to handle his body more efficiently will have carry-over value into the child's pursuit of leisure-time activity, alone or with other individuals. The satisfying of the child's leisure-time needs are an important aspect of his total development if he is to be a part of the world in which he lives.

SELECTED REFERENCES

Ackerman, Jeanne. Using movement exploration in the swimming pool with mentally retarded. *Journal of Health, Physical Education and Recreation,* 1971, **42** (8), 65-68.

Bentley, William G. *Learning to move and moving to learn.* New York: Citation Press, 1970.

Frederick, Joseph B. Balloons, effective teaching materials. *Challenge,* May-June 1970, **5** (5), 1, 9.

Gilliom, Bonnie C. *Basic movement education for children.* Reading, Mass.: Addison-Wesley Publishing Co., 1970.

Hackett, Layne C. *Movement exploration and games for the mentally retarded.* Palo Alto: Peek Publications, 1970.

Havard-Jones, Beti. Fun and games with bean bags. *Challenge,* Sept.-Oct. 1971, **7** (1), 4.

Howard, Shirley. The movement education approach to teaching in English elementary schools. *Journal of Health, Physical Education and Recreation,* 1967, **38** (1), 31-33.

Johnson, Leo J. Parachute play for exercise. *Journal of Health, Physical Education and Recreation,* 1967, **38** (4), 26-27.

Kirchner, Glenn, Jean Cunningham and Eileen Warrell. *Introduction to movement education.* Dubuque: William C. Brown Co., Publishers, 1970.

Ludwig, Elizabeth A. Toward an understanding of basic movement education in the elementary schools. *Journal of Health, Physical Education and Recreation,* 1968, **39** (3), 26-29.

Peterson, Marshall. Developmental activities. *Challenge,* May-June 1971, **6** (5), 4-5.

Popen, Sharalyn. Go parachuting. *Journal of Health, Physical Education and Recreation,* 1967, **38** (4), 24-25.

Sweeney, Robert T., ed. *Selected readings in movement education.* Reading, Mass.: Addison-Wesley Publishing Co., 1970.

Chapter **VII**

Music, Rhythms, and Dance

$\mathbf{M}$entally retarded and emotionally disturbed children can profit from meaningful music and music-related experiences. Musical activity promotes group organization and unity, provides a basic form of communication, stimulates creative activity, and lacks the competitive element. The nonthreatening environment, scope, and infinite variety offered by musical experiences, in some form and some degree of refinement, permit these children to elicit basic human responses, physically, mentally, and emotionally, to the elements of music. Everyone can experience some success if he is properly stimulated to interact with this music environment.

Music skills can be developed in the mentally retarded or emotionally disturbed child to the point where listening becomes a pleasurable experience and performing provides satisfaction. Music can alleviate the child's sense of defeat and deprivation and provide him with a vehicle for emotional expression, thus enhancing his well-being and self-respect. The movement and rhythm of music can help him find an acceptable channel for the release of his undesirable impulses. It can help him sublimate his aggressive and destructive urges, channeling this disorganized energy into socially acceptable activity.

Many mentally retarded or emotionally disturbed children who respond to no other medium can be reached through musical activity. Frequently, music is used as therapy with these children. Even the most severely retarded or disturbed child can nod his head, clap his hands, stamp his feet, or simply sway back and forth in rhythm to music. Music and rhythm provide exhilaration, develop harmonious move-ment, and assist in the achievement of muscular control, motor devel-opment, fitness, poise, and balance. Through participation in musical activities tensions and anxieties can be released, feelings can be ex-pressed and communicated to others, social development and adjust-ment can improve, and language development can be accelerated. Dur-ing music participation the passive child can frequently be stimulated and the hyperactive child may find relaxation. Quiet records may be especially useful in promoting a calming effect on the mentally retarded or emotionally disturbed child, especially at the end of a class period.

Although there is no research available on the ability of mentally retarded or emotionally disturbed children to develop musically, they do respond well to the basic features of music and to the elements of rhythm in music. Their progress in music will probably be related to their progress in other subjects.

Teaching Suggestions

1. Music should have a strong beat and easy rhythm.
2. Songs with simple melodies are best. The melody should have intervals limited in size with frequently repeated figures and phrases. It should be well within the child's vocal range.
3. Songs should have simple words which meet the child's devel-opmental level mentally, physically, and socially. In addition, his needs and interests should be considered. Music is an excel-lent form of nonverbal communication. The child is not threat-ened by nonsense syllables in songs and enjoys repeating words, especially familiar words. Care should be taken in the selection of songs with words so that the child is not insulted. This can happen if the child's mental age but not his chrono-logical and social ages are considered.
4. When singing is a part of the musical experience, the singers and nonsingers should be mixed.
5. Each child should experience some form of success during each music, rhythms, or dance class. The child should be protected from embarrassment, frustration, and failure and not be placed in situations beyond his ability. The goal of the rhythms or dance class should be to provide each and every child with active, pleasurable, rewarding, and successful experiences rather than the mastery of intricate dance steps and techniques. Praise should be used as often as possible.
6. Because of the limited ability and attention span of these chil-dren, short, frequent music experiences will be more successful than long, infrequent ones. Frequent rest periods of short dur-ation will also be beneficial.

7. Simple, easy to manipulate instruments should be used when the children are participating in instrument play. These might include triangles, maracas, tambourines, cymbals, and drums.

8. Reinforce musical cues with other sensory cues and experiences which will be appropriately motivating to the children. If the children are involved in instrument play or simple rhythmic movement, the teacher can clap his hands to the rhythm so the children can see and hear the clap, count for the children, or sing the rhythm.

9. Observe simple rules of safety regarding use of space, especially in locomotor rhythmic activities and creative dance.

10. Begin experiences in music, rhythms, and dance with very simple structures which are frequently repeated. To give the child a needed feeling of success and security, use small step sequences to build these simple structures slowly into more complex rhythms and movements. Frequent repetition is a necessary reinforcement.

11. Use demonstrations frequently. They are more meaningful than verbal explanations. If verbal explanations and suggestions are used, they should be clear, simple, and geared to the child's level of comprehension.

12. Rhythm and dance activities selected should be of short duration with much repetition. They should be within the intellectual comprehension and work tolerance level of the child, based on his mental age, needs, interests, and developmental level.

13. The teacher should assume a structuring, dynamic role in the class. Teaching techniques should be widely diversified, using such methods as mirror image, kinesthesis, and special learning cues. Flexibility is important if the needs and interests of each and every child are to be met.

14. When presenting new musical experiences to the child, first permit him to listen to the entire dance record or musical sequence. Next, have him clap out the rhythm and then perform the required actions. If there is more than one part to the desirable experience, teach each part separately and then combine them into the whole sequence.

15. If necessary, decrease the tempo of the music, especially when teaching the fundamentals of a dance step or pattern.

16. Simplify and modify rhythmic activities as necessary. Swaying, swinging, walking, sliding, or balance steps can be substituted for complex dance steps and patterns.

17. When teaching square dancing, an experienced caller who can follow the speed of the group is ideal. Records with singing calls are frequently difficult for the children to understand and follow. Masking tape can be used on the floor to mark square

dance positions and provide a basis for dance movements and patterns.

18. Creative dance should help the child explore as he learns to move unhampered by set restrictions, words, or rules. The environment should encourage the child to change directions, alter levels, and react to objects upon the suggestions, guidance, or commands of the instructor or the rhythm of the music.

Music

Basic Music Elements

Meter refers to time in music or the grouping of beats to form the underlying rhythm within a measure. Meter can be recognized by listening for the accent on the first beat. In the following examples the ⁄ refers to the accent, which aids in recognizing the meter of the music.

Meter

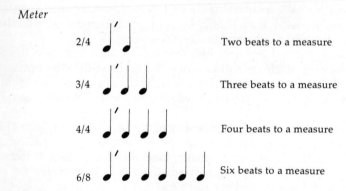

Note Values refer to the length of time given to a note of music. A whole note is held longer than a half note, a half note longer than a quarter note, et cetera.

Note Value

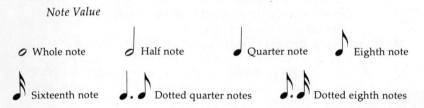

Dotted notes take half value for the next note in the measure. These are found in uneven rhythmic patterns.

Underlying Beat refers to the basic rhythm, the pulse, the beat, the "keeping of time." It is the steady sound that goes throughout a rhythmical sequence and serves as the underlying constant unit of measure upon which all rhythmic structure or relationship depends. The constant, steady pulsation which exists in all movement is the underlying beat. It has equal force and time and serves as the underlying fundamental sound in music.

Rhythmic Pattern refers to a definite grouping of sounds of equal or unequal duration which are heard as being equal or unequal. It is the melody of a song. The rhythmic pattern relates directly to the underlying beat in that a particular pattern of sounds may fit with a unit of underlying beats.

Rhythmic Pattern

Example of a rhythmic pattern in 4/4 time:

Melody or rhythmic pattern
Meter or underlying beat

Even Rhythm refers to a rhythmic pattern in which all beats get equal or full note value. These beats can be either all long or all short. The walk, run, hop, jump, leap, waltz, and schottische are all performed to an even rhythm.

Even Rhythm

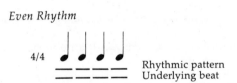

Rhythmic pattern
Underlying beat

Uneven Rhythm refers to a rhythmic pattern in which all beats do not receive equal or full note value. This rhythm is a combination of long and short beats. The skip, slide, gallop, and two-step are all performed to an uneven rhythm.

Uneven Rhythm

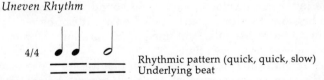

Rhythmic pattern (quick, quick, slow)
Underlying beat

Measure refers to an identical, recurring grouping of underlying beats. Measures are grouped in regular intervals which are separated by a bar.

Phrase refers to a group of measures which give a feeling of unity. In dance it is a movement idea or sequence. Phrases may be long or short. They aid one in knowing when to change movements.

Tempo refers to the rate of speed at which music is played. It is the fast and slow element of music, accompaniment, or movement.

Accent refers to the stress or emphasis given to a sound (beat) or grouping of sounds of underlying beats. The accent gives variety to the otherwise monotonous underlying beat, and groups the sounds of the underlying beats into units. The accent may occur anywhere within the measure. In dance accent is the emphasis placed on certain movements.

Intensity refers to the relative magnitude of force or strength. It is the dynamics of loud and soft, heavy and light, the variation of stress, or the feeling of quality in music.

Related Dance Elements

Rhythm is a binding together of parts into a whole. It is measured energy, action and rest, control and release. The two most important components of rhythm are duration and intensity. Rhythm sustains force and gives it orderly sequence. It is synonymous with form and is the flow of movement.

Spatial Pattern is the organization of movement in relation to the beat, direction, phrase, line, design, et cetera.

Quality of movement refers to its jerky, bumpy, smooth, stiff, loose, hard, soft, or booming force.

Focus is the attention of movements toward a specific spot or point in space.

Direction is the forward, backward, sideward, around pattern the movement follows.

Level refers to the high or low position of the body in movement.

Floor Pattern is the picture, path, or design on the floor that is made while moving. These geometric paths include circles, zigzags, triangles, squares, figure 8s, lines, et cetera.

Time, space, and force are elements found in all movement. They all involve beat, accent, meter, phrasing, rhythmic pattern, tempo, intensity, and spatial pattern.

Time involves movement, sight, and sound. The time of movement can be slow, fast, or a contrast of the two. It can be regular and equal in duration or irregular and unequal in duration. All movement takes place in even or uneven time.

Space refers to the three-dimensional qualities of movement and includes the floor space over which the body moves and the air space through which the body moves. The space used can be large, small, or a contrast of the two. It can be high, low, broad, or narrow. Space involves the position, direction, size, and shape of the body as it is moving. The use of space can involve regular, irregular, frequent, or infrequent changes of direction.

Force refers to the quality of the movement. It is the contrast between tension and relaxation, strong and weak, active and passive, gradual and sudden. The force in movement can be constant or irregular in quality and emphasis.

Listening to and Understanding Music

Music and sound are a way of expressing movement and are an outgrowth of movement. The mentally retarded or emotionally disturbed child responds to the "feel" of the rhythm and the muscle sensations and activity they arouse within his body. The children may be awkward at first, but once they understand the timing and values of intensity they will become more efficient, and skillful movement will result.

Beginning with simple music, have the children clap to the underlying beat. If this is too difficult for some of the children, use a simple rhythmic verse for handclapping. Later, simple body movements can be combined with the handclapping. Next, progress to having the children clap their hands and then move to the rhythmic pattern. When the children can identify the underlying beat and rhythmic pattern, begin clapping the hands or stamping the feet to the accent only. Movement can be added and the children can change the direction of their movement on the accent. A variation of handclapping on the accent can include a loud clap on the accent and light claps on the other musical beats.

Instrument Play

The mentally retarded or emotionally disturbed child can learn the basic elements of music through simple instrument play. Musical instruments which are easily manipulated reinforce the child's concentration and facilitate learning. Once the fundamentals are learned, the children will derive a great deal of satisfaction from making their own music. Simple instruments such as triangles, tambourines, cymbals, drums, shakers, rhythm sticks, bells, maracas, and sand blocks can be made by the children for use in instrument play. Information on how to make these simple instruments can be found in Chapter XII, Innovative Equipment.

Instrument play can begin by having the children clap their hands to a simple drumbeat. Later, they can clap to a simple piece of music being played on a record player. When the children exhibit a basic knowledge of the rhythm of the music, they can begin playing their own homemade instruments to the beat of the record player.

A simple game to play with the children at this time, to teach them to stop playing their instruments when the music stops, is **music** elimination. Anyone who does not stop playing his instrument when the music stops is eliminated from the game. This game can also be adapted to the skills of handclapping and moving to basic rhythms. The children "freeze" when the music stops. The children can learn shapes and symbols in this game if it is varied so they are asked to stand or sit on specific shapes or symbols, which have been assigned to them, when the music stops.

Directionality can be developed through instrument play. Begin by having the children beat a drum with alternating hands — right-left-right-left or right-right-left-left. Then have the feet tap the floor in the same alternate right-left pattern. Later, combine the hand and foot actions.

While involved in instrument play the mentally retarded or emotionally disturbed child can be taught the basic elements of tempo, accent, intensity, phrasing, and rhythmic pattern. He can learn to count on the beats of the music. Eventually, some of the children in the group will be able to progress to part playing with records.

Instrument play can teach the mentally retarded or emotionally disturbed child how to listen to and appreciate music. It will prepare him for participation in singing games, fundamental rhythms, and dance.

Fundamental and Creative Rhythms

Fundamental rhythms are basic, natural, flowing, balanced movements of the child's body. They can be structured or creative. Fundamental rhythms provide the child with the tools necessary for understanding basic movement and the working vocabulary for all forms of dance. These rhythmic activities and movement patterns provide the mentally retarded or emotionally disturbed child with experience in fundamental locomotor, nonlocomotor, and manipulative activity. As structured or creative activities, they all involve time, space, and force. Fundamental rhythms are necessary prerequisites for the child's success in his later structured or creative dance experiences.

When teaching these activities to the mentally retarded or emotionally disturbed child, the teacher should begin with structured, fundamental rhythmic patterns performed to simple music. After basic movement patterns have been developed, the child can begin to explore and create his own rhythmic patterns.

Locomotor Rhythms

Locomotor patterns are classified as being either even or uneven in rhythm. The walk, run, jump, hop, and leap are even in rhythm. The skip, slide, and gallop are uneven in rhythm. Most children will be able to perform these fundamental locomotor patterns by the time they enter school. The mentally retarded or emotionally disturbed child, however, might have to be taught these fundamental skills.

Walk, Run, Hop, Jump, Leap
Even rhythm 2/4, 3/4, or 4/4 time

Skip, Slide, Gallop
Uneven Rhythm 2/4, 3/4, 4/4, or 6/8 time

In the skip, slide, and gallop the step or leap is taken on the slow count and the hop is taken on the quick count.

Walk, Run

Recommended Mental Age: Two to three years.
Record: Educational Activities Album K 3090.

The walk and run, two most significant locomotor activities in daily life, are described in Chapter IV, Basic Motor Patterns and Skills. They are equally important in both structured and creative dance experiences. In ordinary situations one walks to arrive at a destination or runs to get there in a hurry. In dance one may walk to feel a relation to space or run to suggest a sense of hurry. The walk and run can be performed in all qualities of movement and all styles, on any directional line, at any level, with any degree of force or volume, and with varied emotion.

When teaching these fundamental locomotor movements to the mentally retarded or emotionally disturbed child, begin by having him move to a simple drumbeat played by the teacher. A simple record can also be used for this purpose. Walking music should have a moderate, even rhythm in 2/4, 3/4, or 4/4 time. The music should have a staccato, well-accented quality. The run is also performed to a moderate tempo of even rhythm in 2/4, 3/4, or 4/4 time. The music is staccato and the beat can be divided evenly or in triplets.

After the children have learned to walk and run correctly and in rhythm with the music, they can add variety to their walk. The children can walk, changing direction after every musical phrase; walk forward, backward, or sideward; walk to various musical tempos; combine walking with handclapping to the beat; walk on the heels or toes; walk with a heavy tramp or smoothly and silently. Next, the creative element can be added to these simple locomotor patterns. The teacher might make stimulating suggestions to the children. They might be asked to walk as if they were tired, proud, lazy, sad, or happy. They might imitate their mother's or father's walk or a doll, tin soldier, spaceman, giant, or elf. If they are familiar with marching bands, they can walk as if they were in such a band. Later, the children can create their own walk and the other members of the group can try to guess what they are imitating.

The same suggestions for walking can be applied to running. The run can be combined with the walk. Teacher suggestions to develop creativity might include running like a train. The children might all get in line and represent different parts of the train as they run. They can be asked to run at different speeds, in place or moving, in different floor patterns, or by changing the length of their stride. They could run as if they were trying to catch a bus or create their own run variations.

Hop

Recommended Mental Age: Four to five years.
Record: Educational Activities Album K 3090.

Hopping as a locomotor skill is described in Chapter IV, Basic Motor Patterns and Skills. As a rhythmic activity the hop is performed to a moderate, even rhythm in 2/4, 3/4, or 4/4 time. The music has a staccato, well-accented quality.

As a creative activity the hop can be used alone or in combination with other locomotor patterns. In structured dance experiences it is frequently used in combination with a running or walking step. Music can be used to stimulate creative hopping patterns. The child can hop on one foot as if he were a bird, a bouncing ball, or popcorn. The size of the hop, floor pattern followed, and musical speed and quality can be varied in both creative and structured hopping experiences.

Jump

Recommended Mental Age: Four to five years.
Record: Educational Activities Album HYP 29.

The jump as a locomotor skill is described in Chapter IV, Basic Motor Patterns and Skills. As a rhythmic activity the jump is performed to a moderate, even rhythm in 2/4, 3/4, or 4/4 time. The music has a staccato, well-accented quality.

As a structured dance skill the jump is used in combination with other fundamental locomotor patterns. Music can be used to stimulate creativity in jumping. The children can jump continuously in a forward pattern as if they were a bouncing ball, a rabbit, a jack-in-the-box, a fire cracker, a jumping bean, or a grasshopper. Or, the children can create their own jumping variations to solve specific problems presented for solution.

Leap

Recommended Mental Age: Seven to eight years.
Record: Educational Activities Album HYP 7.

Leaping as a locomotor skill is described in Chapter IV, Basic Motor Patterns and Skills. As a rhythmic activity the leap is performed to a moderate, even rhythm in 2/4, 3/4, or 4/4 time. The music has a staccato, well-accented quality.

As a dance skill the leap is usually used in combination with other locomotor patterns. Music can stimulate creativity in leaping. A good record for leaping practice is "Pop Goes the Weasel." The children can leap on "pop" in the song. A variety of floor patterns or combinations of leaping and other familiar steps will add variety and interest to practice. The child can pretend to be leaping over puddles or short bushes. He can leap as if he were lightning or a deer, or he can create his own leap variations.

Skip, Slide, Gallop

Recommended Mental Age: Four to five years.
Record: Educational Activities Album HYP 7.

The skip, slide, and gallop as locomotor skills are described in Chapter IV, Basic Motor Patterns and Skills. Rhythmically, all three of these movement patterns are performed to a moderate tempo of uneven rhythm in 2/4, 3/4, 4/4, or 6/8 time. The music has a staccato, well-accented quality. The skip has a springy, joyful, carefree quality. The slide has a smooth, flowing quality. The gallop has a forceful, sharp quality.

These steps are frequently used in dance in their pure form. Musical accompaniment can facilitate learning and stimulate creativity in the use of the skip, slide, and gallop. Creativity can be added to skipping by accenting the arm lift, skipping for height or distance, or by

following a variety of geometric floor patterns. Variety can be added
to the slide by changing the size, direction, and speed of the movements. Or, the children can slide in a circle as if they were on a merry-
go-round. Creativity can be added to the gallop by having the children
imitate a farmer's horse, a parade horse, a frisky horse, or a race horse.
During the gallop the arms can be held as if the child were holding the
reins of a horse. Music can be used as the children create their own
skip, slide, or gallop variations.

Nonlocomotor Rhythms

Fundamental nonlocomotor rhythmic activities include those body
movements which can be performed while the feet remain in place.
They involve movements of the head, torso, arms, and legs and include
bending, stretching, swinging, twisting, swaying, raising, lowering,
circling, and rotating these various parts of the body. Large, free
movements to the full range of flexibility should be the goal when
teaching nonlocomotor skills to the mentally retarded or emotionally
disturbed child. Once this has been achieved, the creative element can
be introduced. Later, nonlocomotor movements can be combined with
locomotor movements.

The best music for use with nonlocomotor movements would be
of a moderate tempo in 3/4, 4/4, or 6/8 time. The music should have
a smooth, sustained, legato quality.

Beginning work in nonlocomotor activities with the mentally retarded or emotionally disturbed child should be from a fixed base position lying on the back. As movement experience is acquired, the child
should progress to a fixed base sitting, a fixed base kneeling, and then
a fixed base standing position.

Identification of body parts may be a necessary prerequisite to
beginning nonlocomotor movement experiences with the mentally retarded or emotionally disturbed child. From a back lying position the
child can begin to explore and discover the movement possibilities of
the various parts of his body. This would include movements of the
head, neck, fingers, hands, elbows, shoulders, entire arms, spine, hips,
knees, ankles, toes, entire legs, and various movement combinations of
body parts. Teacher suggestions can be used to stimulate movement
sequences. At first it may be necessary to touch a part of the body and
ask the child to move it in as many ways as possible. If additional help
is needed by the child, the teacher might suggest how the part can be
moved or even move the body part for the child. If the teacher intends
to touch the child, he should tell him before actually touching his
body.

From a sitting position the child can begin to rediscover and increase the many possible movements he can make with his neck—for-

ward, backward, sideward, and in combination. Teacher suggestions and/or demonstrations may be necessary, especially with the more severely handicapped child. Next, movements of the fingers, wrists, elbows, shoulders, and spine should be explored. The child should be encouraged to move in as many ways as he possibly can, with or without teacher suggestions and/or demonstrations. Having the child mirror movements made by the teacher may be a good stimulus for this activity.

From a kneeling position the movements performed while sitting can be repeated. Hip movements and a combination of arm and trunk movements can be added. From a standing position swinging and rotating movements of alternate legs can be added to the movements performed while kneeling. Music can be used to add stimulation to these nonlocomotor rhythmic activities.

After the children have developed some freedom of movement in these various positions, they can experiment with moving from one to the other. They can go from a standing position to a lying or sitting position, from a kneeling position to a sitting position, et cetera.

The creative element can be added to nonlocomotor rhythmic activities by using stimulating music and teacher suggestions. If emphasis is placed on feeling, the child will not be self-conscious, freer movement will result, a sense of quality in movement will be established, and a more expressive body will be developed.

Complete flexion and extension can be practiced as the child pretends to be a flower growing, a water fountain, a jack-in-the-box, a butterfly emerging from a cocoon, or an elevator. Side-bending practice would include pretending to be flowers in the wind, bells ringing, or a teeter-totter. Forward bending could include pretending to be planting seeds, washing cloths, or picking flowers. Back flexion and extension would include pretending to be London Bridge, a cat's back, or a balloon.

When working on the skills of rotation or twisting and turning the children can pretend to be a weather vane, a rotating electric fan, or a water sprinkler. Pendular or swinging and swaying movements can be practiced as the child pretends to be a windshield wiper, a swing, a tree swaying in the wind, or a field of grain blowing in the wind. Striking movements can be practiced as the child pretends to be beating a drum, to be the clapper of a bell, or to be killing flies with a fly swatter.

Additional suggestions for creativity would include changes in music time factors and intensity. The children can experiment with various space patterns. Locomotor movements can be added to the nonlocomotor movements of the body. Eventually, the mentally retarded or emotionally disturbed child will be able to make free and informal movements to the music used.

Manipulative Rhythms

Manipulative rhythmic activities include those various skills in which the hands use such items as ropes, balls, wands, and hoops in time with music. These skills can be performed with or without locomotion. Manipulative rhythmic activities are included in Chapter VI, Movement Education.

Singing, Action Songs, Singing Games

Singing

Singing can be an effective method of reaching the mentally retarded or emotionally disturbed child. It provides relaxation and enjoyable entertainment. In addition, singing teaches the child to use words and word sequences as he gains control and strength in his breathing. Skill in singing will make it easier for the child to enjoy participation in action songs and singing games. Singing practice can begin by having the children sing the beat of the music. A simple word such as "go" can be repeated on the beat. Next, the children can progress to singing the syllables. One-syllable words such as red or blue and two-syllable words such as yellow and purple can be used for this practice. Later, the children can progress to singing simple songs such as "Row, Row Your Boat."

Row, Row, Row Your Boat

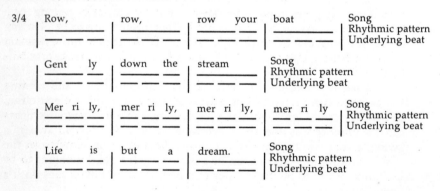

Action Songs and Singing Games

Action songs are rhythmic activities in which words are expressed through body movements. These movements, which accompany the words, facilitate learning by giving the child a more complete understanding of the meaning of the words used. Action songs are especially good as the mentally retarded or emotionally disturbed child's first movement experience in rhythms because these activities usually require that all participants perform the same actions at the same time. Awareness and acceptance of body parts can be realized through such action songs as "Looby Lou," "Hokey Pokey," and "Heads and Shoulders, Knees and Toes." If the words are sung in an action song it can also be considered a singing game.

A singing game can be described as a dance in which the children sing verses which give direction to the movements. Singing games are usually interpretations of old stories, fables, or adult-type tasks. Considerable variation is possible in the movement patterns of singing games, depending on how the children follow and interpret the action picture of the words used in the songs. It is frequently difficult to distinguish the fine line of difference between singing games and simple folk dances. This is partly due to the fact that many singing games are early forms of folk dances.

When action songs and singing games are first introduced to the mentally retarded or emotionally disturbed child, a record or the teacher can provide the singing. As soon as possible, the children should be encouraged to sing along with the music. Begin with simple songs and activities in which all of the children do the same thing at the same time. If music is part of the child's daily activity, the songs used can be taught to the children in music class.

After the children have become accustomed to group participation, action songs and singing games with partners or with an element of choice can be introduced. Songs and games selected should use only those skills in which the children possess a reasonable degree of proficiency. Remember that the fun element is more important than the learning of complex patterns and forms. Review of the basic skills used in each activity should be included at the beginning of each class period.

Because of the varied interests and experiences of the mentally retarded or emotionally disturbed child, it is difficult to assign a definite age level to action songs, singing games, and folk dances. The recommended mental age listed for each activity should only be considered a guide. Ideally, a gradual progression of rhythmic activities should be included in the child's physical education program.

The following action songs and singing games can be taught successfully to the mentally retarded or emotionally disturbed child. Additional action songs and singing games, which can be modified for use with these children, can be found in most elementary dance and elementary physical education textbooks.

I'm a Little Teapot

Recommended Mental Age
Three to four years.

Verse
1. I'm a little teapot short and stout.
2. Here is my handle, here is my spout.
3. I can change my handle and my spout!
4. Tip me over and pour me out!

Formation
Semicircle, facing teacher or leader.

Action
1. Stand straight and tall, hands at sides.
2. Place left hand on left hip to form handle, right arm forms spout by flexing elbow and wrist.
3. Place right hand on right hip to form handle, left arm forms spout by flexing elbow and wrist.
4. Bend sideways to the left, as if pouring the tea.

Heads and Shoulders, Knees and Toes

Recommended Mental Age
Three to four years.

Record
Victor 20806.

Verse

> Heads and shoulders, knees and toes.
> Heads and knees, shoulders and toes.
> Heads and toes, knees and shoulders.
> Heads and shoulders, knees and toes.

Formation

> Single circle, all facing in. Or, semicircle, facing teacher or leader.

Action

> As each part of the body is named, the child touches that part of his body with both hands. This action song is performed to the tune of "Here We Go Round the Mulberry Bush."

One Finger, One Thumb

Recommended Mental Age
Three to four years.

Verse
1. One finger, one thumb keep moving
   One finger, one thumb keep moving
   One finger, one thumb keep moving
   And we'll all be happy and gay.
2. Two fingers, two thumbs keep moving (repeat
   three times)
   And we'll all be happy and gay.
3. Two fingers, two thumbs, one leg keep moving
   (repeat three times)
   And we'll all be happy and gay.
4. Two fingers, two thumbs, two legs keep moving
   (repeat three times)
   And we'll all be happy and gay.
5. Two fingers, two thumbs, two legs, stand up, sit
   down keep moving (repeat three times)
   And we'll all be happy and gay.
6. Two fingers, two thumbs, two legs, stand up, turn
   around, sit down keep moving (repeat three times)
   And we'll all be happy and gay.

Formation
   Semicircle, facing teacher or leader. Everyone is
   sitting on the floor.

Action
   The words of the song are accompanied by appropriate gestures of the body parts mentioned. Each
   verse progressively adds one new action. These actions include moving fingers, thumbs, stamping of
   feet, standing up, turning around, and sitting
   down.

Twinkle, Twinkle, Little Star

Recommended Mental Age
Four to six years.

Record
Childcraft EP-C4.

Verse
1. Twinkle, twinkle, little star
2. How I wonder what you are.
3. Up above the world so high
4. Like a diamond in the sky.
5. Twinkle, twinkle, little star
6. How I wonder what you are.

Formation
Single circle, all facing center.

Action
1. With arms extended overhead, fingers extended and moving, children take seven tiptoe steps toward the center of the circle.
2. Make a full turn in place with seven tiptoe steps.
3. Making a circle with their arms and hands, children rock back and forth.
4. Children form a diamond shape with their fingers in front of their face.
5. Repeat actions of line 1, moving backward.
6. Repeat actions of line 2.

Baa Baa Blacksheep

Recommended Mental Age
Four to six years.

Records
Folkraft V20987, Russell 700A.

Verse
1. Baa Baa Blacksheep, have you any wool?
2. Yes sir, yes sir, three bags full.
3. One for my master and one for my dame,
4. And one for the little boy who lives down the lane.

Formation
        Single circle, all facing center.

Action
1. Stamp feet three times, shake forefinger three times.
2. Nod head twice and hold up three fingers.
3. Bow to the person on the right and then to the person on the left.
4. Hold one finger up high, walk around in a tiny circle, finish facing the center.

Farmer in the Dell

Recommended Mental Age
Four to six years.

Records
Victor 22760, Folkraft 1182.

Verses
1. The farmer in the dell
   The farmer in the dell
   Heigh-O! the dairy-O!
   The farmer in the dell.
2. The farmer takes a wife, etc.
3. The wife takes a child, etc.
4. The child takes a nurse, etc.
5. The nurse takes a dog, etc.
6. The dog takes a cat, etc.
7. The cat takes a rat, etc.
8. The rat takes the cheese, etc.
9. The cheese stands alone, etc.

Formation
Children are in a single circle, facing the center with hands joined. One child, the farmer, stands inside the circle.

Action
1. The circle players walk to the left, with hands joined, while the farmer is deciding on a child to be selected for his "wife."
2. The farmer chooses another child who is led to the center and becomes his wife. The child selected joins hands with him, and they walk around the inside of the circle in the opposite direction from which the circle players are moving.
3-8. Each child selected in turn joins with the center group.
9. All children in the center, with the exception of the child who is the "cheese," return to the circle. The circle stops and the children face the center clap-

ping hands over the head of the child who is the cheese. The cheese becomes the new farmer when the game is repeated.

Teaching Suggestion

The first time this singing game is played it may be necessary for the teacher to be in the center of the circle to assist the children.

The Thread Follows the Needle

Recommended Mental Age
Four to six years.

Record
Victor 22760.

Verse
> The thread follows the needle
> The thread follows the needle
> In and out the needle goes
> As mother mends the children's clothes.

Formation
A single line of about eight children is formed. Hands are joined and each child is numbered.

Action
The first child is the needle, the last child is the knot, and the remaining children in between are the thread. The needle leads the children to the left, forming stitches until the entire line has been sewn. When the music starts, the needle leads the line under the raised arms of the last two children (seven and eight). When the line has passed under their arms, they turn and face in the opposite direction with their arms folded across their chests. This forms the stitch.

The leader now repeats the movement and passes under the next pair of raised arms (six and seven). Number six is now added to the stitch when he reverses his direction. This is repeated until the entire line has been stitched, with the leader turning under his own arm to complete the last stitch.

To "rip" the stitch, children raise their arms overhead and turn back to the original positions. This turn is to the left under their top arm. The game can be repeated with a new leader.

Teaching Suggestions

A good demonstration is essential. The first few times this singing game is played it may be necessary for the teacher to lead the needle through the required actions. If the children cannot rip the stitch as described above, they can release hands and turn back around.

Oats, Peas, Beans, and Barley Grow

Recommended Mental Age
Four to six years.

Record
Victor 20214.

Verses
1. Oats, peas, beans, and barley grow,
   Oats, peas, beans, and barley grow.
   You and I, or anyone else know
   Oats, peas, beans, and barley grow.

2. First, the farmer sows the seed,
   Then he stands and takes his ease,
   He stamps his foot and claps his hands
   And turns around to view the lands.

3. Waiting for a partner,
   Waiting for a partner,
   Open the ring and choose one in
   While we all gaily dance and sing.

4. Now you're married, you must obey.
   You must be kind in all you say.
   You must be kind, you must be good.
   And keep your wife in kindling wood.

Formation
Single circle with a farmer in the center.

Action
1. All children walk clockwise around the farmer.
2. All stand in place and follow actions suggested by words of verse.
3. Circle players again move clockwise while the farmer chooses a partner, which should be done before the end of the verse.
4. Everyone skips during this verse. The circle continues in the same direction clockwise, the farmer and his partner (wife) skip in the opposite direction counterclockwise.

Teaching Suggestion

If the children cannot remember the words to this song, the actions can be performed without the children singing the verses.

Jolly Is the Miller

Recommended Mental Age
Five to six years.

Records
Victor 20214, Folkraft 1192, Columbia A3078.

Verse
1. Jolly is the miller who lives by the mill,
2. The wheel goes around with a right good will,
3. One hand in the hopper and the other in the sack,
4. The right skips forward and left skips back.

Formation
> Double circle, partners side by side and facing counterclockwise. Their inside hands are joined. One child is in the center of the circle.

Action
> During lines 1-3 of the verse all children walk or skip around the circle.

> During line 4 of the verse the inside partner steps or skips backward and the outside partner steps or skips forward, changing partners. The child in the center, who is the "miller" tries to get a partner, leaving one odd person in the center.

Teaching Suggestion
> If necessary, the teacher should help the child in the center get a new partner.

Looby Lou

Recommended Mental Age
Five to six years.

Records
Folkraft F1102, Victor 20214.

Chorus
Repeated before each verse.

> Here we dance looby lou
> Here we dance looby light
> Here we dance looby lou
> All on a Saturday night.

Verses
1. I put my right hand in
   I take my right hand out
   I give my right hand a shake, shake, shake,
   And turn myself about.
2. I put my left hand in, etc.
3. I put my right foot in, etc.
4. I put my left foot in, etc.
5. I put my head way in, etc.
6. I put my whole self in, etc.

Formation
Single circle, all facing left with hands joined.

Action
During the chorus the children skip, slide, walk, or run around the circle to the left. During the verse the children stand motionless facing the center and follow the directions of the words. On line 3 of the verse the movement is made only three times and on the words "shake, shake, shake." On line 4 of the verse the children clap their hands four times as a complete turn with four running steps is made. All movements should be definite, large, and vigorous. On the last verse, the child jumps with both feet together into the circle, then out, shakes himself vigorously, and then turns about.

Did You Ever See a Lassie

Recommended Mental Age
Five to six years.

Records
Folkraft 1183, Victor 21618.

Verse

Did you ever see a lassie, a lassie, a lassie?
Did you ever see a lassie do this way and that?
Do this way and that way, and this way and that way.
Did you ever see a lassie do this way and that.
NOTE: The word "laddie" should be substituted if the center person is a boy.

Formation

Single circle, facing left, hands joined. One child is in the center.

Action

All children skip around singing until they reach the words "Do this way." The child in the center performs some type of movement such as jumping in place. All the children in the circle face the center and perform the actions of the center child. As the verse starts over, the center child selects another to change places with him.

Here We Go Round the Mulberry Bush

Recommended Mental Age
Five to six years.

Records
Victor 20806, Columbia A-3149.

Chorus
Repeated after each verse. Action song begins with chorus.

> Here we go round the mulberry bush,
> The mulberry bush, the mulberry bush,
> Here we go round the mulberry bush
> So early in the morning.

Verses
1. This is the way we wash our clothes,
   Wash our clothes, wash our clothes,
   This is the way we wash our clothes
   So early Monday morning.
2. This is the way we iron our clothes, etc.
   So early Tuesday morning.
3. This is the way we mend our clothes, etc.
   So early Wednesday morning.
4. This is the way we sweep our floor, etc.
   So early Thursday morning.
5. This is the way we scrub our floor, etc.
   So early Friday morning.
6. This is the way we make a cake, etc.
   So early Saturday morning.
7. This is the way we go to church, etc.
   So early Sunday morning.

Formation
Single circle, facing center, hands joined.

Action
As each chorus is sung, the children, with joined hands, walk or skip around the circle to the right. The arms can swing in and out during this action. On the words "so early in the morning" each child

drops hands and makes a complete turn in place. During the verses, the children pantomime the actions suggested by the words. They should be encouraged to use large, vigorous movements.

Hokey Pokey

Recommended Mental Age
Six to seven years.

Record
Capitol 1496.

Verses
1. You put your right hand in,
    You take your right hand out,
    You put your right hand in,
    And you shake it all about,
    You do the Hokey Pokey and turn yourself about,
    That's what it's all about — Yeah!

2. You put your left hand in, etc.
3. You put your right elbow in, etc.
4. You put your left elbow in, etc.
5. You put your right shoulder in, etc.
6. You put your left shoulder in, etc.
7. You put your right hip in, etc.
8. You put your left hip in, etc.
9. You put your head in, etc.
10. You put your whole self in, etc.

11. You do the Hokey Pokey,
    You do the Hokey Pokey,
    You do the Hokey Pokey,
    That's what it's all about.

Formation
Single circle facing in.

Action
Children perform actions indicated by words. During the verse when the song calls for the "Hokey Pokey" the elbows are bent, the hands are up (palms out), and are wigwagged backward and forward in front of the face. The children take a quick turn clockwise and clap out the rhythm of the song, thrusting the right hand toward the center of the circle at the conclusion.

On the last verse both hands are held high and waved in a trembling motion. Children kneel, slap the floor with both hands, and rise and shout as the music finishes.

Bluebird

Recommended Mental Age
Six to seven years.

Record
Folkraft 1180.

Verse
1. Bluebird, bluebird, in and out my windows,
2. Bluebird, bluebird, in and out my windows,
3. Oh! Johnny, I am tired.

Chorus
Take a little boy and tap him on the shoulders,
Take a little boy and tap him on the shoulders,
Oh! Johnny, I am tired.

Formation
Children are in a single circle, facing the center, with hands joined and held high to make arches. One child, the "bluebird," stands in the center of the circle.

Action
1-2. Bluebird walks around the circle weaving in and out under the arches.
3. Bluebird stops behind a boy.

chorus Bluebird places hands on shoulders of child and taps *lightly* through chorus.

The dance is repeated with the boy becoming the leader and the bluebird following behind with hands on his shoulders. The new person chosen always becomes the new leader, the others follow in line behind him. Continue the game until all are chosen. Substitute "Jenny" for Johnny when girls are chosen.

Teaching Suggestion
The first time this singing game is played it may be necessary for the teacher to assist the bluebird as he performs his actions.

Dance

Traditional Dance Steps

Traditional dance steps have their foundation in fundamental rhythms. These steps occur almost universally and are found in the folk dance and social dance of many nations. If properly taught, most mentally retarded or emotionally disturbed children can learn these dance step patterns and enjoy many pleasurable experiences from their use. After they have been learned, these dance steps can be enjoyed for themselves or in combination with other movements and in simple dance sequences.

The mentally retarded or emotionally disturbed child will derive a great deal of pleasure from performing simple traditional dance steps alone or with a partner. They can be performed in a circle or straight line. When first introducing these steps to the children, they should be in a line or semicircle facing the teacher. The children can then mirror the foot patterns used by the teacher.

Step-Point

Recommended Mental Age: Five years.

The step-point is a simple dance step performed to an even rhythm in 4/4 time. This step can be used in folk dances as a pure step or in combination with other movement patterns. The child steps forward on the left foot, then he points the right foot forward. Body weight is not transferred on the point. The action is then repeated with the right foot. All movements receive equal musical time: Count 1—step forward on left foot. Count 2—point right foot forward. Count 3—step forward on right foot. Count 4—point left foot forward.

When teaching this simple step, color-coded foot markings on the floor may prove beneficial. The step can be performed to any moderate music in 4/4 time. The step-point is an excellent lead-up for the "Varsouvianna." In its pure form it is used in "Dance of Greeting."

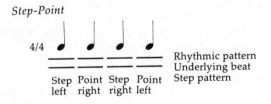

Step-Hop

Recommended Mental Age: Five years.

The step-hop, when performed to an even rhythm, is an excellent lead-up step for the schottische. Because this step is even in rhythm, the quality of the movement is different from that of the skip. The step-hop can be used in folk dances as a pure step or in combination with other movement patterns.

The child steps forward on the left foot, then hops on the left foot. This action is repeated on the right foot with a step followed by a hop. All movements receive equal musical time: Count 1—step forward on the left foot. Count 2—hop on the left foot. Count 3—step forward on the right foot. Count 4—hop on the right foot.

When first learning this step, the mentally retarded or emotionally disturbed child should practice entirely with one foot. This can be accomplished by stepping forward on the left foot, hopping on the left foot, pausing with both feet together, and then repeating the sequence. This procedure should be repeated with the right foot. After the child can step and hop with each foot, the alternate step-hop pattern can be produced at a slow tempo. Increase the tempo as the child's proficiency improves. Color-coded foot markings on the floor may prove beneficial when first attempting the step-hop on alternate feet. This step can be performed to any moderate music in 2/4 or 4/4 time. The step-hop is frequently called a jig step and is used in its pure form in "Seven Jumps," "Milanovo Kolo," "Crested Hen," "Come Let Us Be Joyful," and "Tantoli."

Step-Hop

Step-Swing

Recommended Mental Age: Five years.

The step-swing is a simple dance step performed to an even rhythm in 4/4 time. This step can be used in folk dances as a pure step or in combination with other movement patterns. The child steps forward on the left foot, then swings the right foot across in front of the left foot. In some dances the free foot can swing in any direction, but the swing should come from the hip. The action is then repeated with the opposite foot by stepping forward on the right foot, then swinging the left foot across in front of the right foot. All movements receive equal musical time: Count 1—step forward on left foot. Count 2—swing right foot across in front of left. Count 3—step forward on right foot. Count 4—swing left foot across in front of right.

When teaching this simple step, color-coded foot markings on the floor may prove beneficial. The step can be performed to any moderate music in 4/4 time. In many dances the step-swing is combined with the step-hop. The step-swing is found in the "Hora."

Step-Swing

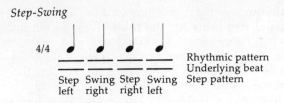

Step-Draw

Recommended Mental Age: Five years.

The step-draw used in folk dancing is a slow slide step usually performed in a sideward direction. Because this is a smooth, slow movement using even rhythmical time, its quality is basically different from the slide described under locomotor patterns.

Using moderate music in 2/4 or 4/4 time, both the step to the side and the draw or close receive equal time. If the mentally retarded or emotionally disturbed child has learned how to slide, this step will be easy for him to learn. Begin with slow music and use color-coded foot markings if the children are having difficulty. The "Kinderpolka" uses the step-draw dance step in its pure form.

Step-Draw

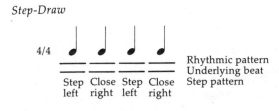

Stamp

Recommended Mental Age: Five years.

The stamp as a dance step is used frequently in many folk dances. It is a step which hits the floor heavily but is quickly lifted so that the stamping foot does not take the body weight. The stamp is usually used in combination with other dance steps and usually requires one beat of music for its execution. "Tropanka" uses the stamp step.

Bleking

Recommended Mental Age: Six to seven years.

Bleking is a relatively simple dance step performed to an even underlying beat in 4/4 time. The rhythmic pattern can be even or uneven, depending on the step combinations used. The folk dance "Bleking" uses a combination of an even and uneven rhythmic pattern. "La Raspa" uses only the uneven rhythmic pattern for the bleking step.

The even rhythmic pattern uses two beats for every body action and includes only two steps or one leg change for one measure of mu-

sic. The uneven rhythmic pattern uses one beat for each of the first
two body actions and two beats for the third. This pattern includes
three steps or two leg changes for one measure of music.

In the bleking step using an even rhythmic pattern the child hops
on the left foot as he thrusts the right heel forward, keeping the right
leg straight. At the same time the right arm is thrust forward. This action requires two beats of music. Next he hops on the right foot as the
left heel is thrust forward with the left leg straight. At the same time
the left arm is thrust forward. This action requires two beats of music.
The entire pattern requires one measure of music.

In the bleking step using an uneven rhythmic pattern the musical
count is as follows: Count 1—hop on left foot, thrusting right heel
forward with right leg straight, and thrusting right arm forward.
Count 2—hop on right foot, thrusting left heel forward with left leg
straight, and thrusting left arm forward. Counts 3 and 4—hop on left
foot, thrusting right heel forward with right leg straight, and thrusting
right arm forward, hold.

Music should be used when this dance step is being practiced.
This will facilitate learning.

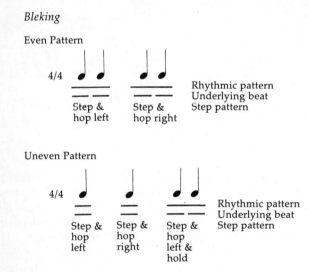

Bleking

Even Pattern

Uneven Pattern

Grapevine

Recommended Mental Age: Seven to eight years.

The grapevine step is used in many folk dances in its pure form or
in combination with other dance steps. It consists of a series of side steps
in which one foot crosses alternately in front of or behind the other
foot. Moderate music in 2/4 or 4/4 time is used for the grapevine step
and all movements receive equal musical time. Count 1—step left to

the side. Count 2—cross right foot in front of left. Count 3—step left to the side. Count 4—cross right foot behind left.

Some mentally retarded or emotionally disturbed children may have difficulty learning the concept of crossing the feet. Teacher assistance and color-coded foot markings on the floor may be beneficial when the children first attempt the grapevine step. Practice can begin without music. After the correct movements have been learned, slow music can be added and the tempo can be gradually increased until it is being played at dance speed. The grapevine step is used in the "Hora."

Grapevine

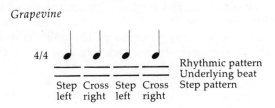

4/4

Step left   Cross right   Step left   Cross right

Rhythmic pattern
Underlying beat
Step pattern

Schottische

Recommended Mental Age: Seven to eight years.

The schottische, an even rhythm consisting of a four-part pattern, can be considered an extension of the basic step-hop. This dance step has a smooth, strong, sturdy, and animated quality. It is a very versatile dance step which can be performed alone, with a partner, or in groups of three or four persons. Variety can be added by changing the tempo, force, or direction of the basic pattern.

The schottische is an even rhythmic pattern performed to 2/4 or 4/4 time. If 2/4 time is used the quality is bouncy, if 4/4 time is used the quality of the movement is smooth. One step pattern is performed to each measure of the music. The schottische dance step consists of three steps followed by a hop. Count 1—step forward on right foot. Count 2—step forward on left foot. Count 3—step forward on right foot. Count 4—hop on right foot. Repeat the pattern beginning with a step on the left foot.

When learning the schottische, the mentally retarded or emotionally disturbed child may find color-coded foot markings on the floor beneficial. Begin by having the children clap the rhythm, then walk to the rhythm, then finally hop. It may be necessary for the teacher to count clearly for the children, especially the first few times they walk through the pattern. The schottische dance step is used frequently in combination with step-hops, two schottische steps followed by four step-hops. The schottische dance step is used in the following simple folk dances: "Tantoli," "Bummel Schottische," "Buggy Schottische," and "Seven Steps."

Schottische

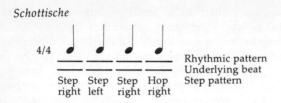

Step   Step   Step   Hop   Step pattern
right   left   right   right

Polka

Recommended Mental Age: Eight to nine years.

The polka dance step consists of an uneven, four-part pattern. It is typically done to 2/4 or 6/8 time and begins with an upbeat which is the hop, followed by three steps. The rhythmic pattern consists of a quick hop followed by a slower step, close, step. The polka is lively and buoyant and is one of the most spirited and vivacious of the traditional dance steps.

The mentally retarded or emotionally disturbed child should have developed skill in performing the skip, slide, and gallop before he is taught the polka dance step. There are many different methods which can be used to teach the polka. By being aware of all of these various methods the teacher can be versatile in his teaching approach. This is important as more than one approach may be necessary when teaching the polka to the mentally retarded or emotionally disturbed child.

One of the easiest methods of learning the polka is from the gallop. Begin by having the children gallop eight times to the left and then eight times to the right. Suggest to them that they hop when they change lead feet and move from the left to the right gallop. It may be necessary for the teacher to count the pattern sequence for the children. When the children have mastered the eight-gallop pattern, reduce the number of gallops before each change to four, and then two. With the change being made on the second gallop, the pattern is the polka step.

The "a" before the following phrases is used to give the feeling of the upbeat. This is important as a polka typically starts with a hop. The polka rhythm can be developed from a combination of a-skip-run-run, a-skip-run-run pattern or a-slide forward and skip, a-slide forward and skip pattern. Another method consists of combining a-gallop and skip, a-gallop and skip pattern into the spirit of the polka. The children can walk out a step-step-step-hold and gradually progress into the uneven quick rhythm of the polka.

If the children have learned the two-step this can be developed into a polka step. Have the children walk out a two-step with a step-close-step-hold. Gradually add a hop on the hold. Begin with a slowed polka record, gradually increasing the tempo until the rhythmic relationship and character of the polka have been achieved.

The mentally retarded or emotionally disturbed child may learn the rhythmic relationship of the step pattern by repeating rhythmic phrases while performing the step pattern. These phrases might include: "a-gallop and skip," "a-skip-run-run," "hop-step-together-step," "a-slide and skip."

After the mentally retarded or emotionally disturbed child has learned to perform a polka step, he can be taught the heel-and-toe polka. With a hop, the child places the heel of the free foot on the floor in front of him; with another hop he extends the toe of the same free foot to the floor behind him. This is followed by a regular polka step. The rhythmic phrase is: "heel-toe, and a-polka step."

A simple polka step is used in "Teton Mountain Stomp." The heel-and-toe polka is used in "Bummel Schottische" and "Tantoli."

If the mentally retarded or emotionally disturbed child cannot perform the polka step with a hop, the step-close-step-hold pattern can be used in most folk dances requiring a polka step. Or, a fast four-count walk can be used. Remember, it is better to substitute a step modification than frustrate the child.

Waltz

Recommended Mental Age: Nine to ten years.

The waltz is one of the most difficult of the traditional dance steps because of the smooth, even, gliding or flowing quality of the step pattern. This dance step is a three-part, even pattern performed to the triple rhythm of 3/4 time. The foot pattern consists of three smooth walking steps to a measure of music. A complete transfer of weight is taken on each step. The ball of the foot should be used for this weight transfer. The first step should be emphasized and be longer in length than the last two. From a position with the feet together, on count 1 the first step is taken either forward or backward. On count 2 the second step is taken diagonally sideward in relation to the first step. On count 3 the first foot is closed to the second foot.

When teaching this step to mentally retarded or emotionally disturbed children, begin by having them clap out the rhythm. Have them accent the first beat with a louder handclap. The waltz music used should be slow and clearly accented. Next, have the children walk in time to the rhythm of the waltz, accenting count 1 with a longer step. When the children can accomplish this with ease, have them try a waltz step: Count 1—step forward left. Count 2—step to side, right. Count 3—close left to right. Count 1—step backward right. Count 2—step to side, left. Count 3—close right to left.

Color-coded foot patterns on the floor may be helpful in teaching this step to the mentally retarded or emotionally disturbed child. To avoid frustrating the child if he cannot master the waltz step, go back to familiar steps in which he can experience success.

Once the child has learned the traditional box waltz, he can be taught the waltz balance. This step is sometimes called a step-balance and can be performed in any direction to any waltz music. Count 1—step forward left. Count 2—close right to left, don't shift weight. Count 3—hold. Count 1—step backward right. Count 2—close left to right, don't shift weight. Count 3—hold.

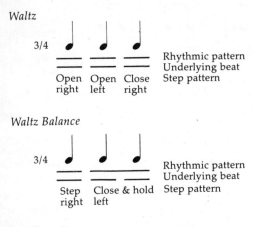

Two-Step

Recommended Mental Age: Nine to ten years.

The two-step is an uneven three-part pattern performed to 2/4 or 4/4 time. The step pattern consists of a step forward or sideward, a close with the other foot, a step forward or sideward again, and a pause. Each new step pattern begins with an alternate foot. One step pattern is performed to each measure of music.

Begin by having the mentally retarded or emotionally disturbed child clap out the rhythm. Then have him step in place to the music: step-step-step (hold). The third step should be accented slightly and the fourth count is held. Color-coded foot patterns on the floor may be helpful when teaching the two-step to the mentally retarded or emotionally disturbed child.

The two-step can be used in simple folk dances or as a social dance.

Two-Step

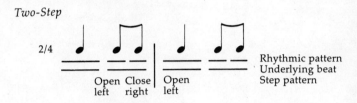

Rhythmic pattern
Underlying beat
Step pattern

Open Close | Open
left right | left

Basic Dance Positions

Single Circle, Facing In

All children form a circle, facing the center of the dance floor, usually with hands joined. They may be with or without partners.

Single Circle, Facing Counterclockwise ·

All children form a circle and turn to their right so they are facing counterclockwise. (Picture, p. 182.)

Single Circle, Facing In

Single Circle, Facing Counterclockwise

Single Circle, Partners Facing

Couples form a single circle, with each girl on the right of her partner. Partners then face each other. (Picture, p. 183.)

Double Circle, Couples Facing Counterclockwise

Couples stand side by side, usually with the girl on her partner's right; they face to the right (counterclockwise). (Picture, p. 183.)

Double Circle, Partners Facing

Usually the boy stands with his back to the center and the girl faces him. (Picture, p. 184.)

Double Circle, Couples Facing

Couples face each other in a double circle, one facing clockwise and the other counterclockwise. (Picture, p. 184.)

Groups of Three

Children stand in three, usually with a boy between two girls or a girl between two boys. They may face the center or, more often, counterclockwise. (Picture, p. 185.)

Single Circle, Partners Facing

Double Circle, Couples Facing Counterclockwise

Double Circle, Partners Facing

Double Circle, Couples Facing

Groups of Three

Longways Formation or Set

A line of boys faces a line of girls, with the "head" or front end of each set near the source of music. (Picture, p. 186.)

Quadrille or Square Formation

For four couples. One couple stands on each side of the square, facing in, with backs parallel to the walls of the room. Head couple has their backs to the music. (Picture, p. 186.)

Closed Dance Position

Partners face each other, with shoulders parallel. Each person shifts slightly to his left, so he can look over his partner's right shoulder. They are somewhat farther apart than in the customary ballroom dance position; arms are higher and more extended. The boy holds the girl's right hand in his left hand, out to the side about shoulder level with the elbows bent. His right hand is on the girl's back just below her left shoulder blade. The girl's left arm rests lightly on the top of his right shoulder and her right hand is resting in his left hand. (Picture, p. 187.)

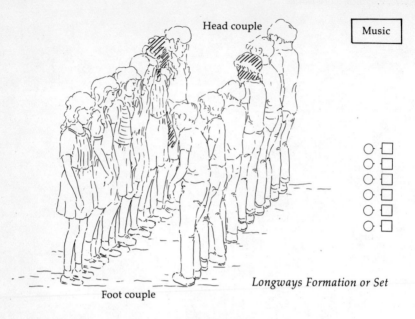

Head couple

Music

Longways Formation or Set

Foot couple

Music

Couple 1 — Head couple

Couple 2 — Side couple

Couple 4 — Side couple

Couple 3 — Head couple

Quadrille or Square Formation

Closed Dance Position

Semiclosed Position

Partners keep the same closed dance hand position but turn to face forward, to the boy's left and the girl's right. His right and her left sides are adjacent. (Picture, p. 188.)

Open Position

Partners stand side by side, with inside hands joined and free hands placed at the waist. In some round dances, the girl holds her skirt with her free hand, and the boy places his free hand behind his back above the hip pocket. (Picture, p. 188.)

Side Position

Partners stand in the closed position. If they shift to their own left, so right sides are adjacent, this is the Banjo Position. If they shift to the right, so left sides are adjacent, it is the Sidecar Position. (Picture, p. 188.)

Semiclosed Position

Open Position

Banjo Position

Sidecar Position

Side Positions

Promenade Position

Partners stand side by side with the girl on her partner's right. Hands are joined (right to right, left to left) with the right arms above the left.

Shoulder-Waist Position or Peasant Position

Partners face; each boy places his hands on his partner's waist, and she places her hands on his shoulders. They lean slightly backward, keeping arms straight.

Varsouviana Position

Partners stand side by side facing the same direction, forward. The boy is on the left and slightly behind his partner. He holds her left hand in his left hand and in front of their waists. She brings her right hand directly back over her right shoulder. The boy reaches behind her back at shoulder height and grasps her right hand in his right hand. (Picture, p. 190.)

Conversation Position

Partners stand side by side, facing forward. The boy's right arm is behind his partner's back, at waist level. Her left hand rests on his right shoulder. Free hands are usually as in Open Position. (Picture, p. 190.)

Promenade Position

Shoulder-Waist or Peasant Position

Varsouviana Position   *Conversation Position*

Folk and Square Dances

A folk dance is considered a traditional dance of a given country and a definite pattern of dance routine is usually set up and followed. The round and square dances of the United States are classified as folk dances.

When teaching folk and square dances to the mentally retarded or emotionally disturbed child, interest can be aroused and concomitant learning can take place if the children are shown pictures of the country and the people related to the folk dance. In addition, information on the customs, food, and climate can be discussed. Short stories about the country and the people may also stimulate interest in the children.

The teaching suggestions outlined at the beginning of this chapter should be observed. The following folk dances are simple enough for most mentally retarded or emotionally disturbed children to perform and enjoy. In some cases, simplifications are suggested to facilitate learning and enjoyment and to avoid frustration. Additional dances can be selected from most folk dance books, if the skill level of the child is considered in their selection.

Shoemaker's Dance

Recommended Mental Age
Four to five years.

Historical Background
Denmark. An ancient occupational dance performed on special holidays.

Records
Victor 20450, Victor 1624, Folkraft 1187.

Verse
1. Wind, wind, wind the bobbin;
2. Wind, wind, wind the bobbin,
3. Pull, pull,
4. Tap, tap, tap!
5-8. Repeat measures 1-4.

Chorus
Tra-la-la-la-la-la-la (sing four times).

Formation
Double circle of couples, partners facing, boys on inside. Hands are placed on hips.

Action

	Verse
meas. 1.	With arms shoulder high and hands clenched in front of chest, roll one arm over the other three times. "Winding the thread."
meas. 2.	Reverse the direction of the arm roll, three times. "Unwinding the thread."
meas. 3.	Pull hands apart and jerk elbows backward twice. "Pulling thread tight."
meas. 4.	Strike clenched left fist with right fist, three times. "Driving the pegs." At the same time, tap right foot forward three times.
meas. 5-8.	Repeat measures 1-4.

Chorus
Partners join inside hands, with free hand on

hip. Skip forward (counterclockwise) sixteen steps. The inside hands can swing forward and backward as the children skip around the circle.

If the children have learned the forward polka step, they can substitute eight polka steps for the skip.

Chimes of Dunkirk

Recommended Mental Age
Four to five years.

Historical Background
France. The dance comes from the coastal region of France and the music depicts the church chimes ringing in Dunkirk.

Records
Folkraft 1159, Victor 1624.

Formation
Couples form a double circle. Partners are facing. Inside partner has his back to the center of the circle; this is the boy.

Action

Part I

meas. 1-2. Stamp feet three times, left-right-left. Hold on count four. During this action boys' arms are crossed in front of their chests and girls' hands are on their hips.

meas. 3-4. Clap hands above own head three times. Hold on count four.

meas. 5-8. Join hands with partner and turn around in place (clockwise) with eight walking steps.

Part II

meas. 1-2. Partners join right hands and place left hand on left hip. They do a step-balance forward on the right foot and a step-balance backward on the left foot.

meas. 3-4. Repeat action of measures 1-2.

meas. 5-8. Partners, with hands joined, circle clockwise (left) with eight steps. On the last count they drop hands and take another step to their left, moving to a new partner to begin the dance again.

Dance of Greeting

Recommended Mental Age
Four to five years.

Historical Background
Denmark. A dance of friendly greeting. The curtseys in the first part of the dance represent a happy greeting. The second part of the dance represents the pleasure of being together.

Records
Victor 20432, Folkraft 1187.

Formation
Single circle of couples, facing center. The boy stands to the left of his partner.

Action

	Part I
meas. 1.	Clap hands twice and then bow or curtsey to partner.
meas. 2.	Clap hands twice and then bow or curtsey to neighbor, turning back to partner.
meas. 3.	Facing center of circle, stamp feet twice in place, right-left.
meas. 4.	With three light running steps, turn away from partner, once around in place and pause.
meas. 5-8.	Measures 1-4 are repeated.
	Part II
meas. 1-4.	All join hands, facing left and starting with the left foot, dance lightly around the circle, making four running steps to each measure. Sixteen running steps.
meas. 5-8.	Repeat actions of measures 1-4, running to the right.

Bleking

Recommended Mental Age
Four to five years.

Historical Background
Sweden. The dance is named after a Swedish province.

Records
Victor 20989, Victor 1622, Folkraft 1188.

Formation
A double circle, partners facing with both hands joined.
Boys have their backs to the center.

Action

Part I

meas. 1. Children hop on the left foot as they thrust the
right foot forward, heel on the floor and toe up.
At the same time they sharply thrust the right
hand forward. This is all done on the first
count. On the second count, the left heel and
hand are thrust forward.

meas. 2. The same action of measure 1 is done three
times quickly, right-left-right, with a hold on
the fourth count.

meas. 3-4. Action of measures 1-2 is repeated with the left
foot leading. Left, right; left-right-left, hold.

meas. 5-8. Action of measures 1-4 is repeated.

Part II

meas. 1-8. Holding partners' hands with arms extended
straight out to the side, the children do sixteen
step-hops turning clockwise as a couple and
traveling counterclockwise around the circle.
These step-hops should be done vigorously
with a rocking side-to-side motion.

Teaching Suggestion
If the children cannot do the turning step-hops in Part II of
the dance, they can join inside hands and do sixteen step-
hops forward around the circle.

The Wheat

Recommended Mental Age
Five to six years.

Historical Background
Czechoslovakia. An easy, but enjoyable dance for three.

Records
Victor 20992, Victor 1625.

Verses
1. From the feast there came a farmer,
    On his back a bag of bran,
    And the bad boys shouted at him,
    "Let those pigeons out, old man,

2. Let those pigeons out, old man,
    Let those pigeons out, old man!"
    And the bad boys shouted at him,
    "Let those pigeons out, old man!"

Formation
Children stand three abreast facing counterclockwise around
the circle. The center player places both hands on his hips
and the outside players place their arms through his arms.
The sets of three are usually formed with one boy and two
girls, or vice versa.

Action

	Part I
meas. 1-8.	All walk forward around the circle, sixteen steps.

	Part II
meas. 1-8.	The center child joins right elbows with the child on his right. They take eight skipping steps clockwise. The center child repeats this action with the child on his left, joining left elbows. They take eight skipping steps counterclockwise.

Teaching Suggestion
The emotionally disturbed child may find security in the
center position in this dance.

Kinderpolka

Recommended Mental Age
Five to six years.

Historical Background
Germany. The name means "children's polka." The dance does not, however, include a polka step.

Records
Victor 45-6179, Victor 1625, Folkraft 1187.

Formation
Single circle of couples. Partners face each other with hands joined and arms extended sideward at shoulder height.

Action

       Part I

meas. 1-2.   Couples take two slides toward center of circle, followed by three light stamps in place. (Step-close, step-close, stamp, stamp, stamp.)

meas. 3-4.   Repeat action of measures 1-2, moving away from center of circle.

meas. 5-8.   Repeat action of measures 1-4.

       Part II

meas. 1-2.   Clap thighs with both hands, then clap own hands slowly. Clap partner's hands three times quickly.

meas. 3-4.   Repeat action of measures 1-2.

meas. 5.   Point right toe forward, place right elbow in left hand and shake finger at partner three times in a "scolding" action.

meas. 6.   Repeat action of measure 5, pointing left toe forward, placing left elbow in right hand, and shaking finger at partner three times.

meas. 7.   Turn a complete circle to the right with three running steps.

meas. 8.   Stamp three times in place.

Broom Dance

Recommended Mental Age
Five to six years.

Historical Background
Germany.

Record
Victor 20448.

Verse
One, two, three, four, five, six, seven,
Where's my partner? Nine, ten, eleven.
In Berlin, in Stettin,
That's the place to find her in.

Chorus
Tra, la, la, la (sing eight times).

Formation
Couples form a double circle facing counterclockwise. One
child is left in the center of the circle with a broom.

Action

> *Verse*
> Couples, holding inside hands, march around
> the room to the music. The child in the center,
> with the broom, gives the broom to someone
> in the circle and takes his place. The broom is
> quickly passed in this manner for eight meas-
> ures of music.
>
> *Chorus*
> The child holding the broom at the end of the
> verse dances with it in the center of the circle.
> Couples skip around the child in the center
> singing the words of the chorus.
> The dance begins again with the center child
> passing the broom on.

Teaching Suggestions
If necessary, teacher assistance should be given to the

broom holder, especially if the child is insecure. Try to avoid having such a child holding the broom during the chorus.

Seven Jumps

Recommended Mental Age
Five to six years.

Historical Background
Denmark. A novelty dance with a follow-the-leader pattern
in which movements are added progressively.

Record
Victor 1623.

Formation
A single circle with hands joined. Partners are not needed.

Action

    Chorus
    The chorus is performed at the beginning, after
    each part of the dance, and again at the end of
    the dance.

meas. 1-8. With hands joined and bodies leaning back-
    ward, children do seven vigorous step-hops to
    the left. They jump on both feet on the eighth
    count.

meas. 9-16. With hands joined and bodies leaning back-
    ward, children do seven vigorous step-hops to
    the right. They jump on both feet on the six-
    teenth count.

    Part I
    Placing hands on hips, each child raises his
    right knee high on the first note of music. On
    the second note, he returns the right leg to the
    floor. He waits on the third, warning note. This
    is followed by the chorus.

    Part II
    The right knee is lifted, then put down. The
    left knee is lifted and put down. The child waits
    during the warning note. This is followed by
    the chorus.

    Part III
    The actions of Part II are repeated — lift right

knee, lift left knee. The child then kneels on
the right knee, rises, waits during the warning
note, and repeats the chorus.

Part IV
The actions of Part III are repeated — lift right
knee, lift left knee, kneel right. The child then
kneels on the left knee, rises, waits during the
warning note, and repeats the chorus.

Part V
The actions of Part IV are repeated — lift right
knee, lift left knee, kneel right, kneel left. The
child then places his right elbow on the floor
and rests his chin on his left hand. He rises,
waits during the warning note, and repeats the
chorus.

Part VI
The actions of Part V are repeated — lift right
knee, lift left knee, kneel right, kneel left, right
elbow. The child then places his left elbow on
the floor, rests his chin on his left hand, rises,
waits during the warning note, and repeats the
chorus.

Part VII
The actions of Part VI are repeated — lift right
knee, lift left knee, kneel right, kneel left, right
elbow, left elbow. The child then places his
forehead on the floor, rises, waits during the
warning note, and repeats the chorus.

NOTE: In Parts I-VII each action should be
held exactly as long as its musical note indicates.

Teaching Suggestions
If the children cannot do a step-hop, the skip or run can be
substituted for this step in the chorus. The teacher should
perform the actions of the various parts of this dance as a
leader for the children to follow.

Carrousel

Recommended Mental Age
Five to six years.

Historical Background
Sweden. The dance suggests a merry-go-round. The inner circle of children is the merry-go-round and the outer circle of children is the riders.

Records
Victor 45-6179, Victor 1625, Folkraft 1183.

Verse
1-8. Little children, sweet and gay,
Carrousel is running.
It will run till evening.
Little ones a nickel,
Big ones a dime.
Hurry up, get on board,
Or you'll surely be too late!

Chorus
1-8. Ha, ha, ha, happy are we,
Anderson and Peterson and Lundstrom and me!
Ha, ha, ha, happy are we,
Anderson and Peterson and Lundstrom and me!

Formation
A double circle of couples facing the center. Inner circle of girls have hands joined. The boys stand behind their partners and place both hands on the girls' shoulders.

Action

Verse
meas. 1-8. All children do sixteen slow sliding steps, or step-draws, to the left. There are two steps for every measure of music.

Chorus
meas. 1-8. The music accelerates and all children do sixteen fast sliding steps to the left. This is double time or four steps for every measure of music.

meas. 1-8.   Actions of measures 1-8 of the chorus are performed to the right. At the end of the sixteenth
step, the boys and girls change places. The entire dance is repeated with the boys in the inner
circle.

Teaching Suggestions

When teaching this dance to the mentally retarded or emotionally disturbed child, practice slowly and carefully, especially the change of direction after measures 1-8 of the
chorus. Encourage the children to take short slide steps
when the movements are fast. If the children cannot change
places with their partners at the end of the chorus, this can
be eliminated from the dance.

I See You

Recommended Mental Age
Six to seven years.

Historical Background
Sweden.

Records
Victor 20432, Victor 1625.

Verses
     I. I see you, I see you, Tra la la la la la.
       I see you, I see you, Tra la la la la la.
    II. You see me and I see you, then you take me and
       I'll take you,
       You see me and I see you, then you take me and
       I'll take you.

Formation
Sets of two couples facing each other about five feet apart.
All sets stand in a line. Girls are in front with hands on
hips. Boys each stand behind partner with hands on her
shoulders.

Action

              Part I

meas. 1-2.   The boy in back bends his head to the right,
              playing "peek-a-boo" with the rear player in
              the opposite set. This action is repeated to the
              left.

meas. 3-4.   Action of measures 1-2 is repeated at double
              time. Right, left, right, hold.

meas. 5-8.   Action of measures 1-4 is repeated, beginning
              left.

              Part II

meas. 1-4.   All children clap hands once. Boys take four
              skipping steps past their partners' left side,
              join hands with the opposite boy and turn with
              four skipping steps.

meas. 5-8.   All children clap hands once. Boys return to

partners with four skipping steps, join hands, and turn with four skipping steps. They resume the original formation but with the boys in front and the girls behind them. The dance is repeated with the girls performing the actions previously performed by the boys.

Teaching Suggestion
During Part I of the dance the teacher should cue the children by calling out: *"Right, left, right-left-right-hold."*

Come Let Us Be Joyful

Recommended Mental Age
Six to seven years.

Historical Background
Germany. An old folk dance which expresses the universal human need — "let us enjoy life."

Records
Victor 1622, Folkraft 1195.

Verses
    I. Come let us be joyful,
        While life is bright and gay,
        Gather its roses,
        Ere they fade away.
   II. We're always making our lives so blue,
        We look for thorns and find them too,
        And leave the violets quite unseen,
        That bloom along the wayside.

Formation
Children are in lines of three, facing lines of three around a circle, like spokes of a wheel. Each group of three stands side by side with inside hands joined at shoulder height, free hands on hips.

Action

                Part I

meas. 1-2. Each group of three walks forward three steps and bows or curtseys on the fourth count.

meas. 3-4. They walk backward to place with three steps, bringing the feet together on the fourth count.

meas. 5-8. Actions of measures 1-4 are repeated.

                Part II

meas. 1-2. Using four skipping steps, the center child turns the partner on his right with a right elbow turn. The child who is not being turned turns about in place with four skips.

meas. 3-4. Using four skipping steps, the center child turns the partner on his left with a left elbow turn. The child who is not being turned turns about in place with four skips.

meas. 5-8.   Actions of measures 1-4 are repeated.

Part I

Music repeated.

meas. 1-4.   Actions of measures 1-4, Part I are repeated.

meas. 5-8.   Children drop hands. Each line of three walks forward and passes through the opposite line of three. Children pass right shoulders. Each set of three faces a new set of three for repetition of the dance. Children take four walking steps for this change.

Bunny Hop

Recommended Mental Age
Six to seven years.

Historical Background
United States. American line dance.

Record
MacGregor 699.

Formation
Children form a conga line which is a single line in single file. The children connect by holding the waist of the person in front of them with both hands.

Action

meas. 1-2.   Starting with both feet together, extend the right foot and leg out to the right side, then bring it back in next to the left leg. Repeat this same action one more time.

meas. 3-4.   Extend the left foot and leg out to the left side, then bring it back in next to the right leg. Repeat this same action one more time.

meas. 5-8.   With both feet together, hop forward once, slowly. Hop backward once, slowly. Hop forward three times, quickly.

This step sequence is repeated throughout the entire dance.

Tropanka

Recommended Mental Age
Six to seven years.

Historical Background
Bulgaria. A circle stamping dance.

Records
The Folk Dancer MH 1020B, Disc Album 635.

Formation
A single circle, all hands joined with elbows bent. Partners are not necessary.

Action

Part I

meas. 1-2. Beginning on the right foot, take five running steps to the right, cross the left foot over the right, and stamp twice in place with the left foot. Pause. Turn.

meas. 3-4. Beginning on the left foot, take five running steps to the left, cross the right foot over the left, and stamp twice in place with the right foot. Pause.

meas. 1-4. Repeat action of measures 1-4.

Part II

meas. 5. Facing the center of the circle, step and hop on the right foot, swinging the left foot in front of the right. Step and hop on the left foot, swinging the right foot in front of the left.

meas. 6. Step on the right foot, cross the left foot over the right, stamp twice with the left foot, and pause.

meas. 7-8. Repeat action of measures 5-6 beginning with the left foot.

Part III

meas. 5. Moving toward the center of the circle and raising hands, step and hop right, step and hop left.

meas. 6. Step forward right and stamp twice with the left foot. Pause.

meas. 7-8.   Repeat actions of measures 5-6, moving backward and lowering hands. Begin with the left
foot.

meas. 9-16. Repeat measures 1-8, Parts I and II of the
dance.

Teaching Suggestion

If the children cannot cross their feet on the stamp or swing
their free leg on the step-hop, this can be eliminated without
destroying the quality of the dance.

Glowworm Mixer

Recommended Mental Age
Six to seven years.

Historical Background
United States. A very simple couple mixer.

Records
Imperial 1044A, MacGregor 310.

Formation
Couples, in promenade position, face counterclockwise in a double circle. Boys are on the inside. Footwork is the same for both partners.

Action

meas. 1.	Beginning with the left foot, walk four steps forward.
meas. 2.	Releasing hands, partners face each other. Boys take four steps backward toward the center of the circle. At the same time, girls take four steps backward away from the center of the circle.
meas. 3.	Each child walks four steps forward, moving diagonally to the left, to meet a new partner.
meas. 4.	New partners join hands and turn once clockwise with four steps. When joining hands, the right is crossed over the left. The children should finish their four walking steps, facing counterclockwise to repeat the dance from the beginning.

Cshebogar

Recommended Mental Age
Six to seven years.

Historical Background
Hungary. A circle dance which means "the beetle."

Records
Victor 1624, Folkraft 1196.

Formation
Couples join hands in a single circle facing the center. The girl is on the right of her partner.

Action

Part I
meas. 1-4. Children take eight sliding steps to the left.
meas. 5-8. Children take eight sliding steps to the right.

Part II
meas. 1-4. Children take three steps forward, raising arms, then stamp on the fourth count. They take three steps backward, lowering arms and stamping on the fourth count.
meas. 5-8. Partners face, join right elbows, and turn in place with eight skipping steps.

Part III
meas. 1-4. Partners face each other in a single circle with hands joined and arms extended sideward. The arms rock up and down as they take four slow step-draw steps (step-close) toward the center, moving to the boy's left and the girl's right. Weight is not transferred on the last step.
meas. 5-8. Each couple takes four step-draw steps away from the center. Weight is not transferred on the last step.

Part IV
meas. 1-4. Each couple takes two step-draw steps toward the center, and two away.
meas. 5-8. Repeat action of measures 5-8, Part II.

The Crested Hen

Recommended Mental Age
Six to seven years.

Historical Background
Denmark. A dance for three people, two women and one man. The man wears a red stocking cap. During the second part of the dance the women try to snatch the man's cap. If one of them is successful, she dons it, thus becoming a "crested hen."

Records
Victor 45-6175, Folkraft 1194.

Formation
Sets of three, one boy with a girl on either side.

Action

Part I

meas. 1-8. Children join hands in a circle of three. Leaning backward, they stamp the left foot and do eight step-hops clockwise (left) around the circle.

meas. 1-8. Repeat action of measures 1-8 moving counterclockwise (right) around the circle.

Part II

meas. 1-2. The two girls drop hands and place their free hands on their hips. The boy or center child never releases his hands. The girl at the left of the boy dances, with four step-hops, in front of him and under the arch made by the raised hands of the boy and the girl on the right. At the same time the girl on the right and the boy dance four step-hops in place.

meas. 3-4. The boy follows the girl through the same arch, turning in place under his own arm. This action takes four step-hops. The two girls take four step-hops in place.

meas. 5-8. The actions of measures 1-4 are repeated with

the girl at the right of the boy dancing under the arch.

meas. 1-8. Repeat actions of measures 1-8.

Gustaf's Skoal

Recommended Mental Age
Six to seven years.

Historical Background
Sweden. A simple square dance in which the dancers pay homage to King Gustaf. The first part of the dance is dignified as though in a court paying homage to King Gustaf. The second part of the dance is lively and free as all rejoice at the King's ball.

Records
Victor 45-6170, Victor 1622, Folkraft 1175.

Verses
  I. A toast we pledge, to Gustaf who is brave and true,
    A toast we pledge, to Gustaf brave and true.
    A toast we pledge, to Gustaf who is brave and true,
    A toast we pledge, to Gustaf brave and true.
  II. Fa-la-la-la-la-la-la-la-la, Fa-la-la-la-la-la-la-la-la,
    Fa-la-la-la-la-la-la-la-la, Fa-la-la-la.
    Fa-la-la-la-la-la-la-la-la, Fa-la-la-la-la-la-la-la-la,
    Fa-la-la-la-la-la-la-la-la, Fa-la-la-la.

Formation
Square set of four couples, with girl on boy's right.

Action

        Part I

meas. 1-4. With inside hands joined and free hands on hips, the head couples walk forward with three steps, singing. They bow deeply on the fourth count ("pledge"), then walk back four steps to place.

meas. 5-8. Side couples perform action of measures 1-4.

meas. 1-8. Action of measures 1-8 is repeated.

        Part II

meas. 1-8. As the side couples raise their joined inside hands to make arches, the head couples take four skips forward, release their partners' hands, and turn away toward the arches (girl to right, boy to left). Holding the opposite persons' hands briefly, they skip under the arch, release the hands, clap their own hands, and return to original places. Joining both hands with their partners, the head couples swing once around with four skipping steps. The entire action takes sixteen continuous skipping steps.

meas. 1-8. Head couples make arches and side couples repeat action of measures 1-8.

Teaching Suggestions

It may be necessary for the teacher to lead the children through the simple direction changes performed in Part II of this dance, especially the first time the dance is attempted. Or, arrows can be placed on the floor for the children to follow.

Seven Steps

Recommended Mental Age
Seven to eight years.

Historical Background
Germany. A lively and enjoyable couple dance.

Records
Folk Dancer MH-1048A, Methodist 101B.

Formation
A double circle of couples, facing counterclockwise. Inside hands are joined and free hands are on the waist. Boys are on the inside.

Action

Part I

meas. 1-2. Starting with the outside foot, run forward with seven steps, pause on the eighth count.

meas. 3-4. Starting with the inside foot, run backward with seven steps, pause on the eighth count.

Part II

meas. 1-2. Release partner's hand and place both hands on own waist. Everyone does one schottische step away from his partner, boys move left, girls move right. This schottische step can be three runs and a hop or a side-close-side, hop. This is followed by one schottische step returning to face partner.

meas. 3-4. In shoulder-waist position or with both hands joined, each couple turns once clockwise with four step-hops. Boys begin with the left foot, girls begin with the right foot.

meas. 5-8. Action of measures 1-4 is repeated.

Circassian Circle

Recommended Mental Age
Seven to eight years.

Historical Background
England. Simple Mixer.

Record
Folkraft 1247.

Formation
Single circle of couples, facing the center with hands joined.

Action

     Part I

meas. 1-4. All children walk four steps toward the center of the circle, bowing or curtseying on the fourth step. They walk backward to place with four steps.

meas. 5-8. Action of measures 1-4 is repeated.

meas. 1-4. Releasing hands, girls walk forward, curtseying on the fourth step. They walk back to place with four steps.

meas. 5-8. Boys walk forward, bowing on the fourth step. They turn and walk back to partner with four steps.

     Part II

meas. 1-8. Join both hands with partner. Swing using sixteen walking or skipping steps.

meas. 1-8. With partner, in promenade position, all couples walk sixteen steps counterclockwise around the circle. Finish facing the center to begin the dance again.

Teton Mountain Stomp

Recommended Mental Age
Seven to eight years.

Historical Background
United States. Simple couple dance and mixer.

Records
Educational Activities Album HYP6, Windsor 7615.

Formation
Double circle, partners facing with both hands joined and arms held at shoulder level. Girls face clockwise, boys face counterclockwise.

Action

meas. 1-2.	Everyone moves toward the center of the circle, beginning with the inside foot. Girls step right, close left foot to right foot, step right, stomp left. Boys step left, close right foot to left foot, step left, stomp right. Body weight is not transferred on the stomp.
meas. 3-4.	Repeat actions of measures 1-2, beginning with the opposite foot and moving away from the center of the circle.
meas. 5-8.	Standing in place, the girls begin with the right foot and the boys begin with the left foot. Everyone performs four step-stomps. Body weight is not transferred on the stomp.
meas. 9-10.	In sidecar position with boys on the outside and girls on the inside of the circle, couples move counterclockwise around the circle. Beginning on the left foot, the boys take four steps forward. Beginning on the right foot, the girls take four steps backward.
meas. 11-12.	In banjo position with boys on the outside and girls on the inside of the circle, couples move clockwise around the circle. Beginning on the left foot the boys take four steps backward. Beginning on the right foot the girls take four steps forward.

meas. 13-14. Repeat actions of measures 9-10.

meas. 15-16. Beginning with the right foot, the girls take four steps in place. Beginning with the left foot, the boys take four steps forward to a new partner. During this part of the dance the girls are facing clockwise and the boys are facing counterclockwise. If the children can perform a polka step, it should be substituted for the walking steps in these two measures.

Virginia Reel

Recommended Mental Age
Seven to eight years.

Historical Background
United States. The most popular all-American country dance.

Record
Victor 1623.

Formation
Four to six couples in longways formation. Partners are facing.

Action

meas. 1-4.	Men join hands in their line and ladies join hands in theirs. All walk or skip forward four steps and backward four steps.
meas. 5-8.	Repeat action of measures 1-4.
meas. 9-12.	All walk or skip forward, honor partner. Boys bow, girls curtsey.
meas. 13-16.	All walk or skip backward to place, honor partner.
meas. 1-4.	All walk forward, join right hands with partners, turn once clockwise, and return to place.
meas. 5-8.	All walk forward, join left hands with partners, turn once counterclockwise, and return to place.
meas. 9-12.	All walk forward, join both hands with partners, and turn once clockwise, returning to place.
meas. 13-16.	All walk or skip forward and do-si-do, passing right shoulders and moving back to back, and passing left shoulders, returning back to place.
meas. 1-8.	The first or head couple in each set join both hands. They slide, or "sashay," eight slide steps down the center of the set and eight slide steps back to place.

meas. 9-12.   All face front. Boys follow head boy as he turns to his left and walks or skips around to the foot of the set. The girls follow the head girl around to the right to the foot of the set.

meas. 13-16. Head couple meet at foot of set, join both hands and hold them high forming an arch. Others join hands with partners at foot of set and walk or skip under the arch to a new place in the set. The dance is repeated from the beginning.

Oh, Susanna

Recommended Mental Age
Seven to eight years.

Historical Background
United States.

Records
Victor 1623, Victor 45-6180.

Formation
Single circle of couples, hands joined, facing the center. The boy is on the left of the girl.

Action

        Part I

meas. 1-4. All children take eight sliding steps to the right.

meas. 5-8. All children take eight sliding steps to the left.

        Part II

meas. 1-4. All children take four skipping steps forward toward the center of the circle, then four skipping steps backward to place.

meas. 5-8. Partners face each other and do a "grand right and left," by taking right hands and walking past their partner, passing right shoulders. They give their left hands to the next person and walk past this person by passing left shoulders. This is continued, alternating right and left hands, until the end of the verse of music. This usually involves meeting four other persons, the last of whom is a new partner.

        Part III

meas. 1-8. Everyone swings their new partner. The simplest method for the children to use for the swing is to join both hands with their partner and skip or walk around each other. If anyone does not have a partner, he should go to the center of the circle, find a partner, and rejoin the group.

Part IV

meas. 1-8.   All children promenade with their partners by taking sixteen walking steps counterclockwise around the circle.

Milanovo Kolo

Recommended Mental Age
Seven to eight years.

Historical Background
Yugoslavia. A simple and spirited kolo.

Record
Victor 1620.

Formation
Single circle, hands joined, facing center. Partners are not needed.

Action

Part I

meas. 1.   Beginning with the right foot and facing to the right, everyone does two step-hops: right-hop, left-hop.

meas. 2.   Facing the center, step to the right with the right foot, cross the left foot behind the right, take three quick steps in place: right-left-right.

meas. 3-4.   Repeat action of measures 1-2, beginning with the left foot and moving to the left: left-hop, right-hop, step to the left, cross right behind, three quick steps left-right-left.

Part II

meas. 1-2.   Facing the center and raising arms forward, move forward with three steps: right-left-right, and pause. Repeat once: left-right-left, and pause.

meas. 3-4.   Repeat action of measures 1-2, moving backward and lowering arms: right-left-right, pause; left-right-left, pause.

Captain Jinks

Recommended Mental Age
Seven to eight years.

Historical Background
American country dance.

Record
Folkraft 1070.

Formation
Single circle facing clockwise. Boys are behind their partners.

Action

meas. 1-4.	Children move forward, clockwise around the circle, with sixteen brisk walking steps.
meas. 5-8.	Girls turn and link right elbows with their partners. They take eight skipping steps, finishing in a double circle with the girls on the outside.
meas. 9-16.	Couples join inside hands. They take sixteen skipping steps clockwise around the circle.
meas. 17.	Stop, face partner. Honor partner.
meas. 18.	Honor neighbor.
meas. 19-20.	Swing neighbor.
meas. 21-24.	Promenade with neighbor. On the last beat the girl steps in front of the boy, forming a single circle. They are now ready to repeat the dance.

Pop Goes the Weasel

Recommended Mental Age
Seven to eight years.

Historical Background
American country dance.

Records
Victor 20151, Victor 45-6180.

Verses
1. All around the chicken-coop
   The monkey chased the weasel;
   That's the way the money goes —
   Pop goes the weasel.

2. A penny for a spool of thread,
   A penny for a needle,
   That's the way the money goes —
   Pop goes the weasel.

Formation
Double circle, couples facing. In each set of two couples, the number one couple is facing clockwise and the number two couple is facing counterclockwise.

Action
meas. 1-4. Couples walk or skip four steps forward and then four steps backward.

meas. 5-6. Each set of two couples joins hands and skips clockwise one full turn.

meas. 7-8. Couple number one lifts joined hands and couple number two skips under to move forward (counterclockwise) to meet the next couple number one. The dance is then repeated with this new couple.

Tantoli

Recommended Mental Age
Seven to eight years.

Historical Background
Sweden. Swedish couple dance.

Records
Victor 20992, Victor 45-6183.

Formation
Double circle, girl on right of partner. Boy puts his right arm around the girl's waist, and the girl puts her left hand on the boy's right shoulder. Outside hands are on hips. Everyone is facing counterclockwise.

Action

Part I

meas. 1-2. Place heel of outside foot forward with toe raised and body leaning backward. Place toe of outside foot backward and lean body forward. Do one polka step forward. (Heel-toe, polka step.)

meas. 3-4. Repeat action of measures 1-2, starting with inside foot.

meas. 5-8. Repeat action of measures 1-4.

Part II

meas. 1-4. With inside hands joined, partners take eight step-hops forward. Inside arms swing back and forth.

meas. 5-8. In shoulder-waist position, partners turn clockwise with eight step-hops. The boy starts on the left foot, the girl on the right foot.

La Raspa

Recommended Mental Age
Eight to nine years.

Historical Background
Mexico. A simple novelty dance based on a Mexican folk
tune.

Records
Folkraft 1119, Victor 1623.

Formation
Couples, holding hands, form a double circle. Boys have
their backs to the center.

Action

Part I

meas. 1-2. Holding hands, the children hop in place on the
left foot, simultaneously thrusting the right
foot and right arm sharply forward. Bringing
the right foot back to place and hopping on it,
each child thrusts the left foot and arm forward. Bringing the left foot back to place and
hopping on it, the child thrusts the right foot
and arm forward. The position is held for one
count.

meas. 3-8 The entire action of measures 1-2 is repeated
three times, leading with alternate feet.

Part II

meas. 1-4. Each child claps his own hands once, hooks
right elbows with his partner, and skips around
with eight steps. They clap their own hands
once, hook left elbows, and skip around with
eight steps.

meas. 5-8. The action of measures 1-4 is repeated.

Troika

Recommended Mental Age
Eight to nine years.

Historical Background
Russia. The title means "three horses" and the dance movements suggest a team of horses pulling a sleigh rapidly.

Records
Folkraft 1170, Kismet S112.

Formation
Groups of three, all facing counterclockwise. Inside hands
are joined at shoulder height, free hands are on hips. The
dance is usually performed with a boy in the center and one
girl on each side.

Action

Part I

meas. 1.   Starting with right foot, take four long running
            steps diagonally forward and to the right.
meas. 2.   Starting with left foot, take four long running
            steps diagonally forward and to the left.
meas. 3-4. Starting with right foot, take eight long run-
            ning steps forward around the circle.

Part II

meas. 1-2. Keeping hands joined, the person on the right
            runs in front of the center person, under an
            arch formed by the joined hands of the center
            person and left-hand partner, and returns to
            place. Eight running steps are used. At the
            same time, the center person turns left, follow-
            ing the person on the right around, under the
            joined hands.
meas. 3-4. Left-hand person repeats this action, running
            with eight steps under the arch formed by the
            center person and the right-hand partner, and
            back to place. The center person does a right-
            face turn under the joined hands.

Part III

meas. 1-4. Each group of three joins hands in a small circle and runs twelve steps to the left (clockwise). They then stamp their feet three times in place (right-left-right) and pause.

meas. 5-8. Action of measures 1-4 is repeated with the group circling right, or counterclockwise.

Buggy Schottische

Recommended Mental Age
Eight to nine years.

Historical Background
International.

Records
MacGregor 400, Imperial 1046.

Formation
Couples are in sets of four in a double circle, all facing counterclockwise. Couples join inside hands and give the outside
hands to the other couple.

Action

Part I

meas. 1-2.   Beginning with the outside foot, everyone
             takes two schottische steps forward: step-step-
             step-hop, step-step-step-hop.

meas. 3-4.   Beginning with the outside foot, everyone takes
             four step-hops forward.

Part II

meas. 1-2.   Repeat measures 1-2, Part I.

meas. 3-4.   Everyone takes four step-hops. The lead couple
             drops inside hands and step-hops around the
             outside of the back couple, who move forward
             during the step-hops. The lead couple joins
             hands behind the other couple, and the positions are reversed.

Teaching Suggestion
Because the music is identical for both parts of this dance,
if the children have difficulty performing Part II, it can be
eliminated.

Hora

Recommended Mental Age
Eight to nine years.

Historical Background
Israel. The national dance of Israel and a symbol of national strength and spirit.

Records
Folkraft 1110B, Folkraft 1116A, Victor 1623.

Formation
A single circle, facing in, without partners. Dancers connect by joining hands, elbows, or shoulders. Their bodies are turned slightly to the left.

Action
meas. 1.   Step to the left with the left foot. Then, step onto the right foot, crossing it behind the left.
meas. 2.   Step to the left with the left foot. Hop on the left foot and swing the right foot across in front of it.
meas. 3.   Step on the right foot in place. Hop on the right foot and swing the left foot across in front of it. This step (measures 1-3) is repeated throughout the entire dance.

Teaching Suggestions
The mentally retarded or emotionally disturbed child should have learned the basic step swing and grapevine steps before this dance is taught. The concept of crossing the feet, as learned in the grapevine step, is important for success in dancing the hora.

Bummel Schottische

Recommended Mental Age
Eight to nine years.

Historical Background
Germany.

Record
Victor 45-6177.

Formation
Couples in double circle, inside hands joined. Boys are on the inside.

Action

   Part I

meas. 1-8. Everyone takes four heel-toe polka steps around the circle. Heel, toe, step-together-step-hop. Movement is counterclockwise.

   Part II

meas. 9-16. In shoulder-waist position, partners take eight schottische steps turning clockwise in place.

Recreational Aspects

Music and related musical activity are excellent methods for use in orientating a mentally retarded or emotionally disturbed child to "normal" children in a recreational environment. Music is a universal language. All children, regardless of the degree of their handicapping condition, can actively participate in and derive satisfaction from music, rhythms, and dance during their leisure hours. Music can replace lonely and enduring free time for the mentally retarded or emotionally disturbed child.

Music can be used in the presentation of pageants, celebrations, drama, variety, and talent shows. The children can pantomime recorded songs. They can perform action songs even if they cannot sing the words. Singing in rounds can be fun for these children. Simple instrument play or simply listening to music is an excellent recreational pursuit.

Dance, according to Margaret H'Doubler, is an old and deeply rooted human activity whose foundations reside in the nature of man. If a person can think, feel, and move, he can dance.

Dance can be performed as a social activity for pure fun and enjoyment. It is both relaxing and exhilarating. Dance can break down needless inhibitions the mentally retarded or emotionally disturbed child may have, releasing tensions and freeing his personality for a wider and more enriching emotional life. Dance can satisfy and deepen the aesthetic senses and permit the child to express feeling without words. The movement through space which dance provides gives the mentally retarded or emotionally disturbed child an opportunity to understand his physical relationship to the real world.

Dance gives the mentally retarded or emotionally disturbed child an opportunity for group feelings, belonging, and social integration. As he grows socially in a dance environment he also develops social courtesies. Dance opens social and educational doors for him and gives him an opportunity to learn and mix well with his normal contemporaries.

Music, rhythms, and dance offer the mentally retarded or emotionally disturbed child endless opportunities for enjoyment and active participation during his leisure hours.

SELECTED REFERENCES

Burchenal, Elizabeth. *Folk dances and singing games,* Vol. I. New York: G. Schirmer, 1909.

Burchenal, Elizabeth. *Dances of the People,* Vol. II. New York: G. Schirmer, 1913.

Burchenal, Elizabeth. *Folk dances from old homelands,* Vol. III. New York: G. Schirmer, 1922.

Cameron, Rosaline. The use of music to enhance the education of the mentally retarded. *Mental retardation,* February 1970, 32-34.

Canner, Norma and Harriet Klebanoff. . . . *And a time to dance.* Boston: Beacon Press, 1968.

Hickey, Carolyn. Adventures in movement. *Challenge,* 1970, **6** (2), 1, 6.

Holthusen, Roselle. Musical recreation for the mentally retarded. *The best of challenge.* Washington: American Association for Health, Physical Education and Recreation, 1971, 72.

Kletter, Willaby. Music power. *Challenge,* November 1969, 3.

Kraus, Richard G. *Folk dancing.* New York: The Macmillan Co., 1962.

McGlone, Roy and F. William Happ. Singing an effective method for reaching mentally retarded children. *The best of challenge.* Washington: American Association for Health, Physical Education and Recreation, 1971, 74-75.

Peters, Martha L. Music and the exceptional child. *Therapeutic Recreation Journal,* 1968, **2** (3), 3-8.

Pomeroy, Janet. *Recreation for the physically handicapped.* New York: The Macmillan Co., 1964.

Sturdivant, Catharine. The little music makers. *The best of challenge.* Washington: American Association for Health, Physical Education and Recreation, 1971, 71-72.

Chapter VIII

Perceptual-Motor Development

Perception is the interpretation of information (sensory stimuli) monitored by the nervous system. Perceptual-motor efficiency refers to the ability to interpret sensory stimuli as they relate to or result from motor experiences. Perceptual-motor efficiency may involve perceiving through the medium of movement or making appropriate motor responses following the interpretation of sensory input.

It is scarcely possible to overestimate the importance of perceptual awareness in the total development of the human organism. The ability to accurately monitor and interpret information emanating from the environment provides the sole means by which the individual comes to know his world.

Perception is the means by which an individual organizes and systematizes his environment. It helps enable the individual to sense similarities and differences among the countless phenomena which make up his world. It enables him to learn about himself, about his environment, and how the two might most effectively integrate.

Problems in perception may arise because one's ability to perceive sensory occurrences is either nonexistent, inadequate, or inaccurate. The inability to derive meaning from sensory mechanisms for whatever the reason can limit the individual's ability to interact with and formulate appropriate responses to his environment. Proponents of such reasoning consider perceptual competence to be a major facet of the foundation from which stems much of the ability to learn.

Perception is thought to be an action affair, and action connotes movement. An experienced observer will note that an infant's initial interactions with his surroundings are almost exclusively motoric. Motor experiences can be observed as being the primary means by which a child initially gathers perceptual information about his world. In effect, the child moves to perceive, and perception through motion begins to give meaning and order to a world heretofore characterized by sensory chaos.

Perception, being an action affair, also connotes the need for movement experience opportunities. Perceptual motor theory alleges that a child deprived of ample and appropriate movement experiences may be cut off from the primary medium by which perceptual abilities can emerge and mature.

Perceptual inadequacies may be evident in children whose sensory mechanisms are either totally or partially nonfunctioning. Perceptual problems among such children may not stem from deficits in appropriate experiences, but from a limited potential to benefit from such experience. For these children, two courses of action may be considered: (1) Bombard the nonfunctioning or partially functioning sensory mechanism with stimuli in the hope that at least some sensation and subsequent perception might be experienced. This approach may be considered when a sensory mechanism is thought to be harboring untapped potential. It would, of course, not be utilized if the sensory mechanism were known to be totally and permanently inoperative (i.e. permanent, total blindness; permanent, total deafness); (2) Accentuate the positive by emphasizing the development of those sensory modalities known to be strong and functioning. This approach exploits those sensory mechanisms most capable of monitoring extensive, accurate information. The primary objective of this approach is to make up for perceptual deficits by emphasizing perceptual awareness through other sensory mechanisms. A possible third course of action involves the use and integration of both approaches.

There can be no broad application of a single best approach to developing perceptual awareness. The best approach or approaches grow out of thorough knowledge of the individual child's needs, capabilities, and characteristics.

The literature abounds in rationale which suggests probable relationships between certain kinds of motor experiences and the development of perceptual and intellectual capabilities. In recent years, acceptance of the perceptual-motor rationale and allegiance to certain perceptual-motor theorist-programmers has risen to unprecedented levels. Among some educators and parents of handicapped children, the perceptual-motor rationale has become a perceptual-motor panacea. This observation is intended not as an indictment or denial of perceptual-motor theory validity, but as an admonishment to explore and evaluate the perceptual-motor question with scholarly scrutiny.

With this admonishment clearly borne in mind, perceptual-motor theory and perceptual motor programming may be explored.

Perceptual-Motor Theory Rationale

Montessori (1912) was an early proponent of movement experiences as a primary means of enabling the child to become acquainted with his environment. Montessori's initial concern was that the child first become proficient in walking, balancing, and in coordinating movements through movement activities. The Montessori approach to education contends that the child lays the foundations for intelligence development by continually observing, comparing, and judging environmental phenomena. It suggests that sensory experience which purportedly occurs in large measure through movement enables the child to become acquainted with his environment and, in turn, to develop his intelligence.

Piaget (1936) has divided the first eleven years of life into three periods. The first stage of development, termed the sensory-motor period, is principally concerned with the sequence of interrelated sensory-motor experiences purported to be the foundations for perceptual development and for the subsequent development of symbolic fluency. Adequate development during the sensory-motor period is thought by Piaget to be a foundational prerequisite for subsequent forms of development which are primarily cognitive and relatively more complex.

Early research by Gesell (1940) suggests motor aptitude to be an effective determiner of normal child development. Gesell's observations suggest that the acquiring of postural skills enhances the individual's potential for adjustment to new situations, and that the mastery of such skills is an essential prerequisite for the development of more complex and sophisticated skills which appear in subsequent years.

Kephart (1960) has suggested that initial well-integrated patterns of motor behavior are prerequisite to subsequent exploration of the environment and learning. Motor proficiency is suggested as being an essential means of developing perceptual integrities including laterality, directionality, postural flexibility, and body image. It is Kephart's contention that the inadequate development of certain motor proficiencies may tend to inhibit the child's development in later, more sophisticated learning tasks. This belief is based upon the assumption that learning skills are hierarchial in nature and that the development and maturation of advanced learning is dependent upon a foundation of fundamental (motorically based) learnings.

Kephart contends that the separation of perceptual experience from motoric experience is probably not possible. He stresses the need to combine perceptual and motor experiences as a primary means of enabling the child to match perceptual and motor information. Perceptual inefficiency is suggested as an essential explanation for initial failure in school.

Barsch (1968) has reported that perception is the basis of intellect and that intellect owes its functional integrity to the various perceptual processes (auditory, visual, kinesthetic, tactual, gustatory, and olfactory perception). Barsch suggests that perceptual fluency is derived from the mature organization of all defined components of movement efficiency.

Earlier work by Barsch (1965) culminated in his Movigenic Theory. The basic tenets of this theory relate learning to movement efficiency. The Barsch system of Movigenics represents a study of movement patterns, their origin and development, and how said movement patterns relate and contribute to learning.

Movigenic Theory suggests that movement efficiency is the primary principle which underlies the design of the human organism. The theory purports that inefficiency in movement relegates the organism to a dependence upon others for survival. Man learns, and man moves. Man learns to move, and then moves to learn.

Movigenic Theory purports that movement efficiency is a measure of the organism's survival potential. As the organism moves, it matures. Symbolic fluency begins to replace motoric modes of gaining experience and comprehension. According to Movigenic Theory the development of symbolic fluency appears to be dependent upon prerequisite, efficient movement patterns.

Vernon (1962) has alleged perception to be the primary force in the development of knowledge and phenomena identification in the environment. He suggests that the beginnings of perception, at least in part, stem from motor experience. Motoric contact with the world allegedly provides the initial means of experiencing likenesses and differences among environmental phenomena.

Taylor (1962) has suggested that spatial orientation is largely dependent upon organism mobility. He contends that movement through one's environment or space world enables one to see relationships between distances and sizes of objects. He suggests that until the child is able to traverse distances which enable him to experience his environment from a variety of vantage points, his perceptual perspectives remain immature.

This review of perceptual-motor theory rationale provides some insights into the allegation that motoric experience may be a catalyst capable of stimulating the development of a variety of functions. The fact that a vast number of children who encounter learning difficulties also exhibit deficits in perceptual-motor efficiency is sufficiently thought-provoking to consider the merits of perceptual-motor programming when working with the mentally retarded and/or emotionally disturbed child.

Components of Perceptual-Motor Efficiency

Perceptual-motor efficiency, like physical fitness, is a global term. It is an umbrella which covers a broad spectrum of perceptual attributes. Components of perceptual-motor efficiency include:

Postural and locomotor awareness
Auditory perception and auditory spatial awareness
Visual perception and visual spatial awareness
Kinesthetic perception
Tactual perception
Body awareness
Laterality and directionality

Postural and Locomotor Awareness

The human organism has been endowed with the ability, need, and desire to move. Virtually all human functions in one way or another exhibit some movement component. In turn, movement is a primary medium through which the organism may find purpose and achieve its objectives. Barsch (1965) has suggested that the ability to move (locomote) is inseparably entwined with the survival potential of the organism. To the extent that an individual experiences movement deficits, Barsch suggests that the individual may become dependent upon others for survival.

Because perception occurs through movement, development of the ability to select and control one's movement patterns (hence, postural and locomotor awareness) should assume major importance in teaching the mentally retarded and emotionally disturbed. Postural and locomotor awareness activities should represent a concerted effort to assist the individual in realizing his movement potential. The more effectively one moves in a variety of situations, the more one is able to come into direct contact with the varying facets of his environment. Postural and locomotor awareness may be viewed as a facilitator of movement, because it precipitates feelings of ease and comfort as one moves through the environment. Secure, threat-free movement helps minimize stress, thus maximizing opportunities to become perceptually fluent through movement.

The development of postural and locomotor awareness among mentally retarded and emotionally disturbed children begins first with assuring that ample movement opportunities exist. Movement experiences do not often abound for mentally retarded and emotionally disturbed children for a variety of reasons ranging from well-meaning overprotection, to misdirected effort, to ignorance of the child's movement needs.

Postural awareness involves the ability to cope effectively with the force of gravity. The child's control over gravitational force manifests itself in the ability to assume and maintain appropriate postural attitudes over a broad spectrum of motor experiences. Postural awareness is inseparably related to locomotor awareness, because it helps assure total body control throughout the movement repertoire of the child.

Locomotor awareness involves the ability to incorporate effectively all of the skills which facilitate movement through the environment. It involves not only the ability to exhibit such skills, but includes the conceptualization necessary to select the most appropriate motor skill or skills to cope with any given situation. Activities potentially capable of developing postural and locomotor awareness may be found in Chapters IV, Basic Motor Patterns and Skills; VI, Movement Education; VII, Music, Rhythms, and Dance; and IX, Developmental Gymnastics.

Auditory Perception and Auditory Spatial Awareness

Auditory perception is more than hearing. Auditory perception involves the ability to translate what one hears into meaningful information.

The ability to perceive the meaning of sound develops in large measure from the ability to move. Movement produces sound and thus sets the stage for auditory perception development. Movement experiences create opportunities to observe that different movements cause different sounds. The child may soon begin to understand cause-to-effect relationships between the movements which he makes and the sounds which his movement patterns create.

The child may also begin to see similarities and differences in the sounds which emanate from the objects he manipulates. The mass and consistency of various objects in the environment create different sounds when manipulated; however, they remain mute until accidentally or purposefully contacted and manipulated by the individual.

Initially, through active pursuit of experience in the environment, the individual encounters a host of auditory sensations which begin stimulating the development of auditory perception. This perception of sound, inseparably entwined with motoric experiences, emerges as auditory perceptual-motor awareness.

Repeated auditory perceptual-motor experiences eventually enable the individual to make judgments about sounds caused by someone or something other than himself. Having learned through personal (motoric) experience that given circumstances result in given sound emissions, the individual need no longer be the perpetrator of an auditory experience or even in the immediate vicinity of the sound source to make value judgments about the sounds which he hears. Presence of the motoric component in auditory perception begins to become less crucial. The individual's backlog and repertoire of motor experiences now enable the formulation of concepts about sounds merely by hearing them.

The development of auditory spatial awareness is thought to be closely related to and dependent upon movement experiences. One develops percepts and concepts of up-down, near-far, left-right, in back of — in front of as one's movement capabilities facilitate exploration of the space world (environment). The individual soon comes to know that sounds emanate from different parts of the environment. This he knows because his movement patterns have taken him there. He has heard sounds become progressively louder or quieter as his movement patterns have brought him nearer to or farther from many sources of sound. Because the individual has moved through the environment and has perceived many sounds from a variety of vantage points, he becomes adept at judging the distance, direction, and characteristics of the sound source.

The following activities are suggested as bearing potential for the development of auditory perceptual-motor efficiency and auditory spatial orientation.

1. Rhythm band activities promote auditory perceptual motor awareness to the extent that rhythm instruments show cause-to-effect relationships between movement and sound. See Chapter VII (Music, Rhythms, and Dance).

2. Rhythm and dance activities require movement through an environment filled with sound. Moving toward, away from, and around sound sources provides experiences in auditory spatial orientation. See Chapter VII (Music, Rhythms, and Dance).

3. During exercise periods, children may perform exercises keeping in time with an audible cadence.

4. Children may give creative motor responses upon hearing the recorded sounds of various animals.

5. The child may be asked to make an appropriate quantity of motor responses after hearing a given number of sounds. For example, the child may be asked to execute as many hops as he hears drum beats.

6. The child may be asked to make appropriate responses to given sounds (e.g. *"Walk when you hear the bell; stop when you hear the whistle"*).

7. Secure two small paint cans which have been thoroughly cleaned out. Place in one can two marbles, and seal the can lid. Place in the other can one marble, and seal the can lid. Have the children shake and manipulate each can, and attempt to guess how many marbles are in each can.

8. Have the children play with balls which have jingle bells or similar sound producers placed inside. As the ball is manipulated, cause-to-effect relationships may be fostered between movement and sound. Sound emissions from the ball as it rolls and is thrown provide opportunities for auditory mechanisms to track the sound as it moves through space. Tracking the

movement of sound provides experience in the development of auditory spatial orientation.

9. Provide auditory experiences where sounds may range from very quiet to quite loud. Ask children to make themselves as small as possible when sounds are most quiet, then make themselves progressively larger as the sound becomes more intense. Recorded music may be utilized by varying the record player's volume control. A drum, tom-tom, or tambourine may be used by varying the strength with which the instrument is struck.

10. Provide auditory experiences where the pitch of the sound may range from very low to very high. Ask the children to make themselves as small as possible when pitch is lowest and as large as possible when pitch is highest. Notes or chords from a piano are most appropriate for this activity.

Visual Perception and Visual Spatial Awareness

Visual perception is more than seeing; visual perception involves the ability to make value judgments and interpretations about the multitude of things which one sees. Because sight tends to be the most heavily relied upon sensory modality, the ability to derive meaning from the things which one sees (visual perception) is of unparalleled importance.

The development of visual perception is closely aligned with and dependent upon a broad base of motor experiences. Visual perceptual-motor experiences occur when one simultaneously sees and manipulates objects. Manipulation, the motoric component of visual perceptual-motor development, is important because there is relative concreteness in the physical manipulation of objects in the environment. The relative concreteness of physically manipulating an object, when coupled with simultaneous visual experiences, facilitates the development of visual impressions about that object. These impressions and judgments simultaneously stemming from seeing and doing provide a major basis for the development of visual perceptual-motor efficiency.

As visual perception capabilities become more acute and visual impressions of objects in the environment become firmly established, the need for physical manipulation as a necessary adjunct to visual perception becomes less crucial. Repeated visual perceptual-motor experiences eventually render the motoric component of visual perception unnecessary in some cases and less necessary in others. For example, a child may first manipulate a stuffed animal toy. His eyes concentrate upon the toy as he plays. The visual information which he receives about the toy is reinforced and augmented by simultaneously occurring tactual sensations. Eventually, visual information alone with little or no adjunctive motoric components provides sufficient sensory input for the assurance of accurate visual perception.

Movement experiences are considered vital in the development of visual tracking capabilities. Visual tracking involves the ability to willfully direct and focus one's eyes from one visual stimulus to another (e.g. reading from right to left across a page). Another form of visual tracking involves the ability to direct and focus one's eyes upon a single visual stimulus which is moving through the environment (e.g. a moving automobile, a thrown ball). Either of these experiences may be further complicated by the fact that the individual himself may also be moving through the environment at the same time. Yet another form of visual tracking involves the ability to direct and focus one's eyes upon a stationary object when the individual himself is moving. A cursory familiarity with physical education and recreation movement experiences would indicate vast potential for enhancing visual-motor coordination and visual tracking abilities.

Visual spatial awareness is a form of visual perception which gives dimension to visual experiences. It facilitates the determination and conceptualization of distances between and among objects in space. Visual spatial awareness evolves largely as a result of one's concretely experiencing distances as one moves through the space world. Having sufficiently experienced distances in the environment as a concomitant outcome of movement experiences, the individual eventually becomes able to know relative distances without actually having to traverse said distances.

Visual spatial awareness aids in the correct interpretation of perceptual distortions. One's perception of any given phenomenon in the environment changes as one's vantage point changes. For example, a ball at the far end of the gymnasium or play field may look extremely tiny, yet it may be completely identical to a seemingly large ball in the foreground. Visual spatial awareness not only facilitates judgments of the distant ball's characteristics, but equally facilitates one's judgment of his distance from the ball. Numerous parallels to this example exist in many life situations. Physical education and recreation skills, which by their very nature encourage movement through and exploration of the environment, create a climate conducive to the development of visual spatial awareness.

The following activities are suggested as bearing potential for the development of visual perception and visual spatial awareness.

1. Ample opportunities should be provided for children to play with numerous sorts of objects. To the extent possible, children should be permitted to roam through, see, and simultaneously manipulate objects in the environment.

2. Have the child walk across the room while visually spotting a brightly colored picture which has been placed on the wall. Note that pictures can be of the children's own making and that drawing is a visual perceptual-motor experience.

3. Ask the child to finger trace dittos prepared by the teacher. Forms to be traced may first include straight lines followed by

geometric forms. Another example involves a picture of an automobile on one side of a page with a garage on the other side of the page. Parallel lines approximately one inch apart connect the automobile to the garage. Ask the child to trace the path of the car into the garage. Additional similar examples can be created by the teacher.

4. Place large numbers, letters, or geometric forms on the play surface. Ask the child to walk heel-to-toe on the lines which form the figures.

5. Have the child stand at varying distances from a wall and roll, throw, or bounce a brightly colored ball at the wall. The ball should be retrieved by the child. Emphasize visual concentration on the ball.

6. Place a ladder horizontally on the ground or horizontally, but a few inches above the ground. Ask the child to walk the length of the ladder stepping between, but not touching, the ladder rungs.

7. Hold a broomstick at various heights, depending upon the capabilities and characteristics of the child, and ask the child to duck under, step over, or slip around but not touch the stick.

8. Secure a length of rope approximately ten feet in length. Tie the ends of the rope together so that the rope may form a circle. Place the rope circle on the ground. Make believe that the circle is a mud puddle, and ask the children to leap or jump across (but not into) the puddle.

9. Two tightly stretched, parallel ropes held at approximately elbow height and slightly more than shoulder's width apart are held by standards or assistants. Ask the child to walk forward (backward, sideways) between the ropes but not touch either rope.

10. Have the child push a small ball while creeping across and around the playing surface.

Kinesthetic Perception

Kinesthetic perception may be defined as an awareness of one's body position in space. It involves the ability to conceptualize the configurations or shapes which one causes his body to assume and the relationships of those configurations to the rest of the immediate environment. Kinesthetic perception helps enable the individual to make judgments including whether or not one is moving and, if moving, how rapidly. It includes an awareness of the body's form or configuration whether moving or standing still. If moving, kinesthetic perception helps enable the individual to determine whether he is moving forward, backward, sideways, at some other angle, in an arc, or in any combination of the above. If the individual is airborne, kinesthetic perception helps enable him to determine his speed, trajectory, and distance from the surface. In such situations, kinesthetic perception becomes an important safety skill.

Kinesthetic perception is an extension of a previously discussed perceptual-motor attribute, postural and locomotor awareness. To be sure, postural maintenance and the ability to locomote require competence in kinesthetic perception. However, postural and locomotor awareness activities are by their very nature extremely basic. They therefore should not be expected to solely stimulate the development of kinesthetic perception competence.

Virtually any activity which requires an awareness of and control over body position in space may hold potential for stimulating the development of kinesthetic perception. Though an extremely wide variety of activities come under such an umbrella, the activities selected as potential enhancers of kinesthetic perception should be challenging, yet not frustrating to the children involved. The following are examples of motor activities typically utilized to enhance kinesthetic perception.

1. Virtually all of the activities in Chapter IX, Developmental Gymnastics, endeavor to stimulate awareness of body position in space.
2. A variety of activities utilizing reclaimed automobile tires may enhance kinesthetic perception. See Chapter XII, Innovative Equipment.
3. Playground equipment including slides, swings, spring-mounted rocking horses, and jungle gyms stimulate kinesthetic awareness.
4. Have the child attempt to stand on one foot with eyes closed and not to lose his balance. Children exhibiting low levels of kinesthetic perception may have to attempt this stunt with eyes open. Another variation for more highly skilled children involves standing on the tiptoe of the supporting leg. Again, eyes may be either open or closed depending upon which performance level is within the child's grasp.
5. Provide opportunities for the children to crawl and creep through improvised tunnels, and suggest that they try touching neither the top nor sides of the tunnel while moving within the enclosure. More highly skilled children may be able to crawl and creep backward through the tunnel.
6. Have the child hold a twenty-four-inch rope in his hands. The rope should hang in the front of the body as would a jump rope with the lowermost part of the rope approximating knee height. Ask the child to jump forward over the rope so that upon completion of the jump, the child's body is in front of the rope.

7. Have the child walk a circle which has been marked upon the playing surface. After several trials, ask the child to walk the circle without looking at the line. As necessary, the teacher may suggest that the child look at the line for reorientation.
8. Have the child lie on a safety mat with a line drawn down its center. Have the child lie flat on the mat with arms at the sides and body extended. Ask the child to roll his body down the length of the mat. The roll should be straight so that the child rolls to the end of the mat rather than off the side of the mat. Have the child roll both to the left and right.
9. Provide scooter boards which enable the child to propel himself across the playing surface, preferably a smooth floor. The child may sit or lie on the scooter board as he propels himself in any direction.
10. Kinesthetic perception may be enhanced through utilization of the balancing devices suggested in Chapter XII, Innovative Equipment.

Tactual Perception

Tactual perception may be defined as the ability to interpret sensations of touch. Touching, feeling, and manipulating objects in the environment imply a rather heavy dependence upon movement as the primary medium through which tactual sensations are experienced. Of course, tactual sensations are experienced by passive beings as well as by active beings; however, tactual experiences and opportunities to interpret tactual sensations become significantly more abundant when one actively pursues the infinite phenomena which comprise the environment.

The development of tactual perception is an especially important attribute among those whose abilities to work with abstractions are limited. Tactual experiences by their very nature tend to be rather concrete. In experiencing something tactually one may touch, feel, hold, or manipulate the object in question. The concreteness of actual physical contact with the environment provides a most important means of coming to know the world especially among individuals who, of necessity, must cope with the world on relatively concrete terms.

Tactual perception is an important attribute in the development of manual dexterity and fine motor skill. It assists the individual in determining how a particular object has been grasped. If an object has been grasped inopportunely, tactual perception is often the primary informant. Tactual perception is also the primary informant when formulating judgments about objects which cannot be seen.

Tactual perception often functions as an adjunct to visual perception. The combined perceptions which stem from simultaneously seeing and feeling are often more informative than perception stemming from either one of the sensory modalities functioning by itself.

Because tactual perception is an action affair, its development is facilitated by movement experiences which emphasize the sensations of touch. The following activities exemplify the development of tactual perception through the medium of motoric experiences.

1. Place a variety of objects in a paper bag. Objects placed in the bag should be familiar to the children. Have the children reach into the bag and try to identify objects grasped before pulling them from the bag.

2. Fill two pans with water, one warm and one cool. Have the child immerse his hand in one pan then immerse his hand in the other pan. Ask the child to tell which pan of water is the warmer. This activity can be repeated utilizing foot and elbow contacts.

3. Have the child touch things with his feet, and without benefit of visual or other sensory input identify the things which he touches.

4. Permit the child to walk barefooted over a variety of surfaces. Surfaces may be smooth, rough, warm, cool, damp, or dry.

5. Place a length of adhesive or masking tape in a straight line on the floor. Permit the child to walk barefooted. Ask him not to look for the tape, but to feel the tape with his feet. Have him walk the length of the tape only by feeling, not by looking.

6. Place a piece of tape approximately two inches square on the flat surface of a 1x12x12-inch board. Place the board in the child's lap, tape side down. Ask the child to feel the tape side of the board with his fingers, and to stop when he thinks he feels the tape. Have him hold that spot, then turn the board over to see if his fingers have located the tape.

7. Encourage the child to play with a variety of variously shaped and textured toys. Here, the child is encouraged to simultaneously manipulate and see. Tactual sensations supplement and enhance visual perception and vice versa.

8. Have the child string various sets of beads. For children whose manual dexterity and tactual perceptions are somewhat lacking, bolts or blocks of wood with relatively large holes may be strung over rope. As manual dexterity and tactual sensations improve, smaller objects and lighter rope or string may be substituted.

9. Have children roll, crawl, and creep over a variety of variously textured surfaces (e.g. tile floor, lawn, safety mats, gymnasium floor, carpet). If possible, permit the children to roll, crawl, and creep over many surfaces during a relatively short period of time. This experience helps enable a child to perceive tactual sensations with his entire body, rather than just with his hands and/or feet.

10. Place three square blocks of different sizes (or balls of different sizes, but the same texture) inside a bag. Ask the child to reach

into the bag, feel each of the objects, and then pull the largest object from the bag. The child may then empty the bag's remaining contents to see if his choice is correct.

Body Awareness

Body awareness, sometimes called body image, refers to an awareness of body parts and segments. It involves an ability to name or point out body parts and an awareness of the existence of one's body parts as one moves through space.

Body awareness has been hypothesized as being an important initial step in becoming aware of the environment through which one moves. The suggestion is that one must come to know oneself before endeavoring to organize and systematize the external world.

Body awareness activities are designed to focus the individual's attention on body segments and parts. Such activities help the individual come to know that the body has two sides which may work together, in opposition, or individually. Body awareness activities also focus attention on the capabilities and limitations characteristic of the various body parts and segments. The following are examples of motor activities typically utilized in the development of body awareness.

1. Swimming activities may promote body awareness through the sensations resulting from movement through the water.
2. Ask the child to point out his ears, eyes, hips, nose, arms, knees, elbows, toes, ankles, and shoulders.
3. Place a bright-colored ribbon or elastic band on a body part or segment to draw the child's attention to it as he moves about.
4. Attach a jingle bell to an elastic band and wrap the band around various body parts and segments. Movement causes the bell to jingle, thus calling attention to the particular body part or segment. Note that this activity is most successful in working one on one or when working with a small group of children. In larger groups, the noise becomes a distraction.
5. Have the child execute a variety of elementary motor skills while watching his body's image reflected in a mirror.
6. Have the child pose or move before a mirror, then have him attempt to draw a picture of his movement as it appeared in the mirror.
7. Have the children stand facing the teacher. There should be adequate space between children so that movements can be made freely. The teacher says to the children, "Do as I do," and proceeds to move his arms and legs in various combinations. Movements may be unilateral, bilateral, and cross-lateral (e.g. left arm only; right arm, left arm simultaneously; left arm, right leg simultaneously).
8. Have the child lie on his back on the floor. Ask him to move

one or more body segments at a time by sliding them along the floor. Be sure only to point to the body segment or segments to be moved so that the child does not get tactual cues. The child may be asked to make unilateral, bilateral, and cross-lateral movements. Movement patterns experienced in this activity resemble movement patterns experienced when playing angels-in-the-snow.

9. Secure a lightly weighted belt to a body segment while the child participates in a variety of motor experiences. The weight should be heavy enough to create an awareness of the segment to which it is attached, but not so heavy that it inhibits movement. The belt may be moved from segment to segment.

Laterality and Directionality

Laterality is defined as an internal awareness that the body has a left and right side. Directionality is an extension of laterality into the external world. Directionality is thought to develop largely as the result of movement experiences. In the hierarchy of perceptual-motor development, body image or body awareness is thought to emerge first, followed by the emergence of laterality. Laterality development is thought to be a foundational prerequisite for the subsequent emergence of directionality.

The establishment of lateral dominance is thought to be an important facilitator in the development of laterality. Well-established lateral dominance is thought to provide a valuable frame of reference which helps enable the individual to determine differences between left and right. Problems in lateral dominance ranging from no lateral dominance to mixed dominance are thought to be at least partially the cause of certain learning difficulties. A common problem associated with laterality inadequacies includes reversals. Common reversals include the unwitting substitution of a *p* for a *q* and vice versa, or the unwitting substitution of a *b* for a *d* and vice versa. It is hypothesized that a child without a well-established left-right orientation may perceive little or no difference between such letters.

Directionality, an extension of laterality into the external world, helps give dimension to space. A child possessing good directionality development is capable of conceptualizing left-right, above-below, front-behind, and various combinations of such directions.

Directionality and spatial orientation or spatial awareness are closely related perceptual attributes. Each gives dimension to the space world and facilitates the child's determination of where he is in relation to other phenomena in the environment. Motor experiences intended to enhance the development of laterality and directionality include the following.

1. Provide a variety of throwing and kicking experiences which

encourage the selection and use of a dominant or preferred side of the body.

2. Have the child participate in rhythm and dance activities which require movement in many directions.
3. Encourage movement activities in all conceivable directions utilizing each of the basic locomotor skills.
4. Have the child wad up a ten-foot section of rope and throw it high into the air. When the rope lands on the playing surface, have the child walk heel to toe from one end of the rope to the other.
5. Draw or tape geometric figures, letters, numbers, and words on the playing surface. Have the child walk heel to toe along the full length of the lines which comprise each figure.
6. Have the child walk forward and backward on a balance beam. The child may perform before a full length mirror to help him conceptualize changes in direction.
7. Have the child walk in both directions sideways on the balance beam. Be sure he walks with the left foot as the lead foot, then the right foot as the lead foot.
8. Place safety mats on the playing surface, and have the children roll from one end of the mat to the other, rolling both to the left and right.
9. Draw a straight line or lane on the playing surface. Provide the child with an old tire or a hula hoop, and ask him to roll the tire or hoop straight down the line or between the lines which form the lane. The child may walk sideways, forward, or backward in performing this activity.
10. Randomly place brightly colored circles on the floor. Have the child randomly leap, hop, or jump from one circle to another. Encourage the child to move in all directions if he does not do so spontaneously.

Assessing Perceptual-Motor Competence

The belief that perceptual-motor competence is a prerequisite academic achievement has led to the development of perceptual-motor efficiency measures. Among the most commonly incorporated measures of perceptual-motor efficiency is the Purdue Perceptual-Motor Survey (PPMS) (Roach and Kephart, 1966). The PPMS alleges to determine areas of perceptual-motor difficulty typically exhibited by nonachievers in the classroom. The survey consists of twenty-two scored items. The examinee is assigned a score ranging from one (low level performance) to four (high level performance) for each item according to specified performance criteria. Survey items are divided into five broad categories including:

Posture and balance

Body image and differentiation

Perceptual-motor match

Ocular pursuits

Form perception

The PPMS is administered individually. It is relatively easy to administer and in most cases provides precise and explicit scoring instructions.

Items selected for inclusion in the PPMS have been validated against scores attained on the Wide Range Achievement Test (WRAT). During the validation phase of the PPMS, an item was selected for inclusion in the survey when children simultaneously exhibited high (low) scores on a potential survey item and high (low) scores on the WRAT.

SELECTED REFERENCES

Barsch, R. H. *A movigenic curriculum.* Madison, Wis.: Bureau for the Handicapped, 1965.

Barsch, R. H. *Enriching perception and cognition.* Seattle: Special Child Publications, 1968.

Gesell, A. *The first five years of life.* New York: Harper and Row, Publishers, 1940.

Kephart, N. C. *The slow learner in the classroom.* Columbus, Ohio: Charles E. Merrill Publishing Co., 1960.

Montessori, M. *The Montessori method.* New York: Frederic A. Stokes Co., 1912.

Piaget, J. *The origins of intelligence in children.* New York: New York University Press, 1936.

Roach, E. G. and N. C. Kephart. *The Purdue Perceptual-Motor Survey.* Columbus, Ohio: Charles E. Merrill Publishing Co., 1966.

Taylor, J. G. *The behavioral basis of perception.* Baltimore, Md.: Penguin Books, 1962.

Vernon, M. D. *The psychology of perception.* Baltimore, Md.: Penguin Books, 1962.

Chapter IX

Developmental Gymnastics

Developmental gymnastics refers to a phase of the child's physical education and recreation experience which centers around activities of an acrobatic and self-testing nature. Such activities include a broad spectrum of motor experiences which may be classified into three general categories.

Mat and Floor Activities	Light Equipment Activities	Heavy Equipment Activities
Preparatory activities	Ropes	Trampoline
Stunts	Wands	Mini-tramp
Tumbling	Balls	Horizontal bar
		Rings
		Parallel bars
		Balance beam

The gymnastics activities presented may be construed as having specific physical values including:

Agility	Muscular endurance
Balance	Muscular flexibility
Cardiorespiratory endurance	Muscular strength[1]
Muscular coordination	

[1]Refer to Chapter III (Basic Physical and Motor Fitness) for definitions of terms.

Potential cognitive and social values include:

Learning to follow directions

Learning to play and get along with others

Stimulating the thought processes (sequential thinking, motor planning) necessary for completion of activities

Having success experiences capable of self-image enhancement

Enhancing language development, both expressive and receptive, through verbal communication

In teaching developmental gymnastics activities to mentally retarded and/or emotionally disturbed children, evaluation questions will aid in the assessment of program effectiveness.

1. How many skills has the child attempted?
2. How well does the child perform those skills which he has attempted?
3. Is the child better able to pay attention?
4. Is the child better able to follow directions?
5. Has participation produced cardiorespiratory stimulation?
6. Does the child show signs of becoming more flexible?
7. Has the child's muscular endurance improved?
8. Is the child more agile?
9. Has the child's general coordination improved?
10. Has the child's static and dynamic balance improved?
11. Does the child appear to have enjoyed the program?
12. Does the child's overt behavior suggest a possible increased level of self-esteem while participating in the program? If yes, does there appear to be carry-over into other facets of the child's life?
13. Has the child who tends to be nonverbal shown new levels of verbal response during or about his developmental gymnastics participation?
14. Has the child who exhibits hyperactive behavior patterns shown positive (negative) tendencies toward acceptable behavior patterns?
15. Has the child who tends to be withdrawn found an effective means of self-expression and involvement with the external world?
16. Has the child developed a rapport and ability to cooperate with his peers? With the teacher?
17. Has the child demonstrated any concomitant improvement in other forms of learning?
18. Has the program uncovered any previously unnoticed physical deficiencies in the child?
19. Do children who exhibit certain physical, mental, or behavioral characteristics tend to respond better or derive more benefit from the developmental gymnastics program?

20. Does the child enjoy the activities to such an extent that he participates on a self-initiated, recreational basis?

Safety Considerations

Attention to safe programming should always remain foremost in the efforts of the teacher. Gymnastics activity is neither inherently safe, nor is it inherently unsafe. Safe programming is a function of knowledgeable, aware teaching.

Safety Mats

Adequate safety matting is essential in the activity area. Safety mats help provide cushioned contacts with the surface, and are particularly vital in helping to reduce the impact of uncontrolled falls.

Should available space permit, it is most desirable *not* to roll up the safety mats when not in use. Constant rolling and unrolling proves detrimental to a mat's longevity. Rolling is most damaging to hair-filled canvas type mats, as the hair tends to bunch in some spots thus rendering the mat uncomfortably (and dangerously) lumpy. When plastic mats are rolled, the ends tend to curl up and create a safety hazard. Should plastic mats be rolled, however, they should be turned upside down prior to rolling. When unrolled, the mat can be returned right side up, thus causing the mat's ends to safely curl downward against the floor. Some mats now being manufactured can be folded accordian-style. Such mats may be compactly stacked away in a corner when not in use. This style of mat, though relatively expensive, is probably most convenient where space limitations prevail.

Apparel

The type of clothing worn by participants is not critical, provided the clothing in no way hinders participation. Care should be taken to see that clothing is neither too tight (inhibits movement) nor too loose (gets in the way). Also, the teacher should make certain that the participant has nothing in his pockets which might cause injury should he fall. Pencils, pens, yo-yos, and marbles are typical culprits.

Footwear should be light and soft, yet special gymnastics slippers are certainly not required. Stockings are acceptable with the reservation that sometimes they tend not to provide sufficient footing. Performing barefooted is also acceptable, but with a reservation that factors of cleanliness be fully considered. Regular gym shoes may be used, yet some children find them uncomfortably large, heavy, and cumbersome. Use of street shoes should be avoided however, because they may damage safety mats and play surfaces (especially hardwood gymnasium floors), and do not provide adequate footing. Whenever possible, participants should wear a sweatshirt upper garment. The heavy stretch material provides a ready "handle" for the teacher to grasp onto while assisting the child through skill performances.

Spotting

Assisting a participant through skill performances is termed "spotting." Becoming an effective spotter should command high priority in learning to teach gymnastics activities to the mentally retarded and/or emotionally disturbed. Spotting may lend much needed confidence to timid, poorly skilled, and marginally motivated children. Spotting is of paramount importance, especially among children whose behavior tends to be particularly unpredictable, unstable, or erratic. Most of the skills presented herein are relatively elementary and hence easy to spot. Even though various developmental gymnastics skills may be demanding of the child, the simplicity of these skills makes for relatively uncomplicated spotting. The effective spotting of any developmental gymnastics skill necessitates these following minimum considerations:

1. Know the behavior characteristics of the individual in an effort to predict and be prepared for the probable nature of his effort.
2. Be as close to the individual as possible without actually hindering his performance.
3. Know the skill being attempted to the extent that you know what will be required of the performer. This facilitates the spotter's lending assistance at precisely appropriate times.
4. Be sure you know the specific skill to be performed, and that both you and the child are ready at the same time.
5. Experiment with various hand placements when spotting each of the various skills, and select those which most effectively facilitate each performance.

Equipment and Supplies

Any equipment selected for use in a developmental gymnastics program should be scaled to the child's physical size. Generally, smaller children should be provided equipment which has been reduced proportionally in size, height, and weight (e.g. smaller child, smaller ball; smaller child, smaller horizontal bar diameter). One exception to this general rule involves the use of balance apparatus where the smaller, typically less mature children would require broader bases of support (e.g. smaller, typically less mature child, wider balance beam). An abundance of commercially manufactured gymnastic equipment, while desirable, is not always necessary. However, the teacher should become familiar with gymnastics supply catalogs for the twofold purpose of determining what kinds of equipment might be improvised and of becoming a critical buyer when equipment funds are allocated.

Typical playground apparatus can be improvised, and inexpensive equipment can be innovated to help assure full program benefits and participation. For example, various widths and lengths of galvanized pipe can be fashioned into horizontal bars. Balance beams can be constructed from scrap wood or from inexpensive lumber purchased at a local lumber yard. Balls may be improvised from tightly wadded paper which has been firmly taped. For more complete details regarding improvised equipment, see Chapter XII, Innovative Equipment.

Skill Progressions

In each of the developmental gymnastics activity categories, the specific skills presented have been ordered from most easy to most difficult. While a majority of children seem to learn these given skills in the various suggested progressions, such progressions need not be strictly adhered to in individual instances. Many children naturally develop their own unique progressions, and to the extent governed by circumstances, such individual differences should be respected.

Recreational Aspects

Mentally retarded and/or emotionally disturbed children often enjoy developmental gymnastics activities enough to wish to participate on a self-initiated recreational basis. Their interest in such activities stems partially from the fact that the activities require little formal structure and few rules. Participation is readily geared to individual interests and capabilities.

While self-initiated recreational participation in developmental gymnastics activities can and should be encouraged, close supervision is advised. Care should be taken both by parents and teachers to assure that the child's participation is rewarding yet in no way jeopardizes his safety. The safety considerations suggested in this chapter should be adhered to in recreational as well as in instructional situations.

Additional Activities

The specific activities and progressions presented are intended to serve primarily as examples of developmental gymnastic activities. The list is neither exhaustive nor is it extensive. There exists a variety of additional activities to be found in books devoted solely to gymnastics.

Mat and Floor Activities

1. Preparatory activities.
   a. Perform basic body positions from the standing position.

Tuck

Pike
(Jack Knife)

Layout
(Swan)

Straddle
(Spread Eagle)

Variation one

Variation two

Straddle
(Spread Eagle)

Tuck

Pike
(Jack Knife)

Layout
(Swan)

They include the tuck, pike (jackknife), layout (swan), and two variations of the straddle (spread eagle).

b. Perform the basic body positions while lying in various positions.

c. From a standing position: Jump and tuck; jump and pike; jump and lay out; jump and straddle.

d. From a standing position: Jump to half turn; jump to full turn; jump to face a colored disc placed on the floor by the teacher. Land on the balls of the feet with hips and knees slightly flexed to assure a cushioned landing.

Pike

Layout

Straddle

Tuck

Full Turn

Half Turn

Jump to Face the Disc

2. Stunts.
   a. Try different front bridge positions. Can someone go under the bridge?
   b. Try different back bridge positions. Can someone go under the bridge?
   c. Introduce elements of movement (move hands and/or feet) to both front and back bridge positions.

Front Bridges

Back Bridges

d. Assume the airplane position. Bank to the left and right as if turning the airplane. Assume the rocking horse position. Begin rocking back and forth; rock back and forth and around in a circle simultaneously.

e. Alternately assume the "angry cat" and "sway back horse" positions.

f. Rabbit hop in different directions.

g. Mule kick in various directions.

Note: Airplanes can bank and turn

Airplane

Rocking Horse

Angry Cat

Sway Back Horse

Rabbit Hop

Mule Kick

3. Tumbling.
   a. Assume the lying down layout position. Roll to the left. Roll to the right.
   b. Assume the lying tuck position. Begin rocking back and forth.
   c. Perform forward roll to sitting position. Flex the knees to assume a tuck position, and place hands on the mat directly in front of the feet. To initiate the roll, push forward with the feet, elevate the hips, and tuck the head between the arms. As the hips pass over the head, give a final push forward with the hands and continue the roll until reaching the sitting position. It may be necessary for the teacher to lend assistance by simultaneously tucking the child's head with one hand, and lifting his hips upward-forward with the other hand.

Roll Left, Right from Lying Down Layout Position

Rocking

d. Perform a complete forward roll starting and ending in the tuck position. The initiation of this skill and spotting procedures are nearly identical to forward roll to the sitting position. In this skill, however, the child must initiate the roll more forcefully. The additional thrust helps provide the quantity of momentum required to continue the roll to the standing tuck position.

e. Perform a short dive roll ending in the standing tuck position. Note that a forward roll becomes a dive roll if the performer is momentarily in flight. Performing a dive roll requires the performer to extend his body both forward and slightly upward. As the body momentarily leaves the ground, the arms remain outstretched in front of the performer to cushion his landing. As the hands recontact the surface, the head is tucked between the arms, and the skill is completed as if it were a forward roll. The teacher may wish to assist by ensuring that the child tucks his head between his shoulders upon landing. A hand placed behind the child's head during the landing phase effectively serves this purpose.

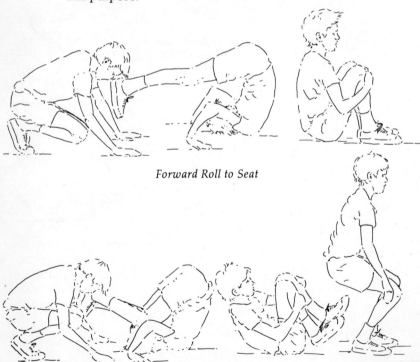

Forward Roll to Seat

Complete Forward Roll

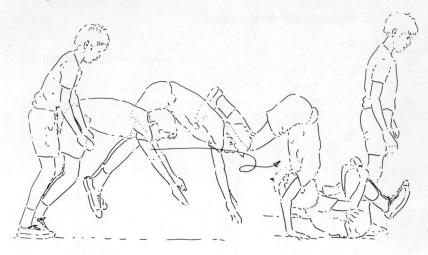

Dive Roll

Backward Roll

f. Perform a backward roll starting and ending in the tuck
position. Initiate the roll by pushing backward with the
hands. Throughout the roll, the chin should remain tucked
in toward the chest. As the hips begin to rise and the shoulders come into contact with the mat, the hands are placed
on the mat (palms down, thumbs toward the ears). At the
moment the hips pass over the top of the head, the arms are
extended to enable the head to clear the mat as the feet return to the surface.

Light Equipment Activities

1. Ropes.
   a. Hang from the rope without touching the ground, and assume the basic body positions.
   b. Grasp rope overhead. Jump to inverted hang position. Wrap legs around rope momentarily for support. Return to stand. Teacher support should be available as needed.

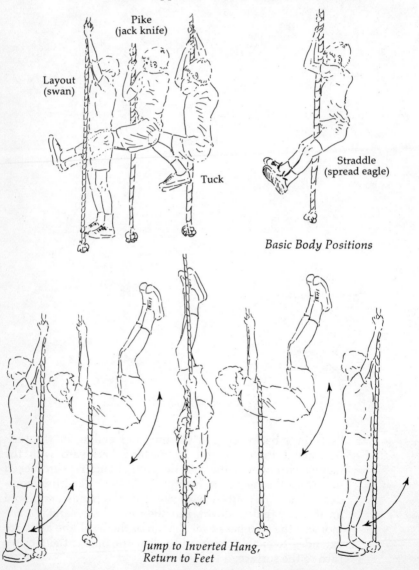

Basic Body Positions

Jump to Inverted Hang,
Return to Feet

c. Swing forward and backward on the rope. Drop to dismount at the end of the back swing.
d. Swing backward and forward on the rope. Kick ball off box at end of the forward swing. Swing backward. Drop to dismount at end of the back swing.

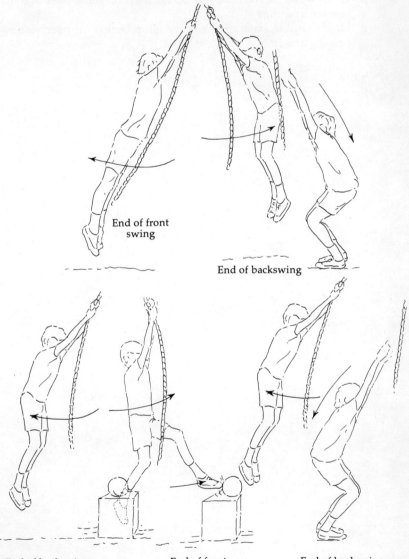

End of front swing

End of backswing

End of backswing

End of front swing and kick

End of backswing

Swinging on Rope

2. Wands.
   a. Place one end of wand on floor. Cup the palm of one hand over the other end. Walk forward in a circle using the wand as the pivot point. Walk backward in a circle using the wand as a pivot point.
   b. Hold wand in front of the body. Step forward over wand one leg at a time.
   c. Hold wand in back of the body. Step backward over wand one leg at a time.

Use Wand as Pivot Point

*Step Forward over
Wand*

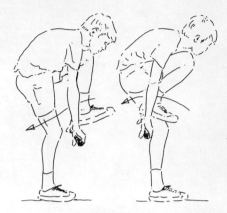

Step Backward
over Wand

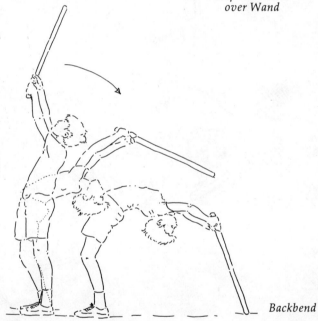

Backbend

d. Hold wand in an upright position. Perform backbend until wand touches the ground.
e. Stand wand on end. Release wand. Perform a full turn to the right. Catch wand before it falls to the ground. Repeat, this time turning to the left.
f. Hold wand in front of the body. Jump over the wand. Land on feet with wand behind the body.

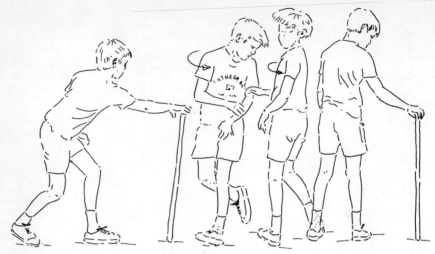

Full Turn

Jump over Wand

3. Balls.
    a. Bounce the ball with both hands (with the right hand, with the left hand).
    b. Pass ball over the head from one hand to the other.
    c. Pass ball around the body from hand to hand at waist height. Reverse the direction.

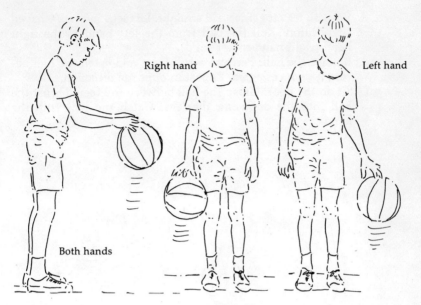

Right hand

Left hand

Both hands

Bounce the Ball

Pass Ball over the Head

d. Sit with legs together and straight. Lift legs into a V-shaped sit position. Roll the ball from the left hand to the right hand (right hand to left hand).

e. Bounce the ball. Perform a full turn, and catch the ball before it bounces again. Repeat in opposite direction.

f. Sit on the floor. Grasp the ball between the feet. Thrust the ball into the air using the legs. Catch the ball with the hands.

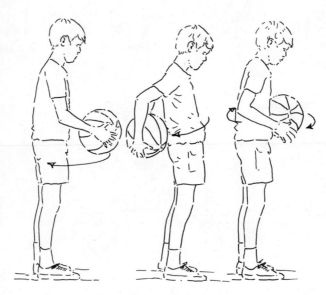

Pass Ball Around the Body

Pass Ball Around the Legs

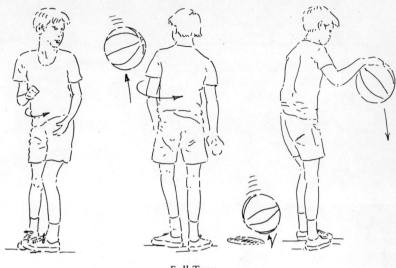

Full Turn

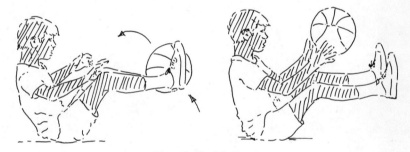

Toss Ball with Feet

Heavy Apparatus

1. Trampoline. (Note: Safety mats should be placed on all sides of the trampoline. Spotters should be stationed on all sides of of the trampoline. The spotter's first responsibility is to the performer. If needed, he should first attempt to push the performer back onto the trampoline bed. That failing, he should endeavor to break the performer's fall.)
   a. Stairway mount (with or without hand assist from the teacher). Step onto the trampoline frame. Step onto the trampoline bed. Walk around the trampoline bed. Step from the trampoline bed to the trampoline frame. Walk down the stairway.

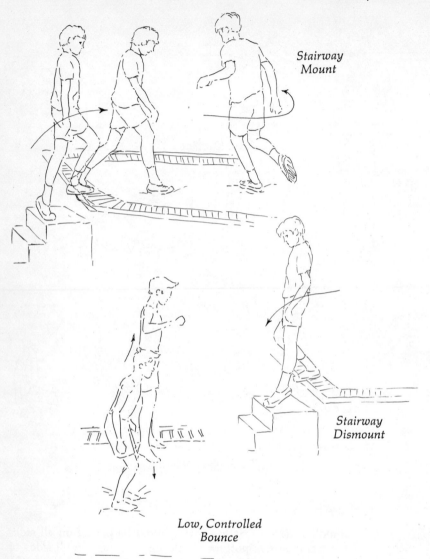

Stairway
Mount

Stairway
Dismount

Low, Controlled
Bounce

b. Perform a low, controlled bounce in the middle of the trampoline. Weight should be carried by the balls of the feet,
and arms should be used to facilitate balance. Terminate
bounce by sharply flexing the knees on bed contact. Emphasis must be on bounce control, NOT upon height, with
all performances beginning and ending as near the center
of the trampoline bed as possible.

c. Bounce to basic body positions.
d. Bounce with half turn. Bounce with full turn.
e. Bounce. Perform hands-and-knees drop (hands and knees strike bed at same time). Push with the arms to assist in returning to the feet.
f. Bounce. Perform seat drop (hips, palms, heels strike bed at same time). Palms contact the bed with thumbs toward the hips. Extend the arms during bed contact to assist in returning to the feet.

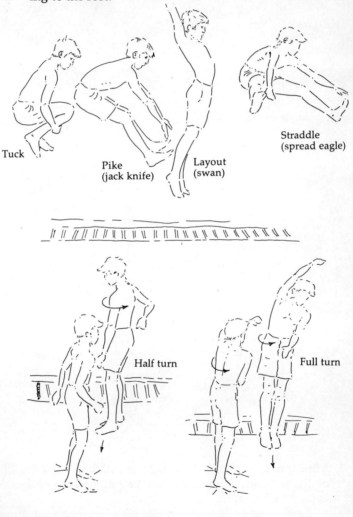

Tuck

Pike
(jack knife)

Layout
(swan)

Straddle
(spread eagle)

Half turn

Full turn

Bounce to Basic Body Positions

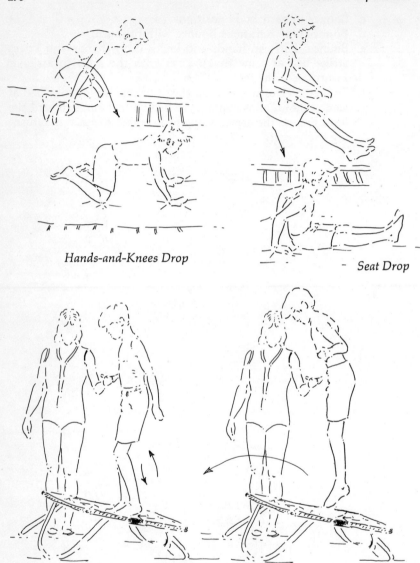

Hands-and-Knees Drop

Seat Drop

Jump on Mini-Tramp

2. Mini-tramp. (Note: Safety mats should be placed on all sides
of the apparatus. Spotters may be necessary both beside the
apparatus and at the point of landing.)
   a. Execute three or four consecutive bounces on the apparatus
   with a handhold assist. Weight should be carried by the
   balls of the feet.

b. Bounce three times with handhold assist. Jump to dismount in front of the apparatus.
c. Run at a comfortable speed to the mini-tramp. Jump mount. Forward jump dismount.
d. Run at a comfortable speed to the mini-tramp. Jump mount. Forward jump dismount. Forward roll.
e. Run at a comfortable speed to the mini-tramp. Jump mount. Forward jump with half-turn dismount.

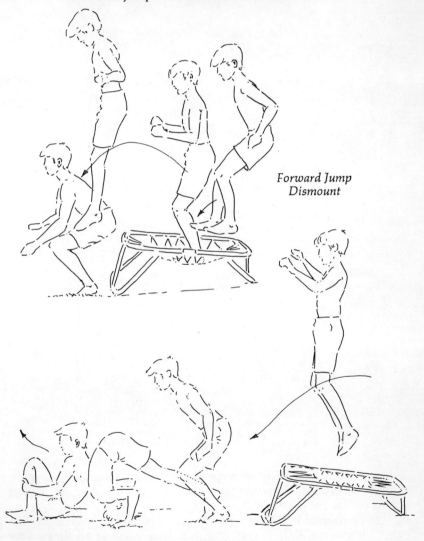

*Forward Jump
Dismount*

Forward Jump Dismount, Forward Roll

Half Turn

Straddle
(spread eagle)

Pike
(jack knife)

Tuck

Layout
(swan)

Forward Dismount in Basic Body Positions

    f. Run at a comfortable speed to the mini-tramp. Jump mount.
       Forward dismount in tuck, pike (jack knife), or layout
       (swan) position.
  3. Horizontal bar. (Note: Safety mats should be placed under the
      horizontal bar. A spotter should be present at all times. Low
      horizontal bar activities may be initiated with feet contact with

the mat. High horizontal bar activities may be initiated from the hanging position. Either starting position can be used at the discretion of the teacher.)

a. Hang from bar with feet not touching the mat.
b. Starting with feet touching the mat, climb over the horizontal bar.
c. Jump to hang. Swing backward and forward. Dismount at end of the backswing.

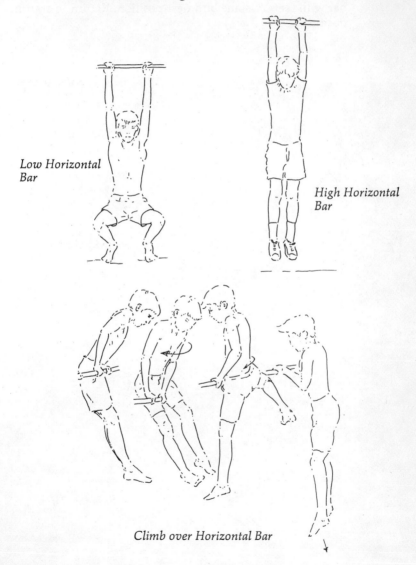

Low Horizontal Bar

High Horizontal Bar

Climb over Horizontal Bar

d. Jump to hang. Draw knees up between hands. Hang by the knees. Return to starting position.

e. Jump to hang. Skin the cat. (Flex the knees and hips, and simultaneously draw the feet between the hands. Allow the feet to pass between the hands and the hips to pass between the elbows. Extend the knees so that the feet hang directly beneath the body.) Release grasp. Land on feet.

f. Jump to hang. Draw knees and feet between arms. Hook bar with feet. Assume bird nest position. Return to starting position.

Hang by the Knees

Swing on Bar

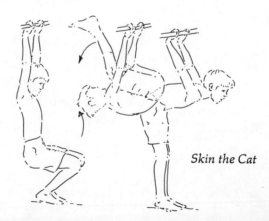

Skin the Cat

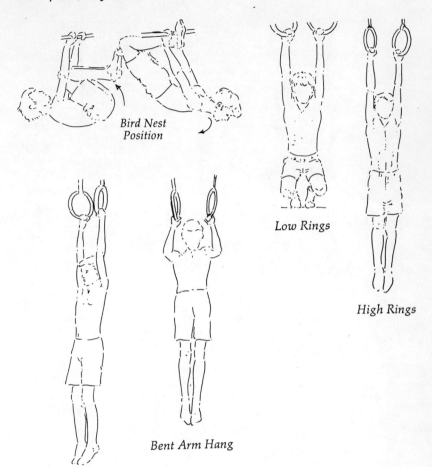

Bird Nest Position

Low Rings

High Rings

Bent Arm Hang

4. Rings. (Note: Safety mats should be placed under the rings. A spotter should be present at all times. Low ring activities may be initiated with the feet in contact with the mat. High ring activities may be initiated from the hanging position. Either starting position may be utilized at the teacher's discretion.)

a. Jump to hang. Release rings. Land on feet.

b. Pull to bent arm hang (with assist if necessary). Return to hang. Release rings. Land on feet.

c. Jump to hang. Swing body backward and forward (rings remain stationary). Release rings at end of backward swing, and land on feet.

d. Jump to hang. Pull to inverted hang. Feet may be wrapped around ring ropes for stability in the inverted hang position

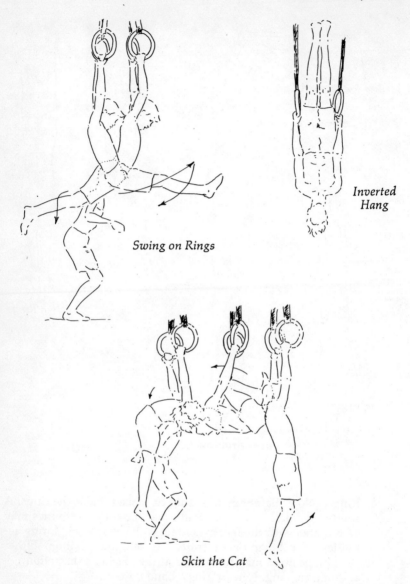

Swing on Rings

*Inverted
Hang*

Skin the Cat

if needed. Return to starting position. Release rings. Land
on feet.

e. Jump to hang. Skin the cat. (Flex the knees and hips, and
simultaneously draw the feet between the rings. Allow the
feet to pass between the rings and the hips to pass between
the arms. Extend the knees so that the feet hang directly
beneath the body.) Release rings. Land on feet.

*Skin the Cat,
Full Turn*

Jump to Support

    f. Jump to hang. Skin the cat. Release *one* hand and perform full turn. Regrasp the released ring with the free hand. Release rings. Land on feet.

5. Parallel bars. (Note: Parallel bars, if adjustable, should be three to four inches below armpit height. This reduces the child's concern over falling between the bars and catching his underarm prior to foot contact with the surface. Safety mats should be placed under and around the apparatus. A spotter should be present at all times.)

    a. Jump to support at end of bars (elbows straight, weight centered between the hands). Return to starting position.

b. Jump to support at end of bars. Swing backward and forward. Dismount at the end of the backward swing.
c. Jump to support. Walk to far end of bars moving first the right hand, then the left hand, etc. Dismount when the far end of the bars has been reached or when fatigued.
d. Go to the middle of the apparatus. Perform a bird nest (spotter may kneel and support the performer's chest and hips from below). Perform an inverted hang (spotter may balance the performer's ankles between his hands). Return to feet.

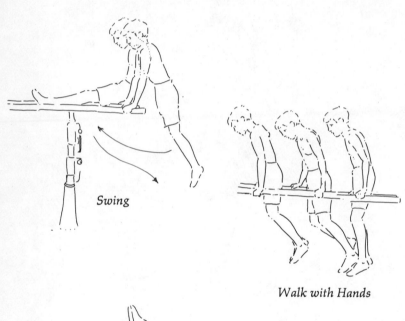

Swing

Walk with Hands

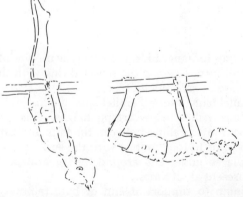

Inverted Hang   *Bird Nest*

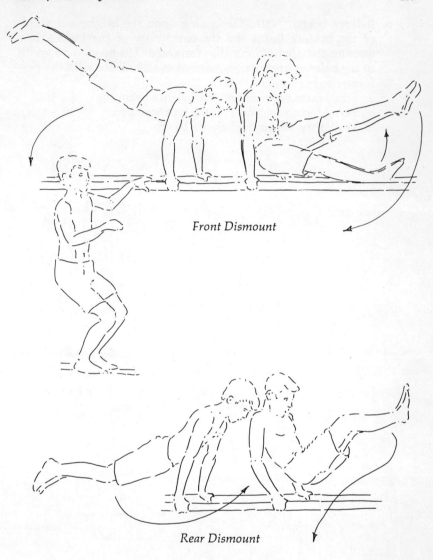

Front Dismount

Rear Dismount

e. Swing back and forth. Perform front dismount. Note that the front dismount is performed at the end of the *backward* swing. It is so called because the front of the body passes directly over the bar.

f. Swing back and forth. Perform rear dismount. Note that the rear dismount is performed at the end of the forward swing. It is so called because buttocks passes directly over the bar.

6. Balance beam. (Note: Depending upon the height and width of the balance beam and the complexity of the task, safety matting and spotting may be warranted. The height and width of the balance beam can be altered in accordance with the performer's skill level.)
   a. Stand facing forward on the balance beam.
   b. Stand facing sideways on the balance beam.
   c. Walk forward on the balance beam.

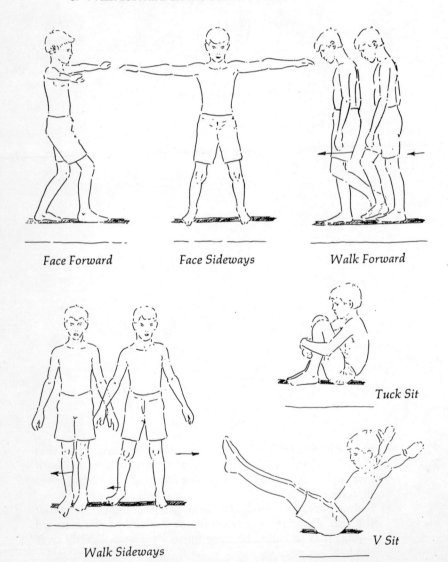

Face Forward   Face Sideways   Walk Forward

Walk Sideways

Tuck Sit

V Sit

  d. Walk sideways on the balance beam. Walk with the left
   foot leading. Walk with the right foot leading.
  e. Perform a tuck sit on the balance beam. Perform a V sit on
   the balance beam.
  f. Walk backward on the balance beam.
  g. Walk forward on the balance beam. Step over (duck under)
   a wand, and continue walking to the opposite end.

Walk Backward

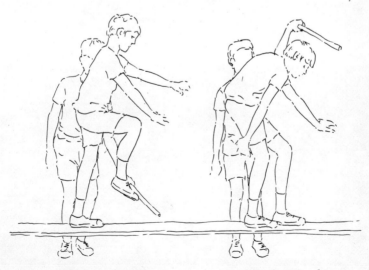

Step over Wand   *Duck under Wand*

Chapter X

Swimming and Water-Related Activities

Aquatic activity provides a wide variety of experiences in which the mentally retarded or emotionally disturbed child can achieve worthwhile movement in an environment which broadens his opportunity for satisfying and successful participation. The basic values include physical fitness and motor development, improved body control, recreational skills, and improvement of self-concept and social skills. In addition to its therapeutic and recreational outcomes, playing in water provides the mentally retarded and emotionally disturbed with necessary, positive emotional outlets. The fearful child discovers that he can push the water and it gives way; thus he gains confidence. The overly aggressive child discovers that he can push and punch the water to his heart's content and no one objects. Swimming produces wholesome fatigue conducive to relaxation which aids in the reduction of tension. If mentally retarded and emotionally disturbed children develop swimming skills, they can go to public swimming areas and participate in swimming and other related aquatic activities. In a swimming program, handicapping conditions are less evident and it is extremely difficult to tell if an individual has any disability, thus increasing his social ease in community swimming situations.

Any swimming facility with a shallow area can be used in an instructional program for mentally retarded and emotionally disturbed children. A water temperature between 85° and 90° would be recommended, but not required, for.the beginner. This would prevent chilling and aid in relaxation. Any established swimming pool rules and regulations should be followed by these children.

Suggested Teaching Techniques — General

1. Background information on each pupil should be available to the instructor teaching that particular child. It should include medical, psychological, and sociological information, chronological and mental age, behavior patterns and emotional make-up. The instructor should add to this information an accurate, daily evaluation of student progress. If a medical clearance is required, this should be on file.
2. Innovative and creative teaching approaches are needed to enable the instructor to adapt skills to the pupil's needs and abilities. The teacher should show inventiveness to break skills down into sequential progressions which can be learned quickly, giving the student daily success experiences and a feeling of achievement. A variety of approaches should be used in the teaching of each skill. Review and repetition should be included daily.
3. Whenever possible, a multisensory teaching approach should be used. The simultaneous utilization of two or more senses reinforces learning and makes learning more rapid and more permanent. The use of these various modalities would include combinations of the following:
   a. *Assistive.* The guidance of body parts through desirable movements capitalizes on kinesthetic (proprioceptive) feedback from the muscles to the brain, helping the child feel and sense where his body parts are as they move. An example of the assistive teaching approach would be the turning of the child's head by the teacher as rhythmic breathing is practiced.
   b. *Tactile.* The touching of body parts enables the child to feel the part to be moved, such as the arm to be used in stroking or the leg to be kicked. Tactile reinforcement facilitates visual and/or verbal stimuli.
   c. *Visual Stimulus.* The eyes are stimulated through demonstrations and simple visual aids, and the child reproduces the movement by imitation. Good demonstrations and simple visual aids can be most effective instructional methods.
   d. *Verbal Stimulus.* The ears are stimulated through the spoken word. Simple and accurate word descriptions of the activity to be performed should be utilized. Oral instruction should reflect the language understanding level of the child.

e. *Abstract Stimulus.* The use of various stimuli such as signals, signs, numbers, and colors requires the student to receive, interpret, and translate these stimuli into actions.
4. Teaching aids and assistive devices such as floats, balls, kickboards, tubes, and jackets should be used with care and discretion and only after the child has adjusted physically and mentally to the water. They should be considered instructional aids and dependency upon them should be avoided.
5. Games and fun situations should be combined with all learning experiences.
6. Motivation and reinforcement are essential. Recognize and encourage all progress and skill achievement, however small, with praise or reward.
7. Discipline is essential. The instructor must be firm, but patient. Empathy, not sympathy, should be utilized.
8. Frequently, circuit and interval training can stimulate learning.
9. Specialized techniques and precautions should be followed. The children may not only harm themselves but endanger others if they are not carefully watched. Strict supervision can avert any dangerous situations.
10. Students with special medical problems, such as convulsive seizures, should work only with personnel possessing medical and lifesaving training.

Additional Teaching Techniques — Mentally Retarded

1. Mentally retarded children frequently have low physical vitality and fatigue easily. They should be watched closely and required to rest when it is warranted. Mongoloid children are extremely susceptible to respiratory infections and must be well dried, especially their hair, after each swimming session.
2. Routine, repetition and recall, and relaxation should be stressed. A slower, more repetitious program is necessary. Progressions must be kept simple, and methods of instruction should be adapted to the ability of the individual to understand. Carefully planned and simple explanations and demonstrations should be used. Terminology used should be simple and easy to understand. If necessary, clarification should be given.
3. A close teacher-pupil relationship must be maintained. The instructor and pupil must be compatible if good results are to be achieved. Acceptance, understanding, and love are of the utmost importance. A one-to-one student-teacher relationship is necessary at beginning levels of instruction. This quickly promotes confidence. As soon as possible, however, the chil-

dren should begin to work in small groups. Firmness and
patience are important.

4. The instructor should be flexible and creative. When one approach fails, another should be tried. If no results occur, another skill in which success is guaranteed should be performed.

5. In some cases, competition is good.

Additional Teaching Techniques — Emotionally Disturbed

1. Activities should be kept short and simple. They should be
performed in a calm, structured, and controlled environment.
A routine should be established and followed for each swimming session. This routine should begin when the child enters
the swimming facility and should continue until he leaves.
Authoritarianism and the use of dull or monotonous drills
should be avoided. The child should be totally involved in his
swimming and permitted little time for worry and brooding.
Much patience and diplomacy should be utilized.

2. Direct confrontations with a student over matters of discipline
can and should be avoided by diverting the child's attention or
changing the activity. The impulsive, disorganized, aggressive,
and negativistic behavior of the child should be channeled into
spontaneous, realistic activity which is acceptable.

3. The class environment should be kept friendly and interesting
to aid in the development of security and confidence. In addition, praise and special credit should be given for skill progression. An unhurried teaching approach should be used to
ensure success and a feeling of achievement. When minor
learning problems are encountered or when the child feels he
is not progressing as rapidly as others in the group, encourage-
ment should be given.

4. Both individual and group teaching techniques are effective
methods of instruction. Each child should, however, receive
some individual attention during each class period.

5. High levels of competition or frustration should be avoided.

Mechanical Principles

A basic knowledge and understanding of the mechanical principles
involved in movement in and through the water is essential in the
teaching of swimming skills to the mentally retarded or emotionally
disturbed child. Movement in and through water differs from movement on land because of the nature of the water itself. All fluids exert
an upward or buoyant force upon bodies immersed in them, which
counteracts the force of gravity on land. Water exerts equal pressure

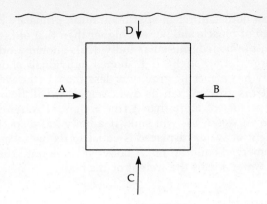

Forces A and B — Equal and opposing forces, cancel each other out.
Force C — Greater than Force D. This upward force is buoyancy.

in all directions at all times, and this pressure increases with the depth of submersion. The pressures exerted about the sides of the body cancel out one another. But, because the bottom surface of the body is deeper in the water than the top surface, the upward pressure upon the bottom surface will exceed the downward pressure upon the top surface and the body will float. This upward pressure or force is buoyancy.

The level at which a body floats is variable and dependent upon the location of the individual's center of buoyancy, center of gravity, and the specific gravity of his body.

Specific Gravity

Specific gravity is simply a comparison of the density of the body with the density of the water, a ratio of body weight to weight of water dis-

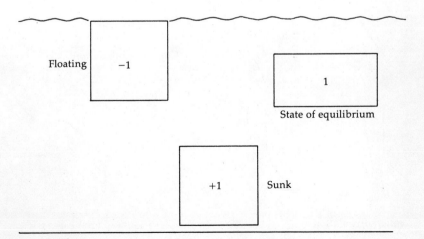

placed. Human bodies differ in specific gravity, primarily because the specific gravity of muscle and bone is higher than that of fat or adipose tissue. Heavy, big boned, muscular individuals should tend to sink in the water. Large, fat, or slight, light-boned individuals should tend to float. If a body has a specific gravity of less than 1 (the weight of the water displaced is greater than its own weight) it will float. If a body has a specific gravity of more than 1 (the weight of water displaced is less than its own weight) it will sink. If a body has a specific gravity of 1 (the weight of water displaced is equal to its own weight) it will remain in submerged equilibrium. A body will sink until the weight of the displaced water equals the weight of the body.

Vital Capacity

Vital capacity is the maximum volume of air taken into the lungs during one inhalation. Although inspiration and expiration, with accompanied rib displacement, insignificantly change the body's specific gravity and center of buoyancy, they do significantly change the location of the body's center of gravity, thus changing the body angle in relation to the surface of the water. Inspiration elevates the rib carriage as the lungs fill with air, increasing body volume without significantly altering weight. It slightly lowers specific gravity and increases buoyancy by changing the location of the individual's center of grav-

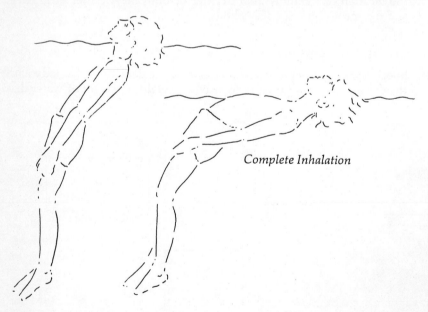

Complete Inhalation

Complete Exhalation

ity, thus causing a greater volume of the body to be pushed above the water. Likewise, expiration and its accompanied compression of the rib carriage reduce volume, slightly raising specific gravity and decreasing buoyancy, thus causing a greater volume of the body to be pushed under water.

The individual with a greater lung capacity would float higher in the water than the individual with a small lung capacity, providing both were using their lungs to full capacity. An essential factor in effective flotation for many individuals is maximum displacement with maximum submersion, necessitating proper breath control when floating. The individual who has a tendency to sink when his lungs are not filled with air must learn to exhale quickly and follow this exhalation by a rapid and complete inhalation, thus minimizing the length of time his specific gravity is increased and his center of gravity is lowered.

Center of Buoyancy and Center of Gravity

Center of buoyancy is the point around which the upward buoying force of the water is equally distributed or balanced. Center of gravity is the point around which the downward pull of gravity is equally distributed or balanced. The location of an individual's center of gravity and center of buoyancy and their relationship to each other influence the position in which his body floats. When his center of gravity and center of buoyancy coincide, a horizontal floating position will result. The buoyancy and gravital forces will become equal if the body floats, because buoyancy will force the body out of the water until it is reduced to an equal gravital force. A body does not float when the gravital force is greater than the buoyancy force, but this is not common and most individuals can be taught to float by learning to balance their body in the water. If the center of gravity is in vertical alignment exactly below (or above) the center of buoyancy, there are no turning moments and a state of equilibrium exists. But, if the center of gravity is even slightly off the vertical line through the center of buoyancy, downward rotation of the lower limbs will cause a change in position until equilibrium is achieved. The sum of the moments or turning effect of the forces acting (about the fulcrum) on the body must be zero, and a body will rotate like a teeter-totter until equilibrium is reached.

The center of buoyancy is normally located in the chest region. The center of gravity is normally located in the pelvic region and toward the feet in relation to the fulcrum and center of buoyancy. The reason for this is the fact that the chest and lung area is larger and less dense than the lower limbs which contain a higher percent of bone and muscle, thus making them heavier than the displaced water. It should be noted, however, that no one has ever really located the

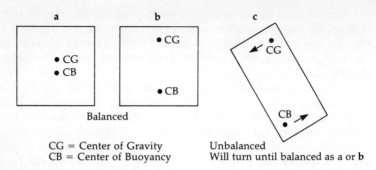

Balanced

CG = Center of Gravity
CB = Center of Buoyancy

Unbalanced
Will turn until balanced as a or b

center of buoyancy in any position except to say that it should be in a vertical line with the center of gravity.

In learning to float, the greater the distance of the body weight from the center of buoyancy (fulcrum) the greater its effect on the angle of flotation. Normally, the leg of the body lever (distance from the chest area or center of buoyancy to the toes) is longer than the head end of the body lever (distance from the chest to the top of the head). This causes the body to be overbalanced at the leg end and to rotate around the chest as the fulcrum. The legs sink and change the center of buoyancy by altering the volume of the body that is underwater. Rotation continues until the center of gravity is below the center of buoyancy and a balanced position is achieved.

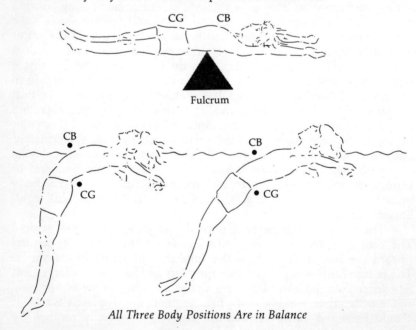

All Three Body Positions Are in Balance

Because of the acceleration caused by the force of gravity, legs gather momentum as they sink in the water. If the buoying force is NOT great enough to overcome this momentum, the individual can be pulled underwater, resulting in his center of buoyancy moving to the opposite side of his body. Inertia must be overcome each time available force is lost. The body will gradually reduce its amount of rocking until it becomes imperceptible and the body is "at rest," "in balance," or "steady." If the back float is started in the vertical position so that the legs have no downward momentum for the buoying force to overcome, the body will be lifted to its point of balance. This is, therefore, the most effective method of beginning a stationary back float.

Any changes in the relative position of the body segments (weight redistribution) which move the center of gravity closer to the head will bring the center of gravity and center of buoyancy closer together and lessen the angle of the body in relation to the surface of the water. Examples: raising the arms overhead to an extended position beyond the head and in line with the trunk; flexing the knees; combining both movements.

If an individual has a tendency to float high in the water with the legs close to the surface, his biggest problem will be standing from the float position. By shortening both ends of his body lever (bringing the knees and head toward the chest) he will remove the mechanical advantage gained by the force of buoyancy, making it easier for his hips

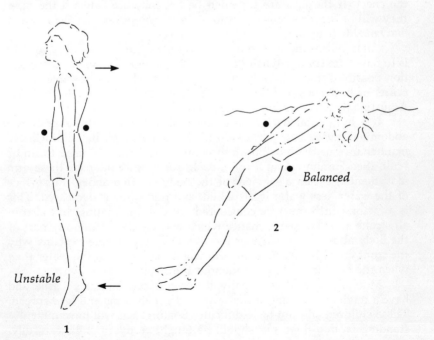

Unstable

Balanced

1

2

a— Raising arms overhead
b— Flexing knees
c— Combining movements a and
   b— arms overhead, knees flexed

to rotate downward through the force applied by the arms. In standing, the pull of the arms should be down and back toward the bottom of the pool and the legs should be extended when the hips are beneath the chest. If the legs are extended before they are beneath the hips, they will be diagonally in the water above the bottom and the force of buoyancy will again lift them to the surface.

An excellent method to use in checking a student's ability to float is to have him try a jellyfish float. This is the most buoyant body position possible, since all body segments are as close as possible to the center of buoyancy and the lungs are filled with air. (See Basic Water Adjustment Activities for a description of the jellyfish float.)

If a horizontal back float is desirable, strong contraction of the abdominal muscles and a forward tilt of the pelvic girdle will facilitate maintenance of this position, especially if the arms are used to fin or scull. (See Finning; Arm Stroke, Back, for a description of these arm movements.) When a segment of the body is lifted above the surface of the water, less water is displaced, and buoyancy is decreased. This is a factor which must be considered not only in floating, but also in all stroke and skill performance which necessitates lifting any part of the body above the surface of the water. This principle explains why the front crawl is easier to perform when the face is in the water than when the head is held up throughout the stroke.

Mongoloid children usually have an excess of fatty tissue and have a tendency to float in the water with their arms and legs spread. These children will not have difficulty floating, but will have difficulty standing from a float and should be taught recovery skills carefully.

The hydrocephalic child, if his head is greatly enlarged, will also have difficulty standing from a float and may not be successful in a back float position because of the inability to keep his nose and mouth out of the water. In performing back float skills these children may need a small flotation device, such as water wings, under the neck. Once fears are removed, the remaining group of mentally retarded and emotionally disturbed children should have no specific flotation problems.

Propulsion

All movement is dependent upon the application of force against resistance. Because water offers less resistance than a hard surface, progress through water is slower and requires more effort than progress on land. But it is this resistance of the water to force which is the basis for all movement in and through the water.

Once a force acts upon a body to put it in motion, that body will remain in motion unless and until acted upon by external forces such as waves or water resistance (Newton's Law of Inertia). This infers that, unless continuous force is applied in swimming, the body will not remain in motion. Resistance is greater during the attempt to gain momentum than during the maintenance of this momentum. Therefore, each time the body stops moving or slows down, inertia must be overcome to increase speed.

When a force of a given value is applied to a body to move it through water, the velocity or speed of the body will gradually increase until it reaches a certain limiting value at which the resistance due to friction is equal to the applied force. After that value has been reached, the velocity will remain constant as long as the same force is applied (Newton's Law of Acceleration).

To every action there is an equal and opposite reaction (Newton's Third Law). When a swimmer pushes against the water, movement occurs in the opposite direction. If the push is backward, movement is forward. If the push is directly downward, the resultant reaction pushes the swimmer directly upwards, and vice versa. To get the most effective use of the available force in a stroke, the direction of movement of arms and feet should be to the rear, pushing directly back against the water. The action then will be forward and equal to the push backward (minus friction).

Maximum force is attained in the propulsive movements of the limbs by presenting as broad a surface and exerting backward pressure through as great a distance as possible, provided undesirable forces are not introduced. If force is used at unproductive angles, resistance results, and there may be opposition to the intended direction of motion. For example, if the beginner attempting the front crawl keeps the arms straight, more pressure is exerted downward than backward and an undesirable lifting effect occurs. Fear and tension, with their accompanying jerky or sudden movements, can also cause resistance. To eliminate excessive resistance, the body should be kept streamlined in the water and undesirable, unproductive movements of the limbs, head, and trunk should be avoided. The body should be relaxed. Additional information on the reduction of resistance can be found in the materials describing the various specific skills and techniques which should be used in the teaching of swimming to the mentally retarded or emotionally disturbed child.

Basic Water Adjustment Activities

Basic water adjustment activities are essential in aiding the mentally retarded or emotionally disturbed child in acclimating to the effects of the water temperature, pressure, and buoyancy. All aquatic activity which is not classified as an actual swimming stroke can be considered a basic water adjustment activity. The mastery of these skills assists the child in overcoming fear. Thus, he acquires greater comfort, confidence, mobility, and safety in the water. Each skill should be correctly demonstrated and explained in simple terms by the teacher before it is attempted by the child.

Physical Adjustment

Physical adjustment to water contact and temperature is necessary for most mentally retarded or emotionally disturbed children. The average pool temperature is 16° to 20° cooler than normal body temperature. Some individuals are very sensitive to this sudden change, and the feeling of water against the skin may be uncomfortable. Physiologically and psychologically, a gradual temperature change is better than a sudden one.

. Adjustment should begin with a cool or cold shower just prior to entry into the pool room. If the pool has a gradual slope, ramp, or steps, the child can wade with the teacher to about thigh-deep water. He should then scoop up water with his hands, putting handsful on his arms, chest, neck, and face, gradually increasing the amounts of water applied until he is wet all over. If a regular pool is used, the child should sit on the edge of the deck at the shallow end with his feet dangling in the water. From this position, with the teacher in the water assisting, water should be scooped with the hands and put on the child's face, neck, arms, chest, back, and legs until he is wet all over. At this point, young children should be lifted into the pool and older children should be assisted in their entry. The body should be gradually immersed in the water. Next, the child, with the teacher or unassisted, should begin moving about, walking, jumping up and down, and splashing with the arms. Any splashing should be kept under control to prevent frightening the timid learner. Holding the nose, and practicing frequently, the child should next submerge.

Simple water games which do not involve breathing skills or which permit the child to hold his nose should be played. Drop-the-handkerchief can be adapted to the water by using a puck or plastic toy as the handkerchief. Other simple games such as a walking relay race or dodge ball with a rubber ball are also effective in facilitating water adjustment. Additional games include:

Cork Scramble

With two teams on either side of the pool, the children (walking) retrieve corks from the center of the pool, one at a time, to their respective sides. The individual or team with the most corks is the winner.

Circle Pass

The children are in a circle in the water. They pass a ball or other object around the circle as many times as possible within a given time limit. Progressive attempts are made to set a new record.

Walking or Hopping Race

Divide the children into two groups, one on each side of the pool. At a given signal one child enters the water from each side, walks or hops to the other side, and returns. The others in the group follow as they are touched off. This race should be performed in shallow water.

Cat and Mouse

One child is a mouse, another is the cat, and remaining children are in a circle. The game begins with the mouse inside and the cat outside the circle. The circle helps the mouse and hinders the cat from catching him.

Breathing, Breath Holding, Rhythmic Breathing

Fear in swimming can often be traced to an inability to keep water out of the nose and mouth when the face is near the water. Ease in breathing is an important factor in creating satisfactory physical and mental adjustment to swimming. Therefore, breath holding and breathing skill should be developed immediately after the initial adjustment to water contact and temperature has been accomplished.

Frequently, the child is very hesitant and fearful when he puts his face in the water. Very slow progressions and simple games can be of great value in teaching breathing, breath holding, and rhythmic breathing skills to mentally retarded or emotionally disturbed children.

Breathing, breath holding, and rhythmic breathing skills should be practiced with the child standing in waist-deep water, his legs spread a comfortable distance apart. From this position, the child can bend forward to put his face in the water and, if necessary, the teacher can make him feel more secure by holding his hand or waist.

Breath holding should be practiced with the face out of the water, then in the water. The child should take a normal breath, close the mouth, and slowly lower his head until it is submerged at least up to the ears. If the child is hesitant, the teacher should have him cup water in his hands and then wash and rinse his face with the water. This should be repeated, putting the face closer and closer to the water until the face is in the water rather than just in the hands. Breath holding should be practiced until the child can hold his head underwater for progressively longer periods of time without discomfort.

The child should next learn to exhale in the water. Have him begin by cupping water in his hands and blowing it off. Blowing ping-pong balls on the surface of the water is helpful for the child having difficulty. Next, have the child exhale with his face in the water. If necessary, he can continue to blow water off his hands, gradually putting the face closer and closer to the water until he is exhaling underwater rather than just blowing water off the hands.

Practice in opening the eyes underwater should be interspersed with breath control skills. Simple games such as counting the teacher's extended fingers and locating and retrieving objects in shallow water can be used in the practice of this skill.

Quoit or Puck Tag

Quoit or Puck Tag is a good game adaptable to these skills. The child who is IT must duck to the bottom of the pool and pick up a quoit before he can tag anyone.

Hat Relay

The children are in two lines. The first child in each line, wearing a straw hat, walks to a designated spot where he ducks out from under the hat and returns to the end of his line. The next child in line walks out and gets under the hat by ducking and returns to the line wearing it. This continues until all children have had a turn. If assistance is needed, the teacher can walk along with the child, holding his hand. This may be necessary with some of the mentally retarded or severely disturbed children, especially the first time the game is played.

Rhythmic breathing consists of breathing in a specific rhythm or series. Air is inhaled through the mouth when the face is turned to the side out of the water, and exhaled through the mouth and nose as the face is turned downward into the water. Because this is a difficult skill to learn, it should be started early and practiced frequently. Rhythmic breathing should be practiced with the child standing in waist-deep water, his feet well apart, the upper body almost parallel to the surface of the water, and the hands on the knees. Starting with the head turned to either the right or left side and the cheek in the water, the child should inhale, then turn his head slowly and smoothly into the water to a face down position. He then exhales through his nose and mouth, blowing bubbles. The head is then turned back to the starting side for his next inhalation. This skill should be repeated an increasing number of times as experience is gained and a smooth, steady rhythm is achieved.

Bobbing

For variety in learning breathing, breath holding, and rhythmic breathing, the child can practice bobbing up and down in waist-deep water, completely submerging. This can be practiced holding the hands of the teacher or a partner and alternating, first one, then the other going underwater. Emphasis should be placed on inhaling as the mouth clears the surface of the water and exhaling as the head goes below the surface, underwater. When the child becomes more proficient at breath holding, he can practice bobbing unassisted and begin to establish a definite rhythm. Bobbing practice should be continued through the swimming lessons, so that eventually the child will be proficient at bobbing safely in increasingly deeper water.

Bobbing is a safety skill of great value to the poor swimmer who accidentally gets into water beyond his depth. Skillful bobbing consists of dropping the body in a vertical position to the bottom of the pool so the feet touch, the body then tucks, the head is brought forward, and the body is pushed vigorously up and forward. When the head comes out of the water a quick breath is taken, the body assumes a vertical position and drops down again to touch the bottom. By using this alternate up-and-forward, then drop procedure, a swimmer not skilled in stroking can progress from water whose depth is a foot or two over his head to shallow water without using arm action to help. If the arms are used, however, they should extend forward as the swimmer begins his forward, upward push from the bottom. As the body nears the surface the arms pull simultaneously and strongly down and back. The arms remain at the sides or overhead as the body drops in the water. When a reasonable degree of proficiency has been achieved, a bobbing relay might be tried in which the child bobs across the pool and back to the end of his team's line.

Jellyfish and Turtle Floats

The jellyfish and turtle floats aid the mentally retarded and emotionally disturbed child in learning about the buoyant effect of the water, aid in fear reduction, are basic to the learning of the prone float, and are fundamental to survival floating. These skills are so named because the position of the body in the water as the child is performing the floats looks similar to that of a jellyfish and turtle.

As confidence maneuvers, these floats are most effective in teaching the child that his body will float and balance, if given time, even though his feet are not on the bottom for support. These skills are essential to early water adjustment and safety. They should be demonstrated and explained by the teacher and tried and practiced by the child as soon as the skill of breath holding with the face in the water is mastered.

From a standing position in waist-deep water with the feet a comfortable distance apart for balance, the upper body almost parallel to the surface of the water, and the hands on the knees, the child should inhale and put his face in the water. He slides the right hand down outside of the right leg to the ankle, moving slowly. He next slides the right hand up to a position at the knee, lifts his face out of the water, exhaling through the nose and mouth. This is repeated with the hand moving down the outside of the left leg. Continue repeating this procedure until the child is able to perform it with ease. Then slowly slide both hands a few inches down both legs (not yet floating) and practice standing by slowly lifting the head and sliding the hands up. When the face is above the water, the hands just above the knees, and the feet secure on the bottom, the child stands.

The child is now ready to try the float. If necessary, the teacher can give some support around the waist the first time the float is attempted. This is especially important if assistance is needed in standing from the float. Assuming the starting position, the child should inhale, put his face in the water, and slide both hands slowly down to his ankles. He should hold the position as he floats free of the bottom and his body balances with a portion of the rounded back above the

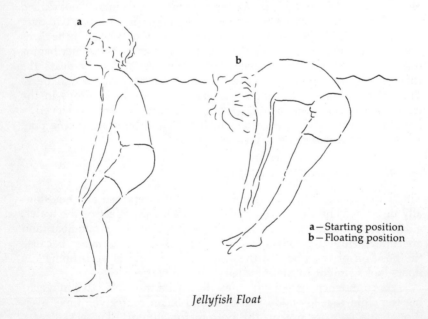

a—Starting position
b—Floating position

Jellyfish Float

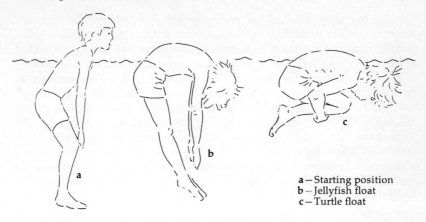

a — Starting position
b — Jellyfish float
c — Turtle float

Turtle Float

water. When ready to stand, he should slowly slide his hands up to his knees, lifting his head and allowing his feet to drop to the bottom of the pool. It should be emphasized that all movements are done slowly and that standing should NOT be attempted until the feet are securely placed on the bottom and the body is balanced over them.

The turtle float is begun from the jellyfish float position. The child then draws his knees to his chest, assuming a tuck position, and moves his arms and hands to clasp around his legs at about midcalf position. Before performing this skill the child should be told that his body will rock forward and backward (toward head, then hips) until it balances and a portion of the back is above the water. Let him observe this in your body before he tries the float. When ready to stand, the legs should be extended downward toward the bottom of the pool, the hands should slide up the legs, and the head should be lifted. When the feet touch the bottom and are secure, the child should exhale and stand. If necessary, support can be given as in the jellyfish float.

Simple contests can be held to see how long the child can hold the jellyfish or turtle float position, either competing against his own past performance or that of others in the group.

Prone Float and Stand, Prone Glide, Prone Kick Glide

The prone float is performed in a semihorizontal to horizontal position with the body on or near the surface of the water. The face is down and the arms and legs are extended. (See Mechanical Principles for additional information.) The prone float, like the jellyfish and turtle floats, has definite value as a confidence maneuver. Development of proficiency in this skill is basic to forward movement through the water.

An excellent method for teaching this skill to mentally retarded and emotionally disturbed children is from a balanced turtle float position. When this position is assumed, the arms are slowly extended forward and the legs are opened from the tuck position and slowly extended backward. The body is then balanced in the new position. A demonstration should precede the trial by the child. The first attempt to stand from this position should use the known procedures of standing from the turtle float, the child returning from the prone to the turtle float and standing. When skill is acquired, the child should be taught to stand by pulling down toward the bottom with his arms and hands, bringing his knees and legs under his body and lifting his head. Although these movements can be performed sequentially, in skillful performance they should be done simultaneously, slowly, and smoothly.

To perform the prone glide, the child should begin by standing at the side of the pool with his back to the wall. He should assume a turtle float position, extend his arms forward slowly, and open his legs from the tuck position, extending them slowly backward until they touch the wall. He should push easily away from the wall, glide until momentum stops, and then stand. A demonstration should precede the trial by the child. As skill and confidence in the glide are developed, the child will be able to begin the skill with a push from the bottom of the pool. Simple contests can be held to see how far the child can glide, either competing against his own past performance or that of others in the group.

An elementary flutter kick should be taught and practiced with the arms in a bracket position at the side of the pool, with the hands held by the teacher, or with the teacher holding the child under the chest region. This kick should be executed by swinging the legs up and down through the water. The swing should come from the hips

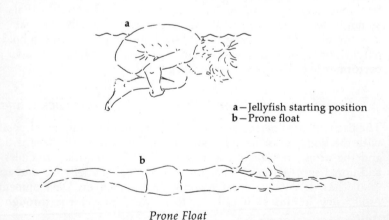

a—Jellyfish starting position
b—Prone float

Prone Float

a — *Flutter Kick, Bracket Position at Wall*

b — *Flutter Kick, Teacher Holding Student's Hands*

c — *Flutter Kick, Teacher Support at Shoulders*

with the knees relatively straight, the ankle extended, and the entire foot and leg under the surface of the water. The primary purpose of this elementary kick is to enable the child to move forward through the water under his own power.

After assuming the prone glide position, the child should begin kicking his legs. When he needs air, he should stand as from the prone float. Kickboards can be used to practice this elementary flutter kick. Contests can be held to see how far the child can kick, either competing against his own past performance or that of others in the group.

a — Prone Glide

b — Prone Kick Glide

Back Float and Stand, Back Glide, Back Kick Glide

Many mentally retarded and emotionally disturbed children feel very insecure in a back float position. The hydrocephalic child, if his head is greatly enlarged, may not be successful in this position because of his inability to keep his nose and mouth out of the water. (See Mechanical Principles for additional information.)

In a back float position the body lies in the water in a semihorizontal (even vertical) to horizontal position. The nose and mouth should be sufficiently clear of the water to permit necessary breathing. For added comfort, the face and chest should be well above the surface of the water. In initial practice, this skill should be performed with the teacher giving assistance.

Standing in waist- to chest-deep water with the arms extended out to the side at shoulder height, the knees and hips are tucked until the shoulders are submerged and the arms rest easily on the surface of the water. The teacher stands behind the child with his hands in position to rest just under the head and upper back. The child slowly moves his head backward until it rests in the water on the teacher's hands. His chest comes up and his back arches. With the eyes looking directly up to the ceiling and the hips fully extended, the lower and upper back should continue to arch and the legs should hang down easily with the toes being the last part of the body to leave the bottom of the pool. No push off or lift of the legs should be attempted. In some cases the feet may be resting on the bottom, but most of the body weight will be supported by the water.

Beginning at shoulder height, the arms, with elbows easily bent, should move slowly toward the head. This will help counterbalance the weight of the lower body in the water and help the child achieve a more horizontal floating position. A good demonstration should precede practice.

To stand from the back float position, the arms are pulled strongly to the sides, the hips are tucked (as if to sit in a chair), bringing the legs under the body, and the head is brought forward to the chest. The legs are then extended to rest the feet on the bottom of the pool and the child comes to a standing position. On the first several attempts at standing, the teacher should assist by gently pushing the head and upper chest area forward, keeping contact with the child's body throughout the performance. Some children may find it easier to stand from the back float by assuming a tuck position, rolling forward into a turtle float, and then standing.

The position of the body in the back glide and back kick glide is more horizontal than that of the back float because the body movement tends to lift the legs. The head position must also be adjusted to prevent water from being forced into the nose, eyes, and mouth. Before the child is ready to attempt a back glide, he should learn to assume a

a — *Back Float, Teacher Support*

b — *Back Float, Arms Overhead for More Horizontal Position*

c — *Back Float, Position for Back Glide and Back Kick Glide*

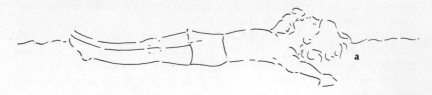

a—Arms at shoulder height
b—Arms raised overhead

position in the water, on the back, with his chin tucked slightly forward, his arms extended and relaxed at his sides, and his hips as close to the surface as possible. Assistance should be given when this streamlined body position is first attempted.

The back glide is begun in chest-deep water with the child submerging until his shoulders are in the water. With his chin tucked in slightly and his arms extended and relaxed along the sides, he pushes gently off the bottom of the pool. The child should stand as from the back float. Any necessary assistance should be given under the head and upper back on both the float and stand. With practice, a more

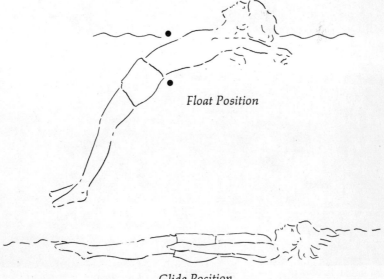

Float Position

Glide Position

vigorous thrust of the legs can be exerted. Once the child can perform a back glide with a push from the bottom of the pool, he should attempt the skill starting from a position at the side of the pool with his hands holding the gutter, his feet against the wall, and his body in a tuck position. The legs should be slowly extended as the child pushes easily away from the wall, assuming a streamlined position with his body.

a — *Back Glide*

b — *Back Kick Glide,*
Arms at Sides

c — *Back Kick Glide, Arms Overhead*

When the child has learned to perform a back glide by pushing off the wall, he can add an elementary flutter kick to the movement. The kick used in the back kick glide should be similar to the front kick glide with the legs kept under the surface of the water. Correct body position and an upward kicking motion of the legs should be stressed. The child should be cautioned not to begin kicking until a streamlined back glide position is assumed. He should stand as from the back float.

Changing Position from Prone Float to Back Float, from Back Float to Prone Float

Although the average swimmer learns by experience to turn from a prone float to a back float and from a back float to a prone float, frequently the mentally retarded and emotionally disturbed child must be taught these skills. They should be carefully demonstrated and the child should be assisted on his first attempts to perform them in the water.

To change from a prone float to a back float, one of the extended arms is pressed firmly downward to the opposite hip and the head is turned sharply toward the direction in which the arm is pulling. If necessary, the stationary arm may be moved behind the back as the pulling arm reaches the hip.

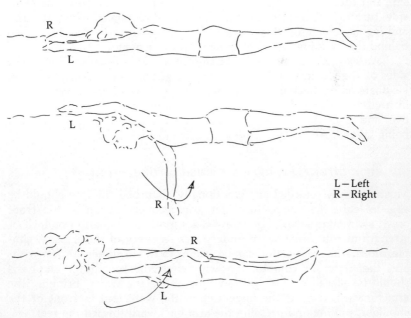

L—Left
R—Right

Changing from a Prone Float to a Back Float

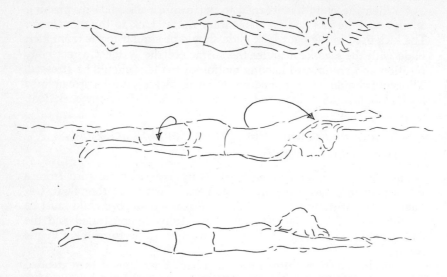

Changing from a Back Float to a Prone Float

To change from a back float to a prone float, reach across the body with one arm (if the arm is overhead, move the arm toward the side and then across the body) and cross with the leg from the same side, turning the head to look in the same direction in which the arm and leg are reaching. If necessary, the stationary arm may be tucked behind the back just after reaching with the arm and leg.

An excellent game for practicing these skills is called "log." The sides of the shallow end of the pool are goals. One player is the log. He floats on his back in the center of the pool. The other players move in a circle around the log. Without warning, the log suddenly rolls over and gives chase. The players try to reach one of the goals without being tagged. Any player who is caught must be the log.

Arm Stroke, Front; Combined Stroke, Front

Most mentally retarded and emotionally disturbed children should be able to learn the above-the-water arm recovery action of the front crawl swimming stroke. In a few cases, poor coordination or lack of strength may necessitate an underwater recovery of the arms. A simple, alternating arm action can be taught to the beginner, at first without, then later in combination with rhythmic breathing. Emphasis should be placed on lifting the elbow above the water, bringing the arm forward, then as the fingers enter the water out in front of the shoulder, pulling and pressing the arm backward toward the feet.

At first, the teacher can stand behind the child, hold his hands,

a   b

c

Arm Stroke Practice, Front Crawl, Standing Position
with Rhythmic Breathing

and guide the arms through the proper movements. This should be performed with the child standing in waist- to chest-depth water, his body bent forward at the waist, and his face in the water. Once the proper arm movements are felt by the child, he can try them unassisted. It should be remembered that many mentally retarded and emotionally disturbed children will forget skills learned in previous lessons. Constant review is important, especially when new skills are added to already acquired movements.

When these simple arm-stroking movements can be performed automatically and in an acceptable, continuous, and alternate rhythm, the child can begin to combine them with other previously acquired skills. In the standing position used to practice the basic arm-stroking movements, rhythmic breathing can be added. From a prone float, first the flutter kick then the arm movements can be added. Later, all three skills, rhythmic breathing, arm movements, and flutter kick, can be combined into a simple front crawl swimming stroke.

Combined Stroke, Front, Front Crawl

Finning; Arm Stroke, Back; Combined Stroke, Back

Finning is a very elementary hand movement executed with the body in a back float position. It is a good stroke for the beginner primarily because it is simple to learn and easy to perform. Both arms move simultaneously through the finning action. The arm action should first be practiced with the swimmer standing in waist-deep water. With both arms fully extended at the sides of the body and with the elbows back, the hands are drawn up toward the waist where they are turned out and then pushed toward the feet in a slightly outward, downward action. Once the arm movements have been learned they should be practiced with a back float glide and a back kick glide. It should be stressed that the arm action is executed completely underwater. Although this combined stroke on the back is very simple, it should be taught to mentally retarded and emotionally disturbed children before either the back crawl or the elementary backstroke.

Combined Stroke,
Back, Finning

Change Direction

Once a simple stroke on the face and back has been accomplished, the child can be taught how to change directions while swimming. This skill, although very simple, should be demonstrated by the teacher. To change direction the child simply turns his head and reaches with his arms in the direction he wants to turn. When the desired new direction has been achieved, the reach should be discontinued and the basic stroke resumed. It should be stressed that the legs must kick slowly and continuously as the change of direction·is executed, assisting in the maintenance of a horizontal body position.

Several games which might be included at this skill level include:

Japanese Tag

Swimming, the child who is IT may tag other children only on a specific part of the body such as the leg, arm, hand, or head.

Nightgown or Other Clothing Relay

The child swims a designated distance in the clothing, climbs out of the pool, changes clothing with a teammate, who repeats the procedure.

Leveling Off, Jumping

If the child has properly mastered the prone glide, prone kick glide, back glide, and back kick glide with a push off from the bottom of the pool, he has experienced the sensation of leveling his body off in the water — going from a vertical to a horizontal position with forward motion following. As a safety skill, leveling off should be practiced by the child, starting in chin-deep water and pushing off into a modified swimming stroke on the face. (See Combined Stroke, Front, for a description of this modified stroke.) When the child shows proficiency at leveling off and swimming in chin-deep water, the skill should be attempted in deep water. In case assistance is needed, the teacher should be in the water with the child when these skills are attempted.

The skill of leveling off and going into a swimming stroke should also be taught from a feet-first jump. Progressions should be gradual as many mentally retarded and emotionally disturbed children will be hesitant when given the task of jumping feet first into the water. Begin by having the child lower himself from a sitting position on the pool deck. Next, practice jumping into chest-deep water from a squatting position. The child can push off from the deck with one or both feet, but should bring the feet together before they hit the water, with the ankles extended and the toes pointing directly downward. When the feet touch the pool bottom, the legs should relax. With arms leading, the child should push up and forward, moving into a swimming

Jump into Deep Water

stroke. Eventually the child will be able to jump from an erect position into deep water, level off, and swim. All necessary safety precautions should be taken when these skills are being practiced. If jumping skills are properly taught and mastered, they will prove beneficial as a lead-up to diving.

Treading

Treading is an extremely valuable safety skill which should be learned after some ability to move about in deep water is acquired. Any action of the legs which creates downward pressure sufficient to keep the head above the water surface can be used. So that previously acquired skill can be relied upon, the mentally retarded and emotionally dis-

a — *Treading Water, Holding Pool Gutter*

b — *Treading Water, Teacher Holding Swimsuit Strap*

c — *Treading Water, Teacher Holding Armpit*

d — *Treading Water, No Support*

turbed child should use either a slow flutter kick or bicycling action of the legs. A simple arm action in which the hands and arms move in small circles, close to the body, pressing water downward, should be combined with the leg action. The arms should be relaxed when they recover to the starting position at the surface. The body should be slightly bent at the trunk and the head should be above the water surface.

When learning to tread, the child can practice the arm movements while standing in neck-deep water. The kick can be practiced in deep water with the child holding the side of the pool. Still holding the side of the pool in deep water, the child can practice using both legs and one arm, reversing his position so that he practices on both sides. The child should begin practice without holding by having the teacher hold a shoulder strap, back of swim trunks, or armpit. When the teacher assists the child in this manner, he should do it from the rear and hold the child just at water level. While giving assistance the teacher can feel the effectiveness of the child's treading action and decrease his support as the child gains skill.

After the child has mastered the skill of treading he should practice moving from a treading position to a prone float and back float.

Sitting Dive from Side of Pool

When the child can handle himself safely in deep water, he is ready to learn diving. Diving skill should be developed progressively, starting with a sitting dive and gradually moving to a standing dive.

The child sits on the side of the pool with his feet resting in the gutter edge. The legs and knees are well apart. The head is between the arms and the arms are resting against the ears. The arms are fully extended in front of the head, thumbs hooked together, fingers of one hand overlapping those of the other hand. The child bends forward from the hips and down between the knees. The fingers are pointed

Sitting Dive,
Starting Position

toward a definite spot on the bottom of the pool far enough out to ensure a safe, shallow entry (about three feet).

When ready to dive, the child takes a breath and rolls into the water by lifting his hips, straightening his legs, and reaching for the bottom of the pool. Many children may need to practice the hip lift from a sitting position on land before attempting the sitting dive. When the dive is first attempted, one assistant should be on land and one in the water. During the dive, the eyes are opened as the head is submerged. When the bottom is reached, the arms and hands are turned up and the head lifts. One foot is dropped to the bottom as the hands touch. The child pushes off the bottom with the foot and pulls with his arms as in the recovery from a face float. When he reaches the surface he begins swimming.

To ensure a successful dive, the eyes should be kept open to judge body location in the water at all times and the arms should be kept in line with the head to control the angle of entry. The child should make a conscious effort to tense or contract the abdominal and leg muscles to get full alignment and extension of body joints to prevent an overthrow or collapse on the entry.

Kneeling Dive from Side of Pool

After the sitting dive has been mastered, the kneeling dive can be taught. The child kneels on one knee at the side of the pool with the arch of the other foot resting on the gutter edge. The calf of the same leg presses against the side of the pool. The head and arm positions are identical to that of the sitting dive. The point of aim, however, is out slightly to ensure a safe, shallow dive. (Picture, p. 326.)

The child pushes against the deck with the foot of the kneeling leg (the toes of which are turned under so the push will be easier to accomplish), lifts the hips, and dives over the knee of the leg resting on the gutter edge, reaching for the bottom. Recovery is as in the sitting dive. The head must be kept in line with the body and the hands in front of the head until the recovery is well started. Repeat the dive with the foot on the deck edge rather than the gutter edge.

Standing Dive from Side of Pool

The standing dive should be taught progressively. With the arms overhead, the child goes from a tip-in dive to a fall-in dive and finally to a dive with a small spring.

To execute the tip-in dive the child stands at the edge of the pool with one foot slightly forward, bends forward at the waist, and puts the arms and head in the same position as in the sitting dive. Keeping the knees straight and the fingers pointing to a definite spot on the bottom far enough out from the side of the pool to ensure a safe entry,

a — Starting position

b — Hip lift

c — Entry (poor)

Kneeling Dive

he pushes forward and lifts with the foot that is back, leaning forward and falling into the pool. The legs trail.

The fall-in dive is performed with the feet together. The procedure of the tip-in dive is followed except the child is standing with both feet at the edge of the pool. The toes are curled over the edge to increase security. As in the tip-in dive, the child leans forward and falls into the pool with the legs trailing.

Standing Tip-In Dive

a — Starting position,
fall-in dive,
knees bent

b — Starting position,
fall-in dive,
knees straight

Standing Fall-In Dive

a – Standing dive side of pool

b – Standing dive from diving board

Standing Dive

The standing dive from the side of the pool with a push or small spring follows the same procedures of the fall-in dive except, just after starting the forward lean, the knees bend, then extend strongly, pushing away from the side. The head is kept in line with the arms and body.

Standing Vertical Dive from Side of Pool

The child stands erect at the deck edge of the pool with his toes curled securely over the edge. The body should be in good standing posture with the arms hanging easily at the sides. The eyes are looking upward from the deck of the pool (the arms help to lift the body upward), the head and arms are dropped, and the hips and legs are lifted. On entry, the body is perpendicular to the surface of the water. The back must be kept straight and the dive should be carried down to the bottom of the pool.

As lead-ups to this vertical entry, the child should practice springing on the deck, pushing up from both feet simultaneously. He should practice a vertical jump and feet-first entry from the deck edge into the water. The body must be kept in good standing posture in this jump. If the head is forward, the child will fall into the water in a semihorizontal position. If the head is back, the child will fall into the water in a semisitting position.

After the mentally retarded or emotionally disturbed child has mastered the above skills, he can be taught the conventional swimming strokes. Descriptions of these strokes can be found in most swimming textbooks.

Recreational Aspects

Once the mentally retarded or emotionally disturbed child has mastered basic swimming and water safety skills, he can participate in a wide variety of water-related recreational activities. These activities would be considered recreational in nature if participation occurred

during one's leisure time, if the activities were chosen freely and according to one's own wishes and personal desires, and if participation in the activity were for the fun, enjoyment, and personal satisfaction derived from such involvement.

The mentally retarded or emotionally disturbed child can accompany his family or friends to school, community, or other public swimming facilities. Swimming in a recreational environment aids in the development of social skills and provides the child with wholesome, vigorous activity and fun.

If proper safety precautions are followed, mentally retarded or emotionally disturbed children can learn to participate in such recreational activities as fishing, rowing, canoeing, and sailing. Approved life jackets should be worn by the children. One qualified lifesaver should accompany every two children in such small craft activity. The American Red Cross *Basic Canoeing*, *Basic Rowing*, and *Basic Sailing* textbooks are excellent references for the teacher interested in giving basic instruction in these activities.

Recreational Water Stunts

Elementary water stunts such as the tuck turn, handstand, front somersault, and back somersault can be taught to the mentally retarded or emotionally disturbed child. These skills can be used in a follow-the-leader game, in an aquatic spell-down, or in simple water routines set to music. A good demonstration should precede practice of these skills by the child.

Tuck, Tuck Turn

Starting in the back glide position, with the arms performing a finning action (as previously described under Finning; Arm Stroke, Back), a

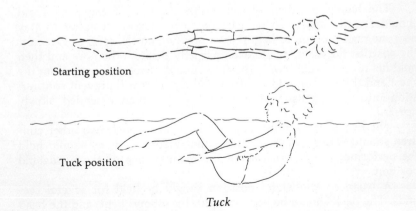

Starting position

Tuck position

Tuck

tuck position is assumed by dropping the hips and drawing the knees toward the head. A continuous, smooth motion of the hands should be stressed to avoid sinking.

From the tuck position, a tuck turn (frequently referred to as a tub or man-in-the-tub) is performed by modifying the finning motion of the arms. Both hands are drawn up toward the waist and then reach out to one side of the body, either right or left. They are then pushed away from the body in the opposite direction of the reach. The arm action is repeated until the body completes a circle on the surface of the water. For variety, the lower legs can perform a slow flutter-kicking action as the body maintains the tuck position and turns. If the children have learned a sculling arm motion, this can be used instead of finning. Using a tuck or a tuck turn, the child can be taught to perform a variety of patterns on the surface of the water and to music.

Handstand

The handstand is considered basic to the effective learning of all other water stunts. It uses the previously learned skills of breathing, breath holding, and the turtle float and stand.

From a standing position in waist-deep water with the feet apart for balance, the child inhales and holds his breath. With the arms at the sides and fully extended, he bends forward until the upper body is parallel to the water surface. The hands and arms are in the water with the palms facing the bottom of the pool and the finger tips pointed back away from the face. The hands are then pressed strongly toward the pool bottom to lift the hips. At the same time the chin is brought toward the chest and the body is tucked into a turtle position. The hands continue pressing downward, moving in a circle, until downward movement of the body is well started. One strong half circle and smaller circling actions with the hands and arms, as needed for balance, should bring the body near the bottom of the pool.

The hands are then placed on the bottom of the pool about shoulder width apart. To reduce buoyancy, making it easier to stay near the pool bottom, to help relieve pressure on the ears, and to clear the nostrils, the child should exhale briefly through the nose and then hold his breath again. Next, the chin should be moved away from the chest and the head should be lifted slightly. This will prevent continuation into a somersault turn. The legs are then extended slowly upward.

The first several times a handstand is attempted, two other children should stand on either side of the performer. They should hold the performer's legs, assisting in the maintenance of the handstand position.

A balanced handstand position should be held for several seconds. The back should be kept straight, the elbows bent, and the head

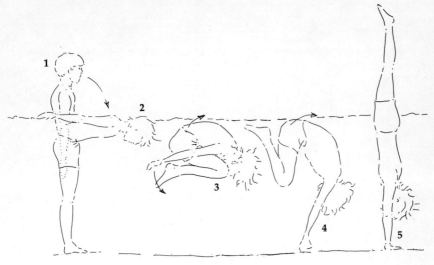

Handstand

held up. This will help counterbalance the weight of the legs. If necessary to stay near the pool bottom, the child should exhale briefly and then hold his breath again.

The child returns to a standing position by bringing the legs back to the tuck position, lifting the head and hands, and standing as from the turtle float. He should exhale as he stands. It should be stressed that all movements should be performed slowly.

Front Somersault

The front somersault as performed in the water is similar to the front somersault performed in gymnastics. This skill can be performed in a tuck position (turtle) or pike position (knees straight and body bent at hips) in shallow or deep water. The front somersault uses the previously learned skills of breathing, breath holding, turtle float and stand, handstand, and finning or sculling. During the performance of a front somersault the child's body makes a complete rotation around its horizontal axis.

The front somersault can first be attempted from the handstand starting position. Instead of placing the hands on the bottom of the pool, the child should continue rotating the arms in a circular motion from the shoulders until the body has completed a circle in the water. Stress should be placed on pressing the arms and hands forward in a clockwise movement (as observed from the performer's left side). When a circle has been completed, the child stands as from the turtle float position.

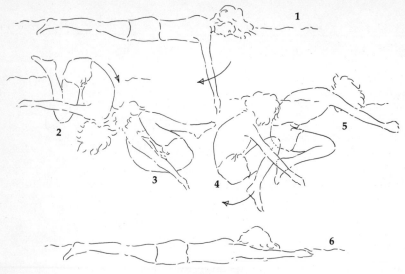

Front Somersault

Next, have the child practice the front somersault, starting and finishing in the turtle float position. Although more difficult to perform, the pike somersault can also be learned and practiced starting in a handstand or jellyfish float position.

When these skills have been mastered, the front somersault, tuck or pike position, should be learned from a prone float starting position. The breath should be held during the performance of the somersault. To keep water out of the nose, the child can exhale slowly through the nose, particularly through the first half of the circle. He should be taught to exhale as he stands from the somersault.

Back Somersault

Like the front somersault, the back somersault involves rotary movement around the performer's horizontal axis. It can be executed with the body in a tuck or pike position, in shallow or deep water. The back somersault is usually started from a back float position. It uses the previously learned skills of breathing, breath holding, turtle float and stand, handstand, and finning or sculling.

From a back float position with the hands finning or sculling, the hips are dropped and the legs are drawn into a tuck position. The child next inhales and tucks his chin to his chest. The arms stop finning or sculling. With the palms facing the bottom of the pool and the arms fully extended, the hands and arms press strongly downward and backward. This pressure lifts the hips upward and starts the body ro-

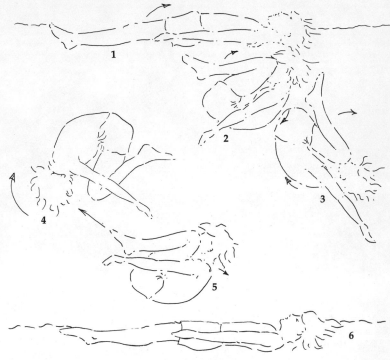

Back Somersault

tation. When the hands are at the bottom of the circle and the fingers are pointing directly toward the bottom of the pool, they are rotated outward. The arms, circling at the shoulders, start moving upward, palms pressing against the water in a counterclockwise circle (as observed from the performer's left side). The head and shoulders are pulled down; the hips come up over the head and shoulders, the weight of which aids in turning the body. During the somersault movements the performer can exhale slowly or hold his breath. The legs should be kept in a tight tuck position and the chin should be kept on the chest. The arms continue circling from the shoulder until a circle is completed. When the body returns to the tuck starting position on the back, the legs are extended to the back float position and the arms begin a finning or sculling motion.

When first attempting the back somersault, one or two partners can assist in lifting the hips into the turn.

The front somersault, back somersault, tuck, and tuck turn can be combined with simple stroking movements and music. These and other simple water stunts will provide the mentally retarded or emotionally disturbed child with a variety of recreational pleasures.

SELECTED REFERENCES

American National Red Cross. *Swimming and water safety.* Washington, D.C.: American National Red Cross, 1968.

Berg, S. H. and W. R. Gardner. Therapeutic pool heals and thrills crippled children. *American School Board Journal,* December 1939, **99**, 23+.

Brent, Irwin E. Hydrotherapy in a Y pool. *Journal of Physical Education,* March-April 1950, **47**, 88.

Brown, Richard L. *Swimming for the mentally retarded.* New York: National Association for Retarded Children (420 Lexington Avenue), 1958.

Bullock, Doris Layson. Some basic skills in the water. *Journal of Health, Physical Education and Recreation,* January 1957, **28**, 27-28.

Carr, Dorothy B., ed. *Sequenced instructional programs in physical education for the handicapped.* Los Angeles: City Schools, 1970.

Council For Exceptional Children and American Association for Health, Physical Education and Recreation. *Recreation and physical activity for the mentally retarded.* Washington, D.C.: American Association for Health, Physical Education and Recreation, 1966.

Council for National Cooperation in Aquatics and American Association for Health, Physical Education and Recreation. *A practical guide for teaching the mentally retarded to swim.* Washington, D.C.: American Association for Health, Physical Education and Recreation, 1969.

Foster, Robert E. Swimming activity opens a new world for retarded youths. *Swimming Pool Age,* September 1967.

Gober, Bill. Swimming for trainable mentally retarded. *Challenge,* May 1968, **3** (5).

Grosse, Susan J. Adapted swimming. *Outlook,* December 1969, **1** (3), 8.

Grove, Frances. Aquatic therapy: A real first step to rehabilitation. *Journal of Health, Physical Education and Recreation,* October 1970, **41** (8), 65-66.

Henning, Harold, Jr., Value of swimming in rehabilitation. *Beach and Pool and Swimming,* May 1946, **20**, 9-10, 19-21, and February 1952, **26**, 7-8, 16-17.

Kamm, A. Swimming as an activity therapy. *Mental Hygiene,* July 1949, **33**, 417-423.

Lowman, Charles L. and Susan G. Roen. *Therapeutic use of pools and tanks.* Philadelphia: W. B. Saunders Co., 1952.

Lowman, Charles. Growth and importance of hydrotherapy. *Beach and Pool,* April 1939, **13**, 8-9, 23-25.

Moran, Joan M. The effects of the front crawl swimming stroke on trainable mentally retarded children. Unpublished doctoral dissertation, University of Utah, 1971.

Mundt, Raymond, Martin Wood and Howard Ludwig. Physical therapy swimming program. *Military Medicine,* August 1965, **130**, 775-778.

Reynolds, Grace. Swimming and recreational programing at the Longview YMCA. *Challenge,* May 1968, **3** (5), 10.

Stewart, Joan E. Participation of mentally retarded children in a swimming program. Unpublished master's thesis, University of Nebraska (Lincoln), January 1966.

Chapter XI

Integrating Movement Experiences with Other School Subjects

Within the past several years a great deal has been written and much thought has been given to the effects of physical activity on the learning capacities of the individual. Many theorists involved in teaching mentally retarded and emotionally disturbed children to function better imply that intellectual and cognitive ability can be developed through perceptual-motor training. In many institutions movement experiences are assuming an increasingly important role in programs designed to enhance the cognitive or intellectual development of the mentally retarded and/or emotionally disturbed child.

Although some evidence suggests that movement experiences may be important in the development of certain perceptual-cognitive behaviors, the research is unsubstantiated in this area. The often generalized assumption that improvement in movement proficiency will always lead to better academic achievement is, therefore, erroneous. Research relating movement and intellectual abilities is discussed in Chapter II, The Status of Physical Education/Recreation for the Mentally Retarded and Emotionally Disturbed.

Motor and perceptual activities can be used successfully to complement or reinforce classroom learning activities and situations. We can only assume, however, that those academic operations directly incorporated into movement games can be improved through such experiences. Games and techniques employing whole-body movements can be particularly helpful for teaching academic skills that involve perception of spatial relationships. The development of the ability to move the body efficiently usually improves the child's self-concept to the extent that the child gains confidence in his ability to succeed in the classroom. This can positively influence the mentally retarded or emotionally disturbed child's total ability to learn. The relief from tension afforded by the opportunity for movement experiences can be especially beneficial for the mentally retarded or emotionally disturbed child who is under strain in the classroom. This release of tension can permit the child to return to the classroom better able to concentrate on academic tasks. In addition, properly planned movement experiences can promote such basic abilities as memory, hand-eye coordination, perceptual and sensory awareness, increased attention span and concentration, body orientation in time and space, and the ability to solve problems. All of these skills underlie the learning process.

Art

The basic concepts of color and form, which are needed in art, can be reinforced through properly structured movement experiences. The mentally retarded or emotionally disturbed child can learn color discrimination and form recognition from participation in the following activities:

Color Relay

One-foot squares of brightly colored cardboard or vinyl (blue, yellow, red, green, white) are placed in a straight line, at least one foot apart, on the floor. It would be best to start with only two colors, such as blue and yellow, then gradually add the remaining colors as the children learn to differentiate between them.

Before the activity begins the teacher should identify the various colors for the children.

The children run down and back, hopping with both feet in the blue squares and one foot in the yellow squares. The first team successfully completing the movements is the winner. If desired, minus points can be given for all incorrect movements and the team with the fewest minus points declared the winner. The game can be repeated by hopping with both feet in the yellow squares and one foot in the blue squares.

When the children develop a reasonable degree of proficiency in this activity, additional colors can be added and different movement skills can be performed in each of the various colored squares. An example would be: Hop with both feet in the yellow squares, hop on the right foot in the blue squares, hop on the left foot in the red squares. In addition, they might be asked to move around in a circle in the white squares and jump twice in the green squares. The children can make up their own sequence of skills to perform in the various colored squares and then try to repeat their own performance. Or a leader can create a movement sequence which the other children must copy. When the mentally retarded or emotionally disturbed child attempts this task of remembering a specific series of movements, he is gaining practice in seriation, one of the component parts of the thinking process.

The complexity of this activity should be dependent upon the child's ability to remember the color code and sequence of actions used.

The element of form recognition can be added to this game by using squares, circles, diamonds, and triangles in the same or different colors and by having the children perform different movements in the various patterns.

Bean Bag Toss

Colored targets are used and the child is asked to toss the bean bag into a specific color. The element of form recognition can be added to this activity by using targets of different colors and shapes. Two points can be awarded for successfully hitting the designated target. Each child tosses three bean bags. The child with the highest score is the winner.

Later, the children can make their own colorful bean bag targets in art class for use in this game.

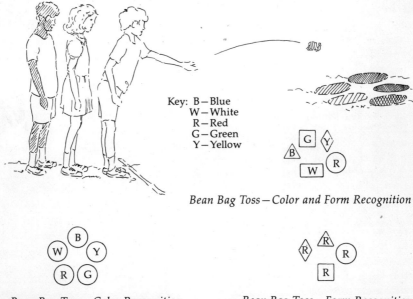

Key: B — Blue
W — White
R — Red
G — Green
Y — Yellow

Bean Bag Toss — Color and Form Recognition

Bean Bag Toss — Color Recognition

Bean Bag Toss — Form Recognition

Traffic Light

A simple game using red, yellow, and green circles can be played to teach color recognition and traffic safety. A circle is held up by the teacher as its color is mentioned. The children move freely around the room on "green." They must begin to slow their body movements on "yellow" and freeze on "red." If desired, the children caught moving after red is called can be eliminated from the game.

Obstacle Course

A simple obstacle course can be built and the children can follow a color-coded pattern as they travel around the course. A variety of color patterns in the shape of feet, hands, and circles can be used. The children can be required to climb, crawl, walk, or run through, over, under, on, or around various obstacles placed on the floor. An example is given below.

Miscellaneous

Additional activity in form recognition can include performing specific skills in, or a variety of locomotor patterns around squares, circles, triangles, rectangles, and diamonds. The teacher or the children can create numerous other games and activities using various colors and shapes to reinforce color and form recognition.

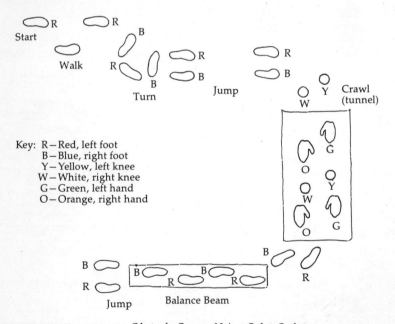

Key: R—Red, left foot
B—Blue, right foot
Y—Yellow, left knee
W—White, right knee
G—Green, left hand
O—Orange, right hand

Obstacle Course Using Color Code

Music

Rhythm is an integral part of movement. By combining body movements with basic rhythmic experiences the child can develop a better understanding and appreciation of rhythm and music. The mentally retarded and/or emotionally disturbed child can be taught many simple rhythmic activities and singing games simultaneously in both his music and physical education classes. Numerous examples using movement to reinforce music and rhythm are included in Chapter VII, Music, Rhythms, and Dance.

Health and Safety

A healthful and safe atmosphere should surround the school environment in which movement experiences are taught. Positive health and safety habits should be a by-product of these experiences. Numerous opportunities for the incidental teaching of health concepts continually arise in movement classes. The mentally retarded and/or emotionally disturbed child can feel the effects of vigorous physical activity on his body. He can be taught that this is necessary for a healthy body, that it stimulates proper growth, makes the body better able to fight disease, and at the same time gets rid of undue emotional stress. The child can also learn that the shower taken after such exercise is healthful and invigorating.

When the mentally retarded and/or emotionally disturbed child is taught how to carry his body in correct posture, he should also be taught that this correct body position is beneficial to the body and enables it to function more efficiently. He should learn that physical examinations are necessary not only to ensure his safe participation in activity classes but also to provide for the early detection and prevention of disease. Another by-product of the child's movement experiences should be an understanding of the part that nutrition and rest play in the healthy functioning of the body.

If the child's movement experiences are properly planned, they will include carry-over activities of a recreational nature. The mentally retarded and/or emotionally disturbed child should understand the value of these leisure skill activities in filling his free-time hours, not only during childhood, but also into his adult life.

Safety and safety factors are important considerations in many movement activities. The mentally retarded and/or emotionally disturbed child should know how to properly set up and take down equipment. He should be able to assist the teacher in checking and inspecting the equipment and facilities used, thus ensuring that these safety standards are always followed.

Relaxation

The teaching of relaxation should be included as a part of the child's movement experiences. The development of the ability to relax will be especially valuable for the hyperactive child, but all of the mentally retarded and emotionally disturbed children in the group will benefit from the experience of becoming aware of and learning how to control the tension in their bodies.

Begin with the children in a comfortable position, preferably on mats, lying on their backs. Have the children think about breathing and breathe slowly and deeply. Next, have them try to make their bodies as "tight" and "hard" as possible. After they have held this "tight" position for several seconds, have them make their bodies "soft" and "light as a feather." This practice in tightening and relaxing the entire body can be practiced with specific muscle groups such as the neck, fist, arms, legs, et cetera. Practice in slow, deep breathing should be alternated with the tightening and relaxing of the muscles.

If this technique is not successful with all of the children, have them very slowly roll their arms in and out while resting on the mat. Repeat this procedure with the legs. Combine slow inward and outward rolling of the arms and legs with slow, deep breathing.

Most mentally retarded and emotionally disturbed children will benefit from spending three to four minutes a day practicing relaxation techniques.

Language Arts

Language is a vital skill which is acquired naturally by normal children as they interact with their environment. Many mentally retarded and emotionally disturbed children need additional stimulation to develop this skill.

Receptive Language

The receptive skills of listening, comprehending, and perceiving are preliminary to the development of language. Movement experiences, if properly planned, can prove to be an excellent vehicle for stimulating and reinforcing the receptive language skills, increasing the child's memory span, and contributing to vocabulary development and an understanding of word concepts.

The teacher should talk to and narrate for the child as he performs motor tasks. He should begin with simple, short directions. The length and complexity of the directions can be increased when the child's attention and comprehension increase. The child can learn to react to directions denoting relationships in time and space. Meaning is ascribed to the words spoken as the child performs the tasks the words represent, such as: *"Hop to the ladder, then crawl under it."* The child will eventually absorb the words through use. At first it may be difficult for many of the children to grasp the entire concept: *"Hop to the ladder, then crawl under it."* For these children it may be necessary to begin with smaller concepts, such as: *"Hop to the ladder."* When the child reaches the ladder, add: *"Crawl under it."* Eventually the teacher will be able to combine the entire phrase.

Receptive language frequently develops as the child develops a kinesthetic understanding of the meaning of the words which describe his movements. When a child is asked to step right, back up, walk forward, walk under an object and he performs the task, the words take on added meaning for him.

Words denoting comparisons are difficult for most mentally retarded and emotionally disturbed children to comprehend because of the relationships they describe. Because movement has temporal and spatial extensions, these experiences can help the child understand such comparisons as slow/fast, wide/narrow, high/low, up/down, in/out, under/over, and around/through. Eventually, considerable contextual variety can be presented in relation to the different tasks expected of the child. This can expose him to a larger vocabulary with many contrasts in concepts.

Movement tasks, as presented in Chapter VI, Movement Education, can stimulate the child and improve his ability to think more efficiently. An example of this would be: *"How many different ways can you move along the balance beam?"* The child has already experienced movement on the balance beam and must now think of new ways of moving or different movement combinations he can use on the beam.

Most games and activities used in physical education classes require the receptive language skills of listening to directions and performing the required verbal commands. "Simon Says" is an example of a simple game using these skills.

Expressive Language

Expressive language skills are more difficult to develop in a movement environment. The following suggestions might be helpful in encouraging vocalization:

1. Ask the child to repeat the directions for the activity or game being used.
2. Rotate using the children as leaders, especially when playing simple games such as "Simon Says."
3. Ask the child to describe the movement he has performed or is going to perform. This would be especially applicable when the movement education approach is used.
4. Ask the child to explain the meaning of the action used in mimetic or other creative play.

Letter Recognition, Spelling, Reading

Simple games and relays can be used to help the mentally retarded and/or emotionally disturbed child recognize the various letters of the alphabet and reinforce his classroom work in spelling and reading. Ideally, the same letters and words should be taught simultaneously in the classroom and physical education class. The following examples are only a few of the many possible games which can be used to reinforce letter recognition, spelling, and reading.

Alphabet or Word Relay

The children are divided into teams, six to eight in each group. Each child is given a letter of the alphabet, which is printed on a card approximately six by eight inches. Matching cards are placed either on a rack or on the floor approximately twenty feet in front of the lines of children.

On the signal "go" the first person in each line runs to the rack, picks out the card matching the one in his hand, and runs to the end of his line after touching the next player, who repeats the process. The game continues until all children have had a turn. Errors are corrected as they occur. The team to finish first is the winner.

For variation, other locomotor movements can be substituted for the run in this relay. The first time the game is played, use only two or three letters. This will make the selection of matching cards easier.

This relay can be played with either upper or lower case letters, or both. Reading can be substituted for letter recognition by substituting simple words printed on cards for the letters. With more advanced students, the words each team gathers can be made into a simple sentence before the team can win.

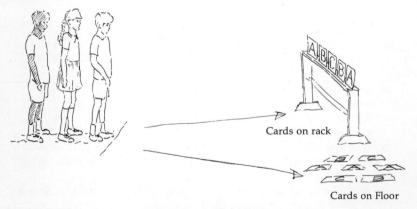

Cards on rack

Cards on Floor

Alphabet or Word Relay

Circle Game

The children are sitting in a circle. Everyone has a letter of the alphabet, which is printed on a card. The teacher calls a letter. The child with that letter must stand up, skip (gallop, run, et cetera) once around the outside of the circle and back to place.

Variation: Music is used and the children skip around the circle. When a letter is called, everyone stops and the child with that letter must repeat the letter and say a word beginning with the letter, such as: "A — apple."

Bean Bag Toss

The bean bag toss game included in this chapter under Art can be played with letters of the alphabet instead of geometric forms.

Hopscotch

A hopscotch variation can be played with the letters of the alphabet. The letters can be arranged in alphabetical order or arranged at random. As the child hops from one to the other he can say the letter, gaining practice in learning the alphabet.

Using this same floor pattern, the children can hop the letter pattern of their first name, last name, or simple words such as *walk, hop*.

Reading and spelling can be introduced into this activity by having the teacher hold up a card on which a simple word is printed, such as *cat*. The child must say the word (it may be necessary for the teacher to say the word first) and then hop out its spelling while repeating the letters *c-a-t*.

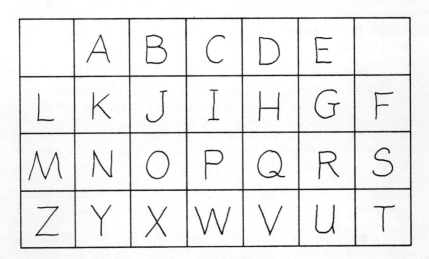

Hopscotch Floor Pattern

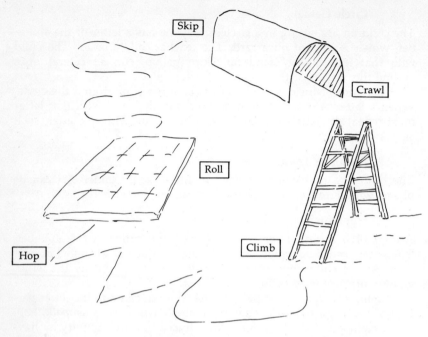

Reading Obstacle Course

Reading Obstacle Course

An obstacle course can be set up with words describing the movements required of the children printed on cards. As the children move through the obstacle course they perform the actions listed on the various cards.

Snatch the Letter or Word

The children are facing each other in two lines about twenty feet apart. The teams are numbered. The teacher calls a letter of the alphabet or a word and then calls a number. The two children with that number each run to the center, try to snatch that letter or word, and carry it safely across his own goal line without being tagged by the other. If the runner carrying the letter or word reaches his goal safely, his team scores one point. If he is tagged, the opponent's team scores one point. If either player touches the letter or word or picks it up and drops it, the opposing player can score a point by tagging him before he reaches the goal. If the players stall and neither one picks up the letter or word, the teacher can call another number for two more children to try to snatch the letter or word. When the children tire of the activity, the team with the highest score is the winner.

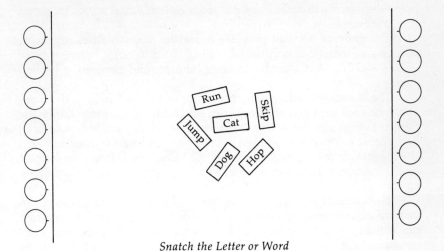

Snatch the Letter or Word

Miscellaneous

A wide variety of games can be created in which the child is required to recognize a letter and write it correctly on the blackboard before he performs a designated movement sequence.

Games and other activities in which the teacher calls the child's name before he performs a required movement sequence can be played with words. Each child's name is printed on a card. Instead of calling the child's name, the teacher holds up the card on which his name is printed.

Actions and movements such as *go, skip, up, run* can be printed on cards. As the card is held up by the teacher, the child performs the correct actions. The first time this activity is played, the teacher should hold up the card and pronounce the word before the child performs the actions. The child can progress to responding to a sequence of cards. As the child is performing the movements of one card, another is held up and he changes his actions accordingly. For more advanced groups, complete sentences, printed on cards, can be held up and the child then performs the movement sequence, such as: "Hop to the ladder."

Arithmetic

Properly selected movement experiences can be used to reinforce numbers, counting, and arithmetic concepts. Numbers are essential for measuring physical performance in which distance (standing broad jump), time (fifty-yard dash), or height (vertical jump) achievement is the goal. Counting is used when the children count the number of times they perform a skill or keep team or individual scores in games and other contests.

The game of softball provides numerous opportunities for incorporating arithmetic concepts — learning the difference between three strikes and four balls, understanding innings, and computing batting averages.

The movement education approach can be used to help the mentally retarded or emotionally disturbed child grasp many arithmetic concepts: *Can you run to the farthest hoop? Who can throw the bean bag closest to the center of the circle? Who can toss the bean bag into the biggest circle? . . . the smallest circle? Can you skip on the longest line? . . . hop on the shortest line? We have four children. How many balls do we need if everyone has his own ball?*

The concept of weights, addition, subtraction, and division can be reinforced through the use of weight-lifting equipment. The children can actually feel the difference between a one-half-pound and one-pound weight. They can feel the change in the weight of the bar as they add or subtract weights from it. Division can be taught as the children learn how to equate the amount of weight on each end of the bar.

Number Relay

The Alphabet Relay included under language arts can be changed to a number relay. Numbers are substituted for the letters of the alphabet.

Snatch the Number

Snatch the Letter can be changed to Snatch the Number.

Bean Bag Toss

At a distance approximately ten feet from a target, the children toss bean bags, attempting to get them in the highest numbers. Each child gets three tosses. The child's score is the number in which his bean bag lands. Scores are written on the blackboard and added. The child with the highest score is the winner. The children should rotate turns so that each child can keep his own score.

Hopscotch

A variety of patterns can be used to give the child practice in using numbers in consecutive order to help him learn seriation.

Arithmetic Game

Using a variation of a hopscotch pattern, the children can hop from number to number adding or subtracting. Example: $1 + 2 = 3$.

The creative teacher will be able to devise numerous additional games which can be used to reinforce the regular classroom learning tasks of the mentally retarded and/or emotionally disturbed child. It

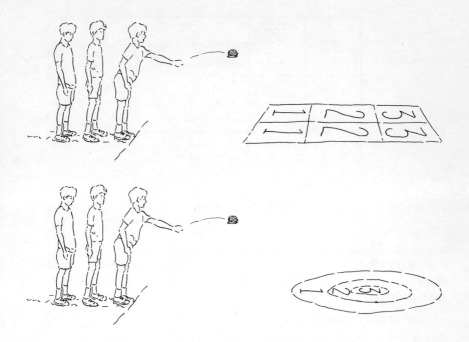

Targets for Bean Bag Toss

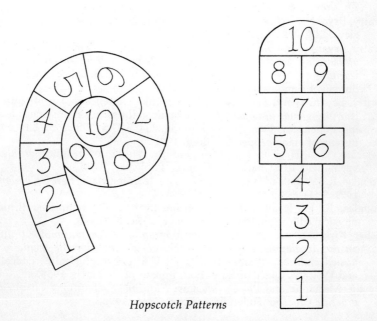

Hopscotch Patterns

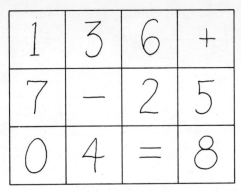

Hopscotch Variation

should be remembered that movement skills and visual, auditory, and kinesthetic stimuli reinforce each other. These learning games should supplement and not replace the standard methods of teaching classroom materials.

SELECTED REFERENCES

Barsch, Ray H. *Achieving perceptual-motor efficiency*, Vol. 1. Seattle: Special Child Publications, 1965.

Corder, W. Owens. Effects of physical education on the intellectual, physical, and social development of educable mentally retarded boys. *Exceptional Children*, 1966, **32**, 357-364.

Cratty, Bryant J. *Active learning: Games to enhance academic abilities*. Englewood Cliffs, N.J.: Prentice-Hall, 1971.

Cratty, Bryant J. and Sister Margaret Mary Martin. *The effects of a program of learning games upon selected academic abilities in children with learning difficulties*, Part I. Washington, D.C.: U.S. Office of Education, Bureau of Handicapped Children, 1970.

Cratty, Bryant J. and Sister Mark Szczepanik. *The effects of a program of learning games upon selected academic abilities in children with learning difficulties*, Part II. Washington, D.C.: U.S. Office of Education, Bureau of Handicapped Children, 1971.

Delacato, Carl H. *The treatment and prevention of reading problems*. Springfield, Ill.: Charles C. Thomas, Publisher, 1959.

Douglas, R. W. It all adds up—Fun ways are learning ways, Part I. *Challenge*, 1971, **7** (1), 6-7, 12.

Douglas, R. W. It all adds up—Arithmetic concepts reinforced through physical education, Part II. *Challenge*, 1971, **7** (2), 6-8.

Fisher, Kirk L. *Effects of a structured program of perceptual-motor training on the development and school achievement of educable mentally retarded children*. Washington, D.C.: U.S. Office of Health, Education and Welfare, Office of Education, Bureau of Research, 1969.

Frostig, Marianne and Phyllis Maslow. *Movement education: Theory and practice*. Chicago: Follett Educational Corp., 1970.

Getman, G. N. The visuomotor complex in the acquisition of learning skills. In *Learning disorders*, Vol. I, ed. J. Hellmuth, pp. 49-76. Seattle: Special Child Publications, 1965.

Harrison, W., H. Lecrone, M. Temerlin and W. Trousdale. Effect of music and exercise on the self-help skills of nonverbal retardates. *American Journal of Mental Deficiency*, 1966, **71**, 279-282.

Humphrey, James H. and Dorothy D. Sullivan. *Teaching slow learners through activity games*. Springfield, Ill.: Charles C. Thomas, Publisher, 1970.

Kephart, Newell C. Perceptual-motor aspects of learning disabilities. *Exceptional Children*, 1964, **31**, 201-206.

Oliver, James N. Effects of physical conditioning exercises and activities on the mental characteristics of educationally sub-normal boys. *British Journal of Educational Psychology*, 1958, **28**, 155-165.

Painter, Genevieve. Effect of a rhythmic and sensory-motor activity program on perceptual-motor-spatial abilities of kindergarten children. *Exceptional Children*, 1966, **33**, 113-116.

Troth, William B. Procedures and generalizations for remediation in motor coordination and perceptual training for the mentally retarded. *Training School Bulletin*, 1967, **64**, 77-80.

Webb, Ruth C. Is movement necessary in the development of cognition? *Mental Retardation*, August 1971, 16-17.

Wedemeyer, Avaril and Joyce Cejka. *Learning games for exceptional children: Arithmetic and language development activities*. Denver: Love Publishing Co., 1971.

Williams, Harriet G. Learning. *Journal of Health, Physical Education and Recreation*, 1968, **39** (9), 28-31.

Chapter XII

Innovative Equipment

Those who teach physical education to and provide recreation for the mentally retarded and/or emotionally disturbed experience varying needs for a diversity of equipment and supplies. Many teachers of the mentally retarded and/or emotionally disturbed have circumvented the relatively high cost of equipment and supplies through resourcefulness and innovation. To be sure, some equipment and supply items should be purchased through commercial sources; however, many items can and should be homemade.

Items to be purchased will be discussed with a view to their proper selection. Items which can be homemade will be discussed with a view to facilitating their proper construction.

When the decision has been made to construct equipment and supply items locally, the teacher may consider allowing the children to assist to the extent of their capabilities. The children may show surprising interest in such activities and take great pride in the results of their efforts.

Because children's needs (hence equipment and supply needs) may tend to vary considerably, a complete résumé of commercially produced and homemade recources would be impractical if not impossible. The following delineation and description of equipment and supply items include those items which have exhibited consistent utility over years of experience.

Suspended horizontal ladder

Child swings from rung to rung with teacher's assistance

Child swings from rung to rung

Ladder as balance beam

Ladder supported between uprights

Adjustable uprights permit child to practice with feet in contact with surface

Horizontal Ladders

Horizontal Ladders

Horizontal ladders of various sizes and lengths may serve a variety of purposes. When suspended at a distance slightly above the child's reach, the child may swing from rung to rung under the ladder. Such activity may be construed as having value in the development of shoulder, arm, forearm, and grip strength. Visual cues which facilitate hand-to-rung contact may enhance hand-eye coordination.

Children who are apprehensive about swinging freely under the ladder may be assisted by the teacher who can support some of the child's weight. Another possibility involves making the ladder's height adjustable so that the child may progress from rung to rung while walking the distance under the ladder.

Horizontal ladders may be placed on the ground or at distances somewhere below knee height. Here the objective is to step between the rungs of the ladder without touching the ladder. Such activity has potential value in the development of foot-eye coordination and in the development of visual spatial awareness.

The horizontal ladder may be placed on its side and supported by two pipes or two heavy pieces of wood at each end. The ladder may now serve as a balance beam. Place the supporting uprights at each end as close together as possible to prevent the ladder from wobbling.

Ladders, whether homemade or of the commercial type, should be fitted with round rungs. One-inch wooden dowels usually provide an appropriate rung size. In any instance, rung size should be compatible with the size of the child's hand.

Suspended Ropes

Suspended ropes may be utilized in a variety of hanging, climbing, and swinging activities. For maximum gripping efficiency, rope size will vary with grip size. However, a one-inch diameter rope should provide a good starting point. Ropes should be knotted or wrapped with adhesive tape at both ends to prevent their unraveling.

The physical values of suspended rope activities are closely aligned with those of the suspended horizontal ladder. The gymnastics-type activities which utilize suspended ropes may be potentially valuable in the enhancement of kinesthetic perception and spatial awareness. Refer to Developmental Gymnastics (Chapter IX) for suggested examples of suspended rope activities.

Slides

Slides are of physical value because the child must climb. It is conceivable that development of the ability to climb, slide, and culminate with a controlled stop enhances the child's self-confidence and sequential thinking ability. Maintaining an awareness of one's body position in space while sliding and properly positioning the feet upon contact with the ground stimulate the visual, kinesthetic, and tactual capabilities of the child.

Teacher assistance may be needed during the initial stages of learning to slide. It may be necessary to assist the child in climbing, to control manually the speed of his descent, and to facilitate his regaining balance upon contact with the ground.

Swings

Swings provide the child with opportunities to move rapidly backward and forward through space at varying speeds and distances above the ground. Potential values in the perceptual-motor realm include the development of visual perception, kinesthetic perception, and visual spatial awareness.

The physical fitness values of swinging are probably negligible because one is sitting down during the activity. However, motor coordination skills are enhanced as the child learns how and when to shift his weight as the primary means of keeping the swing in motion.

Heavy canvas webbing material should be utilized for the swing seat. Metal or wooden swing seats are dangerous because of their firmness and weight. Children have been accidentally struck by swing seats of this sort with resultant serious injury.

It is preferable that the swing seat be suspended with chain rather than rope. Select chain which has been plated so as to resist corrosion and rust when subjected to the elements. The use of rope is inadvisable because of its tendency to rapidly wear. Rapid wear is evident especially when ropes are subjected to a combination of the elements and heavy usage.

Tetherball Poles

Tether poles may be improvised from already existing pipes, poles, or supports of any kind which are free from obstructions. The tetherball itself must be purchased. Tetherball activity can provide mild cardiorespiratory stimulation, agility training, and hand-eye coordination development. Tetherball activity also provides opportunity for two children to interact with each other.

Automobile, Truck, Bicycle, and Tractor Tires

Tires of most any kind may be utilized in numerous situations. The variety of uses to which such tires can be put is limited only by the teacher's imagination. Discarded tires are often free for the asking at many tire dealerships.

Tractor Tire for Climbing

*Automobile Tires
Embedded in Concrete*

A large tractor tire firmly embedded in the ground and fixed to a sturdy tree serves as an excellent climbing apparatus. Climbing the tire may serve a fourfold purpose of enhancing strength, balance, kinesthetic awareness, and self-confidence.

A series of automobile tires placed side by side and partially embedded in concrete may be stepped across. Often such tires may be placed next to a fence, which serves as an aid to balance if needed. The child soon discovers that each of the tires gives differently when stepped upon. As a child traverses the series of tires, he receives and, to the extent possible, utilizes visual, kinesthetic, and tactual cues. He also is dependent upon reaction time in adjusting to the constantly unstable surface upon which he is walking.

Tires may be placed on the ground and stepped into. The potential values of this activity are similar to those of the ground level horizontal ladder. Unlike the ladder, however, the tires may be arranged and rearranged in divergent directions and at varying distances apart. This enables the teacher to establish reasonable challenges for each child. The placement of tires in divergent directions may, in addition to above-stated values, assist in the development of agility.

When the tires are placed somewhat farther apart, the child may zigzag or weave through the maze of tires. The need to change directions rapidly enhances agility and the ability to think prior to and while moving (sequential thinking and motor planning).

A tire may be mounted on a four-by-six-inch wooden support which has been firmly embedded in the ground. A four-by-six-inch hole is cut in the bottom of the tire, thus allowing the support post to

Tires Placed on the Ground

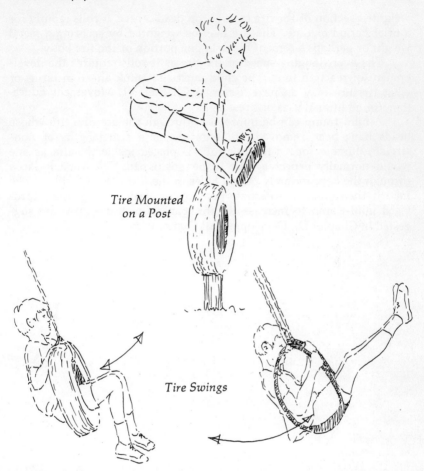

Tire Mounted on a Post

Tire Swings

slide through. The support post comes to rest on the top (inside) of the tire. If needed, nails may be utilized to firmly secure the tire to the post. Utilizing the tire in leapfrog fashion calls upon abilities to run and jump, hand-eye coordination, visual spatial awareness, and kinesthetic awareness.

Though swings have been discussed previously, the possibility of utilizing tires as swings warrants additional mention. In one instance, a tire is merely suspended from a single rope or chain. In another instance, most of the tire is cut away and discarded, leaving only the entire bead and part of the tire body intact. In this instance a separate chain or rope is attached to the uppermost part of each bead.

A tire with an excess amount of weight in one part of the radius results in unexpected surprises when rolled. The tire rolls slowly and laboriously as the weight rises to top dead center. As soon as the weighted section of the tire crosses top dead center, it rolls rapidly for a brief period of time. The tire may be weighted by securing a metal weight or perhaps a cement block in one portion of the tire body.

The everchanging speed of the tire as it rolls requires the development of reaction time. The child must also think ahead in terms of what the tire may do next. Refer to Chapter VI, Movement Education, for additional uses of tires.

A mini-tramp can be improvised through the use of a tire whose beads have been removed, an innertube, and two lengths of non-stretch, durable rope. The innertube is placed inside the tire as one would normally expect a tube to be positioned. The rope is laced through the appropriately placed holes in the tire (on both sides). The tube is then inflated. Alternate jumping on both sides of the improvised mini-tramp to increase its life span. Mini-tramp uses are suggested in Chapter IX, Developmental Gymnastics.

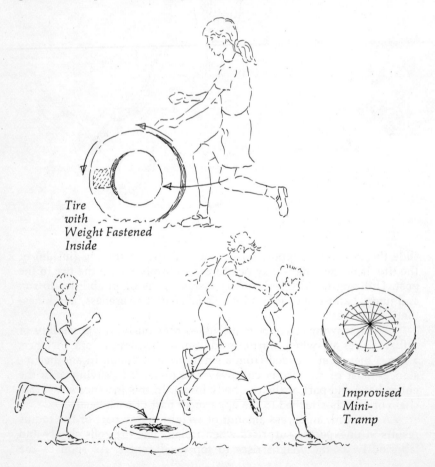

Tire with Weight Fastened Inside

Improvised Mini-Tramp

Bicycle Tires

Bicycle tires may be utilized in various forms of tug-of-war. Tugs-of-war, regardless of variation, generally may be considered as having value in strength development.

Innertube Circles

Innertube circles cut into two-inch widths may be utilized in a variety of strength-building activities. Both teacher and children may invent exercises to be performed with the tube circles. In the event a child invents an exercise, name that exercise after the child. The teacher may subsequently refer to that exercise as "Bobby's exercise" when the tube circles are being used. This is a good motivator since it gives the child recognition and praise for something he has created.

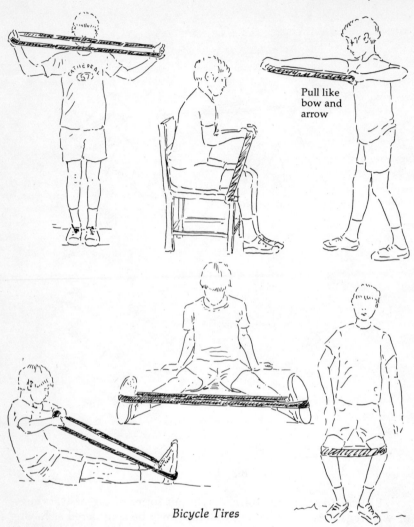

Pull like
bow and
arrow

Bicycle Tires

Large Cardboard Boxes

Heavy corregated cardboard boxes of the type found at appliance
stores may be used to build a "creeper." The creeper is fashioned from
a three-foot tall cardboard box which has both the top and bottom
removed. The finished product takes the shape of an oval or oblong
circle. The creeper may be utilized as a motivating device in getting
children to crawl and creep. The inherent value of crawling and creeping lies in the fact that these are initial skills which facilitate the child's
exploration of his environment or space world.

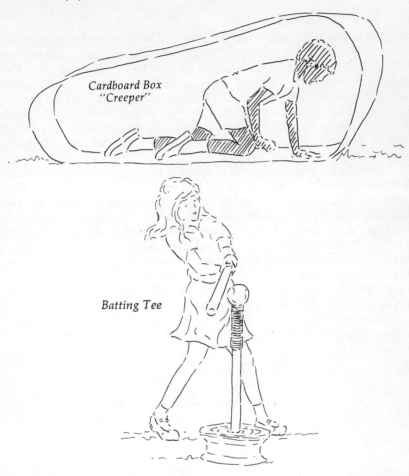

Cardboard Box
"Creeper"

Batting Tee

Batting Tees

A batting tee may be utilized when the child does not have sufficient skill to make contact with a moving ball. Use of the batting tee may help avert the frustration which often arises from failures on initial attempts. Batting tees can be fashioned from a section of pipe, any sufficiently heavy base material (e.g. an automobile wheel), and a length of radiator or similar type hose. The pipe is welded or otherwise fastened to the base. The hose is slipped over the opposite end of the pipe and fixed with a hose clamp if necessary.

Bats and balls of various types, sizes, and weights should be utilized as indicated by the needs of the children. Hollow plastic bats and whiffle balls may be considered for use among children who are lacking in physical stature or strength, or when practicing indoors.

Balance Apparatus

Balance beams of various types, widths, and heights can be improvised from relatively inexpensive pine or plywood. In addition to the previously cited ladder balance beam, a balance beam having three sides may be constructed. This type of balance beam utilizes three widths which can be selected by rotating the beam and placing it on top of the base or in the appropriate notch. This type of balance beam is of particular value because it enables the teacher to accommodate variously skilled children in one place, at one time, and with one piece of apparatus.

A balance beam may be fashioned utilizing four-by-four-inch lumber for the beam and either rubber tires or heavy springs for the supports. Regardless of whether tires or springs are utilized as the base material they should be embedded partially in concrete or otherwise anchored firmly to the surface. The base should bear sufficient strength to prevent the child's weight from bending the supports sideways. The base, however, should be sufficiently resilient to provide an up-and-down bounce as the child traverses the beam. Balance beam activities are suggested in Chapter IX, Developmental Gymnastics and Chapter VI, Movement Education.

The teeter board, like the spring- or tire-mounted balance beam, emphasizes the ability to maintain balance on a unsteady surface.

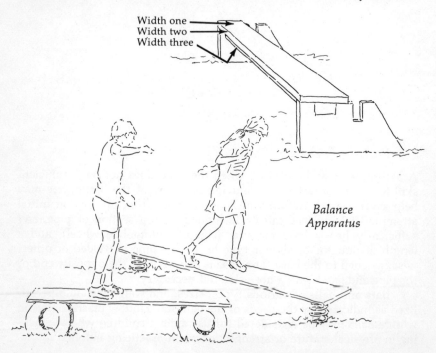

Width one
Width two
Width three

*Balance
Apparatus*

Counterparts to this type of balance in the environment include riding elevators, escalators, buses, or trains.

The teeter board surface should be approximately 2½-feet long by twelve-inches wide by one-inch thick. The teeter board fulcrum should be attached to the underside of the surface board and equidistant from both ends. Three-quartér-inch diameter pipe should suffice as fulcrum material. A base should be constructed which permits the balanced teeter board to hover at a height of approximately six to eight inches from the floor.

Blocks of equal height may be placed on the floor directly under each end of the board surface. This will lend needed confidence to marginally skilled and timid children. As a child's balance improves and confidence is gained, progressively smaller blocks may be used until the need for blocks no longer exists.

Plywood circles approximately fourteen inches in diameter by one-inch thick mounted on heavy springs provide yet another opportunity to practice balance on unstable surfaces. Note that the circular platform is preferable to one which is square because the circle eliminates sharp, pointed edges.

A balance board may be constructed utilizing a sixteen-inch square by one-inch thick board and blocks of various dimensions. Examples of block dimensions include four by four by three inches, three by three by two inches, or two by two by one inches. The various

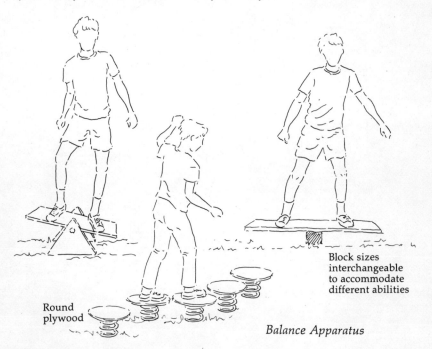

Block sizes interchangeable to accommodate different abilities

Round plywood

Balance Apparatus

blocks are placed in the center (bottom side) of the sixteen-inch square board. The child attempts to stand on the board and balance his weight. The child's weight is balanced if no part of the sixteen-inch square board touches the ground. The difficulty of the balancing task may be varied by changing the dimensions of the block upon which the sixteen-inch square board is placed.

Cardboard Barrels

Cardboard barrels of thirty-to-fifty-gallon capacity can be utilized as improvised targets or baskets. A hole somewhat larger than ball size should be cut in the barrel where the side touches the bottom rim. The top of the barrel is removed and serves as the target at which the ball is thrown. A large piece of plywood wedged diagonally inside the barrel (slanting toward the opening) will cause the on-target ball to roll out of the opening and back to the thrower. It may be preferable to place the barrels against a wall so that missed shots need not be difficult to retrieve. Also, note that the children may enjoy decorating the barrels.

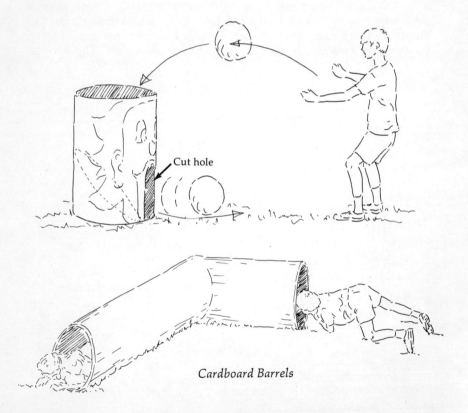

Cardboard Barrels

Large Concrete Pipes

Concrete pipes or culverts approximately three feet in diameter are excellent for crawling, creeping, and climbing experiences. Sections of pipe or culvert may be utilized individually as playground equipment or as part of an obstacle course.

Logs

Sawed logs may be utilized as inexpensive weights in an exercise program. A typical log might measure eight inches in diameter and twelve inches in height. The children can manipulate the logs through a variety of exercises. When the teacher is talking (i.e. giving instructions) the child places the log on end, sits on it, and listens. The weight of the log should be painted on each end of the log for ready identification by the teacher and by those children who are oriented to numbers. The logs also may be color coded for those children who have not yet become familiar with numbers (e.g. red logs equal five pounds, white logs equal eight pounds, blue logs equal ten pounds). Note also that logs may be utilized in an obstacle course.

Vaulting Box

A vaulting box with adjustable heights (i.e. one which has been constructed in sections) may be used in developing abilities to run and jump. Vaulting also requires varying degrees of visual perception, visual

Logs

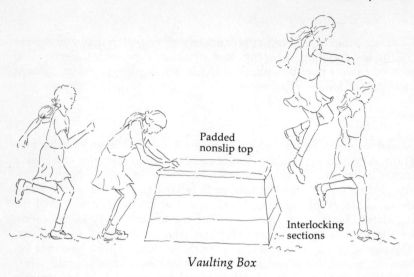

Padded
nonslip top

Interlocking
sections

Vaulting Box

spatial awareness, kinesthetic perception, hand-eye and foot-eye coordination. The vaulting box may also be part of an obstacle course.

If the vaulting box is to be homemade, be sure a system is devised where sections may be interlocked. The top surface should be padded and covered with vinyl or some similar nonslip material. The base of the vaulting box should be somewhat larger than the top surface to assure stability.

Horizontal Bars

Horizontal bars at various heights may provide upper body strength development and enhance kinesthetic awareness. Homemade horizontal bars can be fashioned from galvanized pipe. The uprights should be firmly embedded in concrete or deeply embedded in the soil. Uprights should be approximately 1½ inches in diameter. The crossbars should be approximately one inch in diameter, and may be connected to the uprights by combinations of ninety-degree pipe elbows and tees. Refer to Chapter IX, Developmental Gymnastics, for suggested horizontal bar activities.

Parallel Bars

Parallel bar activity, like horizontal bar activity, emphasizes the development of upper body strength and kinesthetic awareness. Parallel bar activity differs from horizontal bar activity to the extent that parallel bar activities are initiated primarily from a support (shoulders above the bar) position. Note that most horizontal bar activities are initiated

Bars Made from Pipe

primarily from a hanging position or swinging hang (shoulders below the bar) position. This seemingly subtle difference produces sufficiently different developmental outcomes to warrant engaging in both activities.

Homemade parallel bars may be fashioned from galvanized pipe. Firmly emplanted 1½-inch pipe should suffice as upright material. The parallel bars themselves may be fashioned from 1¼-inch pipe. Bars should approximate eight to ten feet in length and should be connected to the uprights with ninety-degree pipe elbows. Refer to Chapter IX, Developmental Gymnastics, for suggested parallel bar activities.

Rings

Ring activities are similar to horizontal bar activities with the exception that the rings are suspended in pendulum fashion and therefore swing, while a horizontal bar remains stable. For this reason, learning ring skills may be somewhat more difficult for the child.

Rings may be made from lengths of chain, wooden dowels one inch in diameter, and eye bolts. Master chain links will be needed where chains connect together and to eye bolts. The rings may be suspended from a sturdy rafter or from a supporting structure of the

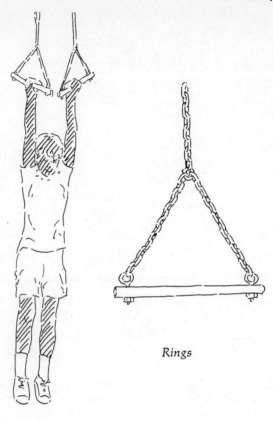

Rings

type used for swings. See Chapter IX, Developmental Gymnastics, for suggested ring activities.

Wands

Wands may be fashioned from old broomsticks, mop handles, rake handles, et cetera. If wooden dowels are to be used, select one-inch stock. Wands should be approximately three to four feet in length. Both ends of the wand should be rounded for safety, and its entire length should be sanded to avoid slivers. Refer to Chapter IX, Developmental Gymnastics, and Chapter VI, Movement Education, for suggested wand activities.

Balls Fashioned from Paper and Tape

Wad paper tightly. Tape is used to encircle the wadded paper until it is firm and round. Depending upon the child's capabilities, he may be able to make the ball, decorate it with paint, and write his name on the finished product.

Playground Balls

Playground (utility) balls are inflatable and are made of rubber. They may be purchased in a variety of sizes depending upon the skills to be taught and the needs of the children.

Playground balls may be utilized extensively during the initial stages of teaching the child to throw, catch, and kick. During these stages it may be desirable to partially deflate the ball. A partially deflated ball is somewhat easier to handle because it conforms to the hand more readily. Being accidentally struck by a partially deflated ball is less traumatic than being struck by one fully inflated. Minimizing the threat of being hurt by the ball assists in motivating the child to learn ball skills. Refer to Chapter IX, Developmental Gymnastics, and Chapter VI, Movement Education, for ball-handling activities.

Whiffle Balls

Whiffle balls are made of perforated, hollow plastic. They come in various sizes and may be used during the initial stages of teaching the child to catch and throw. Whiffle balls, because of their light weight, can reduce the child's fears of being hit should he miss the ball. A whiffle ball may be considered for indoor use or in any situation where a heavier ball might be considered dangerous to the immediate physical surroundings.

Bean Bags

Bean bags can be used in a variety of throwing and catching activities. Generally, a bean bag is easier to catch than a ball because a clutched bean bag readily conforms to a child's hand. Marginally skilled children or children in the initial stages of learning to throw and catch should be provided bean bags as one means of avoiding the frustration which accompanies failure. Refer to Chapter VI, Movement Education, for bean bag activities.

Light Ropes

Ropes of the clothesline variety may be used in jumping, movement education, and self-testing activities. Many elementary physical education and movement education textbooks will provide the teacher with an abundance of light rope activities. Note that light ropes tied in circles may substitute for innertube circles previously mentioned in this chapter. Refer to Chapter IX, Developmental Gymnastics, and Chapter VI, Movement Education, for light rope activities.

Hula Hoops

Hula hoops provide numerous opportunities for individual or group play. They can be rolled by the individual as he walks or runs alongside. They can be rolled from partner to partner. They can be stepped into when laid in sequence on the ground, or leaped through when rolled.

Hula hoops, when purchased commercially, may have beads inside the tube which rattle when the hoop is moved. One may find that several hula hoops rattling in unison can become both annoying and distracting. This problem may be solved by drilling a small hole through the tube, thus allowing the beads to be removed.

Hula hoops can be homemade by utilizing lengths of rubber hose one-half or five-eighths inch in diameter, a six-inch length of similarly diametered wooden dowel, carpet tacks, and vinyl tape. The ends of the hose are slipped over the dowel until the ends touch. The hose is then tacked to the dowel. The vinyl tape is wrapped around the hose covering both the tacks and the joint. Refer to Chapter VI, Movement Education, for hula hoop activities.

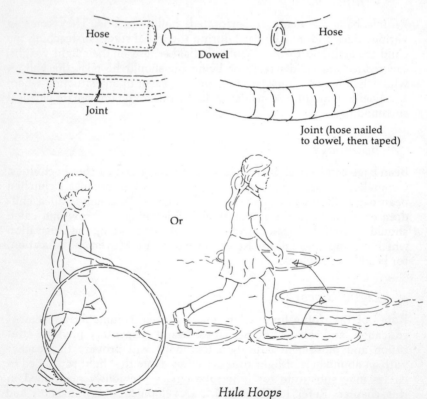

Hula Hoops

Plastic Bleach Bottles

Plastic bleach bottles when filled with sand provide excellent weights for conditioning programs. The amount of sand placed in the bottle may be varied so that a variety of weights are available. The weight may be marked on the outside of the bottle. For children who do not yet recognize numbers, the bottles may be color coded. Note the plastic bleach bottles of the one-gallon capacity variety often have handles which make for easier gripping.

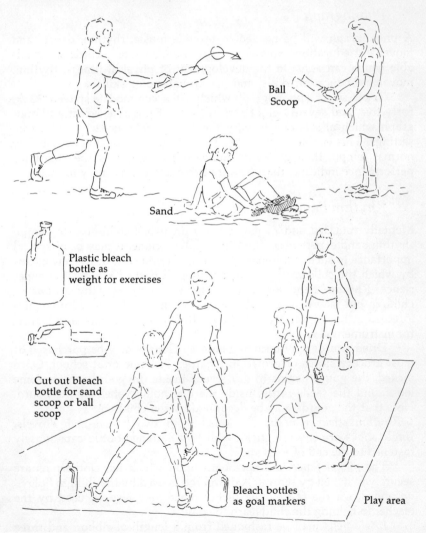

Uses of Bleach Bottles

Be sure that caps are securely fastened. To prevent their coming loose accidentally or being loosened by the children, give the caps an extra twist with a nut cracker or pair of pliers. One may also apply glue to the cap prior to tightening; however, this might permanently fix the cap.

Plastic bleach bottles filled with sand also provide boundary and goal markers for a variety of activities. They may also be partially cut out and used as scoops in sand box play or for catching small balls.

Phonograph

A phonograph will be needed to provide music, rhythm, dance, and movement education experiences. An abundance of records are available which can assist in the development of physical fitness, rhythm, movement education skills, and perceptual-motor skills.

Try to select a phonograph which will accommodate sixteen, 33⅓, forty-five, and seventy-eight rpm records. If possible, select a phonograph which allows one to vary the speed again at each of the rpm settings. This enables the teacher to start the record somewhat below normal tempo, then gradually increase the tempo as the children's performance indicates that they are becoming increasingly proficient.

Rhythm Band Instruments

Mentally retarded and/or emotionally disturbed children often enjoy rhythm band experiences. Rhythm band instruments may be of special importance to such children because they provide one of the few means by which the child may become an integral part of the musical experience. Rhythm band instruments are generally used by groups of children but may be used individually by the child as he accompanies a record at home. Refer to Chapter VII, Music, Rhythms, and Dance, for instrument play.

Dried gourds may become *maracas*. Gourds may be purchased at most grocery stores or grown in a garden at home or at school. Once picked, the gourd begins to dry. Seeds inside the gourd soon become loose, and the seeds rattle inside the dry hollow shell of the gourd. Note that the gourds may be decorated by the children.

Rhythm sticks may be fashioned from two twelve-inch dowels. *Jingle sticks* are rhythm sticks with two flattened bottle caps loosely fastened to the end of each stick.

The *picket fence* is a flat board upon which ten clothespins are securely fastened by screws. A dowel rod is used by the child to "play" up and down the fence. The picket fence may also be used by the teacher in helping the child learn to count.

Jingle bells may be fashioned from a length of ribbon and three small bells. The bells are attached to the ribbon, and the ends of the ribbon are connected.

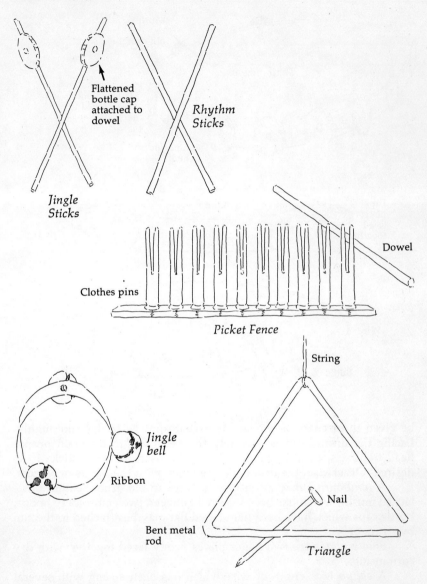

Jingle
Sticks

Flattened
bottle cap
attached to
dowel

*Rhythm
Sticks*

Dowel

Clothes pins

Picket Fence

String

Jingle
bell

Ribbon

Nail

Bent metal
rod

Triangle

Triangles may be improvised from a bent metal rod. The triangle is held by a six-inch string which is attached to one of the bends. This leaves the metal free to vibrate when struck. A three-inch nail held in the other hand serves as the striking implement.

Drums may be improvised from metal cans of various sizes and shapes. Drum heads may be fashioned from circularly cut pieces of rubber innertube. It is also possible to stretch wet muslin over the top of the can, fasten it, and allow it to dry. Once dry, the muslin should

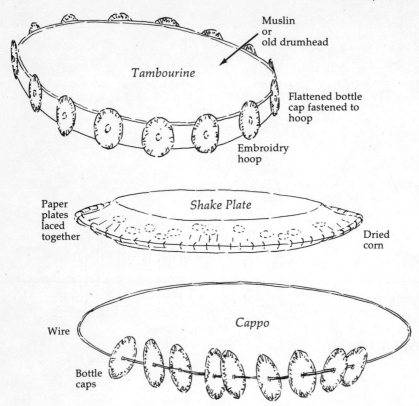

be given three coats of shellac, each coat allowed to dry thoroughly. Lacing the drum head is probably the best way to maintain proper head tightness. Lengths of dowel may be used as drum sticks if so desired. Otherwise, the drum may be stuck with the hands or fingers.

A *tambourine* may be fashioned from an old drum head or shellacked muslin which has been inserted between two embroidery hoops. Bottle caps which have been hammered flat may be attached to the rim by string or wire.

Shake plates are two paper plates firmly laced together with dry corn inside.

A *cappo* is a length of wire which has been strung with several bottle caps. The ends of the wire are twisted together, and tape is utilized to cover the junction.

Clothespin kids utilize a clothespin for the head, body, and legs. The hat is made from a flattened bottle cap which is loosely attached to the top of the pin by means of a wood screw. The clothespins may be painted to look like children. When the clothespin kids are shook, their hats rattle.

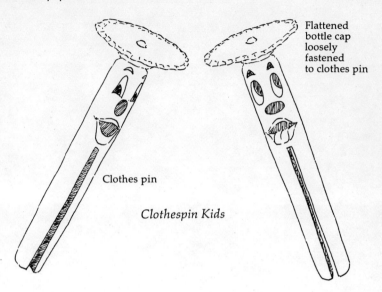

Flattened
bottle cap
loosely
fastened
to clothes pin

Clothes pin

Clothespin Kids

Index

AAHPER, 11, 17
Activity, motor
  and intellectual functioning, 8, 9,
    11-14, 83, 88
  and music, 145-153, 173-234
  and play, 83, 85, 86, 88
  and social competence, 11-15
  see also Education, movement;
    Movement, basic
Aggression
  and music, 139
  and play, 84, 85-87, 90
  and swimming, 291
Agility, 11, 25, 30
  and movement education, 112-114,
    120, 122, 123, 127, 128, 129
American Association on Mental
  Deficiency (AAMD), 6, 7
Andres, 16
Apparel, 257
Aquatics, *see* Swimming
Aquatic skills and games
  balance and buoyancy, 135
  body image, 135, 136
  breath control, 134, 135
  Cat and Mouse, 303

Circle Pass, 303
Cork Scramble, 303
Hat Relay, 304
Japanese Tag, 320
Nightgown Relay, 320
Quoit or Puck Tag, 304
spatial awareness, locomotion and
  force, 136
Walking or Hopping Race, 303
Arithmetic games
  Arithmetic Game, 350-352
  Bean Bag Toss, 350, 351
  Hopscotch, 350-352
  Number Relay, 350
  Snatch the Number, 350
Arithmetic, integration with, 349-352
Art games
  Bean Bag Toss, 341
  Color Relay, 340
  Obstacle Course, 342
  Traffic Light, 342
Art integration with, 340-342
Attention span lengthening, 2, 3
Auditory perception and auditory
  spatial awareness, 241, 242-244
Auxter, Zahar and Ferrini, 15

Aveyron, the Wild Boy of, 9
Awareness, physical
    and music, 150, 152, 153
    in movement education, 112-115,
        131-136
Balance, 11, 25, 30, 112, 113, 120, 123,
    127-129, 132, 135, 140; *see also*
    Balance skills and games
Balance apparàtus, 366-368
Balance beam, 288, 289
Balance skills and games
    balance beams, 127-129
    balance boards, 127
Ball bouncing, 68
Ball games
    Circle Stride Ball, 102, 103
    Teacher Ball, 103, 104
    Toss Ball, 102
    Touch Ball, 103
Balloons, 115
Balls, 117-120
    fashioned from paper and tape,
        372, 373
    games, *see* Games, ball
    playground, 373
    whiffle, 373
Barsch, 240
Batons, 123
Batting tees, 365
Bean bags, 115, 116, 341, 347, 350-352
Beat, *see* Music
BEH, 17
Behavior
    adaptive, 5-7
    emotional, 13, 83-87, 89, 95
    social, *see* Socialization
Bill of Rights of the Handicapped, 10
Bobbing, 305
Body awareness, 241, 250, 251
Breathing, *see* Control, breath
Broadhead, Rarick and Widdop, 11
Broadhead, 13
Broadhead and Rarick, 13
Buck, Pearl S., 4
Buoyancy, 135, 294-301
Caillois, 79
Capacity, vital, 296, 297
Cardboard barrels, 368
Cardboard boxes, large, 364, 365
Cardiovascular endurance, 25, 28, 30
Catching, 71, 72
Central nervous system, 8, 9
Characteristics of M. R./E. D., 5-9
Chasey, 11
Chasey and Wyrick, 13, 14
Classification of M. R., 7-9

Communication, *see* Socialization
Concrete pipes, large, 369
Control, breath
    and movement education, 135
    in swimming, 303-305
Coordination, 11, 25, 32
    and movement education, 114, 115,
        122-134
    and music, 140
    at play, 83, 87
    in swimming, 291
Corder, 11, 12, 15
Cratty, 11
Creeping and crawling, 50-52
Cupp, Leighton, Prince, Philabaum
    and McLarren, 12
Dance
    action songs and singing games,
        152-172
    and recreation, 235
    basic dance positions, 181-190
    basic music elements, 142-145
    folk and square dances, 190-234;
        see also individual listing
    fundamental rhythms
        locomotor, 146-150
        manipulative, 152
        non-locomotor, 150, 151
    teaching suggestions, 140-142
    traditional dance steps, 173-181
Developmental gymnastics
    assessment of program effectiveness,
        256, 257
    physical values, 255
Development, motor, 11, 13, 14, 80-83,
    88, 89, 95, 139, 140, 291
Discipline
    and movement education, 112
    at play, 89
    in swimming, 293
Disturbances, physiological, of M. R., 8
Disturbed, emotionally
    and learning, 339-352
    and movement education, 113-127,
        134, 339
    and music, 139-142, 145-147, 152, 153, 173
    and physical education/recreation,
        9-18, 108, 109, 136, 137, 235
    and swimming, 291-294
    at play, 83-88
    characteristics of, 5, 6
Diving, 324-330
Down's syndrome, 8, 11, 300, 301
Education, academic, 8
    and movement, 339-352
    history, 9

Education, movement, 111-114
  aquatic skills, 134-136
  balance skills, 127-129
  manipulative skills, 114-127
  miscellaneous skills, 129-134
  recreational aspects, 136, 137
  see also Movement, basic; Activity,
    motor; Teaching
Education, physical (1950-1972), 10-16
Educational, physical/recreational
  (1800-1950), 6-10
Endurance, 15, 83, 112, 130
Environment, 5-7
  movement education, 113
  play, 84, 91, 93, 95
Equipment, 258, 259
  instrumental, 152, 153
  movement education, 114, 115,
    117-135
  play, 89-92
Erickson, 79
Etiology of M. R., 8
Experiences, movement, 6, 8, 9
  and music, 146-153, 173-190
  and play, 87, 88
  integration with school subjects,
    339-352
  see also Education, movement;
    Activity, motor
Experiences, sensory, 9, 292, 293
  and play, 95
Exploration, movement, 111, 112;
  see also Education, movement
Explosive strength, 33
Ferrini, Auxter and Zahar, 15
Fitness games and activities, 43-47
Fitness, physical, 11
  and music, 140
  and play, 83, 87
  and swimming, 291
  in movement education, 112, 120
Flexibility, 25, 26, 28
Floats, *see* Flotation
Flotation, 294-301, 305-316
Folk and square dances
  Bleking, 195
  Broom Dance, 198, 199
  Buggy Schottische, 232
  Bummel Schottische, 234
  Bunny Hop, 208
  Captain Jinks, 226
  Carrousel, 202, 203
  Chimes of Dunkirk, 193
  Circassian Circle, 218
  Come Let Us Be Joyful, 206, 207
  Crested Hen, The, 213-214

Cshebogar, 212
  Dance of Greeting, 194
  Glowworm Mixer, 211
  Gustaf's Skoal, 215, 216
  Hora, 233
  I See You, 204, 205
  Kinderpolka, 197
  La Raspa, 229
  Milanovo Kolo, 225
  Oh, Susanna, 223, 224
  Pop Goes the Weasel, 227
  Seven Jumps, 200, 201
  Seven Steps, 217
  Shoemaker's Dance, 191, 192
  Tantoli, 228
  Teton Mountain Stomp, 219, 220
  Troika, 230, 231
  Tropanka, 209, 210
  Virginia Reel, 221, 222
  Wheat, The, 196
Francis and Rarick, 11
Freud, 78, 79
Froebel, 78
Galloping, 60-62
Games, 80-83, 89, 90
  and classroom learning, 340, 341,
    346-348, 350-352
  aquatic, 134-136, 303, 304, 316, 320
  ball, 102, 103
  dancing, 191-234
  group, 97-109
  movement education approach, 112,
    113, 115-136
  relay, 107, 108, 340, 346, 350
  rhythmic, 147-152
  singing, 154-172
  see also individual listings
Gearheart, 11
Gesell, 239
Goodman, Pumphrey, Kidd and Peters, 18
Goodwin, 14, 15
Gravity, center of, 297-301
Gravity, specific, 295, 296
Groos, 78
Group games
  Bean Bag Toss Relay, 107, 108
  Busy Bee, 104
  Catch of Fish, 106, 107
  Cherry Pie, 105
  Circle Stride Ball, 102, 103
  Dodger and Marker, 100, 101
  Hide and Seek, 107
  Inner Tube Tug-of-War, 100
  Nose and Toes Tag, 106
  One Hand Tug-of-War, 100
  Over-Under Relay, 108

Partner Tag, 106
Poison, 104
Posture Tag, 104, 105
Run, Old Bear, 106
Sardine, 107
Sawing Wood, 99
See-Saw, 98
Sit and Stand, 98
Spinning Tops, 99
Teacher Ball, 103
Thread the Needle, 97
Touch Hands and Run, 101
Toss Ball, 102
Touch Ball, 103
Witch's Carpet, 104
See also Arithmetic games, Art
    games, Language Arts games,
    Singing games
Handicapped, incidence, 5; *see also*
    Retarded, mentally; Disturbed,
    emotionally
Harrison, Lecrone, Temerlin and
    Trousdale, 15
Hawthorne effect, 12, 14
Hayden, 12
Health, *see* Safety
Heightened perceptual awareness, 2, 3
Heavy apparatus, *see* Balance beam,
    Horizontal bar, Mini-tramp, Parallel
    bars, Rings, Trampoline
Hillman, 17
History of physical education/
    recreation, 9-18
Hopping, 56-58
Horizontal bars, 280-282, 370, 371
Hospital Improvement Program (HIP),
    17
Howe, 11
Huizinga, 79
Hula hoops, 123-127, 374
Illness, mental, 5; *see also* Retarded,
    mentally
Image, body, 11, 15, 112, 113, 115,
    134-136, 150
Influences
    organic, 5
    environmental/hereditary, 8
Injury, organic brain, 8
Innertube circle, 363, 364
Instruments, *see* Equipment
Integration with other school subjects,
    339-352
Intelligence, 7-9
    and motor activity, 11-14, 83, 88,
    339-352
Itard, J. M., 9

Jumping, 63, 64
Jurcisin, 15
Kephart, 239
Kidd, Goodman, Pumphrey and Peters, 18
Kicking, 65-68
Kinesthetic perception, 241, 246-248
Ladders, 356, 357
Language arts, integration with,
    344-348
Language arts games
    Alphabet or Word Relay, 346
    Bean Bag Toss, 347
    Circle Game, 347
    Hopscotch, 347
    Reading Obstacle Course, 348
    Snatch the Letter or Word, 348
Laterality and directionality, 241, 251, 252
Leaping, 62, 63
Learning, motor, 6, 11, 12
    and play, 81-85, 94, 95
    in other school subjects, 339-352
    see also Education, movement
Lecrone, Harrison, Temerlin and
    Trousdale, 15
Leighton, Cupp, Prince, Philabaum
    and McLarren, 12
Lifting, 73-75
Light equipment activities, 268-275
Logs, 369
Malpass, 11
Manipulative skills games
    balloons, 115
    balls, 117-120
    batons, 123
    bean bags, 115-117
    hula hoops, 123-127
    ropes and rope jumping, 120-123
Marson, 16
Mat and floor activities, 259
McGriff, 17, 18
Measure, *see* Music
Measures of physical fitness, 33-42
Meter, *see* Music
Michelman, 95
Mini-tramp, 278-280
Miscellaneous skills games
    parachutes, 130-132
    scooters, 132-134
    tires, 129, 130
Mongoloids, 8, 10, 300, 301
Montessori, 239
Moran, 12, 14, 15
Motivation, 6, 12, 87, 91, 108, 293
Motor performance, physical fitness
    items, 30
Motor planning, 3

Movement, basic, 111-114
  and rhythm, 146-152, 173-190
  see also Activity, motor; Education, movement
Mumford, 16, 17
Muscular endurance, 25, 28
Music, 15, 139-153
  and dance, 173-234
  and movement, 119, 120, 123, 126, 129, 145-153, 343
  and recreation, 235
  basic elements, 142-145
National Association for Retarded Children, 10, 16
National Recreation Association, 16
Nesbitt, 5
Newton's Laws of Motion, 301
Normalization, 8, 9
Nunley, 14
Oliver, 11, 12
Ontogenic skills, 76
Organic performance, physical fitness items, 26
Overarm throw, 69, 70
Parachutes, 130-132
Parallel bars, 285-287, 370, 371
"Parent Movement," 10
Patterns
  behavior, 5-8; *see also* Behavior
  movement, 6, 12; *see also* Education, movement
  musical
    dance, 144, 145
    rhythmic, 143
Peabody Picture Vocabulary Test, 14
Perception, 13, 14, 83, 95, 132
  and learning, 339
  definition of, 237
Perceptual-motor efficiency, components of, 241
Perceptual-motor theory, rationale, 239, 240
Performance
  academic, 6, 7; *see also* Intelligence; Integration with other school subjects
  motor, 11, 13, 83, 86, 112; *see also* Activity, motor
Peters, 16
Peters, Goodman, Pumphrey and Kidd, 18
Phenylketonuria, 8
Philabaum, Leighton, Cupp, Prince and McLarren, 12
Phonograph, 376
Phylogenetic skills, 50

Piaget, 79, 80, 239
Plastic bleach bottles, 375, 376
Plato, 78
Play
  and motor activity, 83, 85-88
  and recreation, 108, 109
  developmental characteristics, 80-83
  equipment, 89-92, 94, 114-134
  explanations, 77-80
  group, 97-108, 82, 83
  individual, 80, 81, 91-96
  instrument, 145, 146
  of mentally retarded and emotionally disturbed, 85-88
  parallel, 81, 96, 97
  teaching techniques, 88-91
  values and functions, 83-85
Positions, dance, 181-190
Postural and locomotor awareness, 241, 242
Posture, 53, 54, 112, 120, 127
Potential cognitive and social values, 256
Power, 11, 33
Prangle and Solomon, 11, 12
"President's Panel on Mental Retardation," 16
Prince, Leighton, Cupp, Philabaum and McLarren, 12
Principles, mechanical, of swimming, 294-302
Programs
  movement exploration, 14
  physical education/rehabilitation, 9-15
  recreation, 16-18
    play, 89
  see also Education, movement
Pulling, 73
Pumphrey, Goodman, Kidd and Peters, 18
Purdue Perceptual-Motor Survey, 252, 253
Pushing, 72, 73
Rarick and Broadhead, 13
Rarick and Francis, 11
Rarick, Widdop and Broadhead, 11, 13
Reaction time, 25, 32
Recreation, 9, 10
  community, 16-18, 136
  movement education, 136, 137
  music, 235
  play, 108, 109
  research needs, 18
  swimming, 330-335
Rehabilitation, 9, 10

Relationships, interpersonal, 6, 8, 83;
  see also Socialization
Relay games
  Alphabet or Word Relay, 346
  Bean Bag Toss Relay, 107, 108
  Color Relay, 340, 341
  Number Relay, 350
  Over-Under Relay, 108
Research, 15, 18
Responses
  emotional, 6, 83, 84, 87, 93, 94
  motor, 87, 88
Retarded, mentally
  and learning, 339-352
  and motor performance, activity, 11-15
  and movement education, 113-115,
    117-127, 134
  and music, 139-142, 145-147, 152,
    153, 173
  and physical education/recreation,
    9-18, 108, 109, 136, 137, 235
  and play, 83, 85-88
  and swimming, 291-294, 301-335
  characteristics of, 6-9
  classification of, 7, 8
  incidence, 5
Rhythm
  and dance, 173-181
  and movement education, 119, 120,
    123, 130
  see also Music
Rhythm band instruments, 376-379
Rhythmic games
  locomotor
    hop, 148
    jump, 149
    leap, 149
    skip, slide, gallop, 149, 150
    walk, run, 147, 148
  non-locomotor, 150, 151
Rings, 283-285, 371, 372
Ropes, 120, 121, 373
  and rope jumping, 121-123
  suspended, 357
Running, 54-56
Safety (and health)
  at play, 89, 102
  in movement, 343
  water, 293, 331
Safety mats, 257
Schools for mentally retarded, 9
Scooters, 132-134
Seguin, E., 9
Self-concept, 11, 12
  and movement education, 112, 113,
    115, 127, 134, 139, 339, 340

  and play, 84, 87, 93, 94
  and swimming, 291
Self-image enhancement, 2
Sequential thinking, enhancement of,
  2, 3
Shoman, 12, 15
Sidearm throw, 69
Singing, *see* Songs
Singing games
  Baa.Baa Blacksheep, 158
  Bluebird, 172
  Did You Ever See a Lassie, 167
  Farmer in the Dell, 159, 160
  Heads and Shoulders, Knees and
    Toes, 155
  Here We Go Round the Mulberry
    Bush, 168, 169
  Hokey Pokey, 170, 171
  I'm a Little Teapot, 154
  Jolly Is the Miller, 165
  Looby Lou, 166
  Oats, Peas, Beans, and Barley Grow,
    163, 164
  One Finger, One Thumb, 156
  The Thread Follows the Needle,
    161, 162
  Twinkle, Twinkle Little Star, 157
Skill progressions, 259
Skills
  academic, 7, 8, 83, 339-352
  motor, 11
    learning, 339-352
    movement education, 111-137;
    see also Education, movement
    music, 147-152, 173-190
    play, 81-83, 87, 90, 91-108
    swimming, 302-335
  recreational, 136, 137
  social, 5, 6; *see also* Socialization
Skipping, 58, 59
Slides, 357, 358
Sliding, 59, 60
Social development, 2
Socialization, 7, 8, 14, 140
  and motor activity, 11-15
  and movement education, 112, 113,
    115
  in dance, 235
  in play, 83, 84, 86, 87, 92, 93, 108
  in swimming, 291
Socrates, 78
Solomon and Prangle, 11, 13
Songs, 140, 141, 152-172; *see also* Folk
  and square dances
Speed, 11, 25, 30, 32
Spotting, 258

Stanford-Binet Intelligence Test, 7, 8
Stein, 11, 12, 15
Steps, dance
  bleking, 175, 176
  grapevine, 176, 177
  polka, 178, 179
  schottische, 177
  stamp, 175
  step-draw, 175
  step-hop, 173, 174
  step-point, 173
  step-swing, 174
  two-step, 180, 181
  waltz, 179, 180
Strength, 11, 15, 25, 26, 83, 112, 130, 132
Strokes, swimming, 14, 316-320; *see also* Swimming
Stunts, water, 331-335
Swimming
  activities, 291
  and movement education, 134-136
  and recreation, 330-335
  mechanical principles, 294-302
  water adjustment activities, 302-330
  see also Strokes, swimming
Swings, 358
Tactual perception, 241, 248-250
Taylor, 240
Teaching
  movement education, 112-114, 117, 121, 130, 134; *see also* Education, movement
  music, 140-142, 145-153, 173-190
  other school subjects, 340-352
  play, 88-91, 94
  swimming, 291-294, 302, 316-318, 324
Temerlin, Lecrone, Harrison and Trousdale, 15
Tempo, *see* Music
Tetherball poles, 358
Thompson, 16
Throwing, 69, 70
Tires, 129, 130, 358-363
Training, 8, 9
  effect on IQ, 12, 13
Trampoline, 275-277
Trousdale, Lecrone, Harrison and Temerlin, 15
Underarm throw, 69
Vaulting box, 369, 370
Vernon, 240
Vineland Social Maturity Scale, 14
Visual perception and visual spatial awareness, 241, 244-246
Walking, 53, 54
Water adjustment activities, basic
  arm stroke front, combined stroke front, 316-318
  back float, back glide, back kick glide, 312-315
  bobbing, 305
  breath control, 303-305
  changing directions, 320
  changing positions, 315, 316
  diving, 324-330
  finning, arm stroke back, combined stroke back, 319
  jellyfish and turtle floats, 305-307
  leveling off, jumping, 320
  physical adjustment, 302, 303
  prone float, prone glide, prone kick glide, 307-310
  treading, 322, 323
White House Conference on Child Care and Protection, 10
Widdop, Rarick and Broadhead, 11
World War II, 10
Wyrick and Chasey, 13
Zahar, Auxter and Ferrini, 15

DATE DUE

DEC 0 1 1995		
DEC 2 1 1995		